Castles of Northwest Greece

Castles of Northwest Greece

From the early Byzantine Period to the eve of the First World War

Allan Brooks

Aetos Press

Copyright © Allan Brooks 2013

First published 2013 by Aetos Press
36 Moor Lane, Huddersfield, HD8 0QS, UK

All rights reserved. No part of this publication may be reproduced, stored in a retrieval system or transmitted in any form or by any means, electronic, mechanical, photocopying, recording or otherwise, without the prior permission, in writing, of the publisher.

Typeset in Times New Roman 11pt

Maps and plans drawn by the author

All photographs are by the author

ISBN 978-0-9575846-0-0

A catalogue record for this book is available from the British Library.

Aetos Press has no responsibility for the persistence or accuracy of URLs for third-party internet websites referenced in this book, and does not guarantee that any content on these websites is, or will remain, accurate or appropriate.

www.aetospress.co.uk

Contents

List of Figures	vii
List of Maps	xiv
Preface	xvii
Practical Notes	xix

Introduction — 1

1　Aetolia and Akarnania — 16
　Castle and town walls of Nafpaktos — 18
　Castle of Roumeli — 44
　Castle of the Morea — 50
　Mesolonghi — 64
　Anatoliko and Katochi — 67
　Angelokastro — 69
　Dragomestre and Astakos — 72
　Castle of Aetos — 78
　Castle of Barnakas — 81

2　Preveza and Lefkas — 88
　The Fortification of Preveza — 88
　Pantokratoras Fort — 94
　Aktio Forts — 99
　Castle of Santa Maura — 102
　Castle of Grivas — 117
　Fort St. George, Plagia — 122
　Forts Constantine and Alexander — 125
　Nikopolis — 127

Contents

3	**The Gulf of Ambracia**	143
	Castle of Rogoi	145
	Koronisia	155
	Ambrakos	156
	Castle of Arta	157
	Limnaia	167
	Castle of Vonitsa	173
4	**Epiros**	191
	Riniasa (Thomokastro)	193
	Kiafas Castle	198
	Parga	207
	Anthousa	221
	Margariti	229
	Igoumenitsa and Pirgos Ragiou	233
	Paramythia: Castle of Agios Donatos	238
	Fortifications of Ioannina	244
	Bizani Forts	264
	Pente Pigadia	268

Summary	277
Chronology	281
Glossary	292
Bibliography	296
Index	303

Figures

1.1	Nafpaktos: Overall view of harbour.	20
1.2	Nafpaktos: Sea gate in harbour wall.	22
1.3	Nafpaktos: Western harbour defences.	23
1.4	Nafpaktos: Western town gate.	24
1.5	Nafpaktos: Gate from lower to upper town.	25
1.6	Nafpaktos: Clock tower bastion.	26
1.7	Nafpaktos: Eastern walls and the clock tower bastion.	27
1.8	Nafpaktos: Interior of north town gate.	28
1.9	Nafpaktos: Lion of St. Mark.	29
1.10	Nafpaktos: Turkish north town gate.	29
1.11	Nafpaktos: Detached Turkish bastion.	30
1.12	Nafpaktos: Tower with turret in western town wall.	31
1.13	Nafpaktos Castle: Northwestern round towers.	33
1.14	Nafpaktos Castle: Western defences.	33
1.15	Nafpaktos Castle: Interior of second gate.	35
1.16	Nafpaktos Castle: Interior of third gate.	36
1.17	Nafpaktos Castle: Double parapet of tower A.	36
1.18	Nafpaktos Castle: The upper town gate and gun platform.	38
1.19	Nafpaktos Castle: The upper town gate.	39
1.20	Nafpaktos Castle: Western curtain.	40
1.21	Nafpaktos Castle: Gate to middle bailey.	41
1.22	Nafpaktos Castle: The cross wall of the upper bailey.	42
1.23	Nafpaktos Castle: The Turkish citadel.	43
1.24	Castle of Roumeli: North bastion and main gate.	46
1.25	Castle of Roumeli: Southwest walls and west postern gate.	47

Figures

1.26	Castle of Roumeli: View from the southeast.	47
1.27	Castle of Roumeli: The sea bastion and battery.	48
1.28	Castle of Roumeli: The casemates of the sea bastion.	49
1.29	Castle of Roumeli: Interior view to the north.	49
1.30	Castle of the Morea: Southern face of the fortress.	51
1.31	Castle of the Morea: The restored main entrance.	54
1.32	Castle of the Morea: The Turkish double towers.	55
1.33	Castle of the Morea: Interior of the southern walls.	56
1.34	Castle of the Morea: The southeast triangular tower.	57
1.35	Castle of the Morea: The Turkish southwest round tower.	57
1.36	Castle of the Morea: The triple tower with low level gunports.	59
1.37	Castle of the Morea: Triple tower and octagonal magazine.	59
1.38	Castle of the Morea: The Venetian sea battery.	61
1.39	Castle of the Morea: Sea battery from the Rio-Antirio bridge.	62
1.40	Castle of the Morea: The Venetian powder magazine.	62
1.41	Castle of the Morea: The western ravelin.	63
1.42	Mesolonghi: The town gate.	66
1.43	Mesolonghi: Restored Botzaris Bastion.	66
1.44	Katochi: The mediaeval tower.	68
1.45	Angelokastro: The tower from the south.	71
1.46	Angelokastro: The surviving wall section.	71
1.47	Angelokastro: The church of Agios Georgios.	72
1.48	Dragomestre: The west tower of the mediaeval crosswall.	75
1.49	Dragomestre: Southwest section of the mediaeval circuit.	76
1.50	Dragomestre: Early Christian church.	76
1.51	Dragomestre: View of the circuit above the northern cliffs.	77
1.52	Aetos Castle: North flanking tower.	78
1.53	Aetos castle: The southeast hollow tower.	80
1.54	Aetos castle: The western open tower.	80
1.55	Barnakas: Southeast wall and postern gate.	83

Figures

1.56	Barnakas: Northwest walls overlooking the gorge.	83
2.1	Preveza: Castle of St. George.	92
2.2	Preveza: Pefkakia Bastion.	93
2.3	Preveza: Castle of St. Andrew.	93
2.4	Pantokratoras Fort: View from the east.	94
2.5	Pantokratoras Fort: Main gate.	96
2.6	Pantokratoras Fort: Interior courtyard.	97
2.7	Pantokratoras Fort: Sea battery.	98
2.8	Pantokratoras Fort: View from the northwest.	99
2.9	Aktio Fort: Northwest and southwest bastions.	101
2.10	Aktio Fort: View from the north.	101
2.11	Santa Maura: Circular towers of original Turkish fort.	103
2.12	Santa Maura: Venetian east front and moat.	104
2.13	Santa Maura: Turkish west gate.	106
2.14	Santa Maura: Remains of two-storeyed barrack blocks.	107
2.15	Santa Maura: Approach to the west gate.	109
2.16	Santa Maura: Venetian artillery embrasures.	110
2.17	Santa Maura: Restored northeast casemates.	111
2.18	Santa Maura: Gunports of northeast casemates.	111
2.19	Santa Maura: Eastern defences and gate.	112
2.20	Santa Maura: Turkish east gate.	114
2.21	Santa Maura: Entrance to chapel in southeast bastion.	115
2.22	Santa Maura: Southeast bastion and southern outwork.	116
2.23	Santa Maura: Venetian outworks east of the moat.	116
2.24	Castle of Grivas: Northwest tower.	118
2.25	Castle of Grivas: Gate tower.	119
2.26	Castle of Grivas: Interior of fort and magazine.	120
2.27	Castle of Grivas: Overall view from the east.	120
2.28	Castle of Grivas Northeast tower.	121
2.29	Fort St. George: View from the Lefkas shore.	123
2.30	Fort St. George: East tower.	124
2.31	Fort St. George: Unfinished southwest rampart.	124
2.32	Fort Constantine.	126
2.33	Fort Alexander: View from the Lefkas shore.	126
2.34	Nikopolis: East tower of Roman south gate.	130
2.35	Nikopolis: Northern Nymphaeum.	130

Figures

2.36	Nikopolis: Roman north walls and gate.	131
2.37	Nikopolis: Ground plans of the Byzantine towers.	133
2.38	Nikopolis: Byzantine south walls.	133
2.39	Nikopolis: Byzantine south gate.	134
2.40	Nikopolis: Exterior of Byzantine west gate.	135
2.41	Nikopolis: Interior view of Byzantine west gate.	137
2.42	Nikopolis: Monumental stairways to the Byzantine walls.	137
2.43	Nikopolis: Interior of the north tower of the west gate.	138
2.44	Nikopolis: Postern gate.	139
3.1	Rogoi: The River Louros.	148
3.2	Rogoi: Northwest corner tower of ancient Bouchetion.	149
3.3	Rogoi: Postern gate.	150
3.4	Rogoi: View of acropolis from the west.	151
3.5	Rogoi: East wall and tower of upper bailey.	151
3.6	Rogoi: Centre and west towers of upper bailey.	152
3.7	Rogoi: Tower of middle bailey.	153
3.8	Rogoi: West tower of outer bailey.	154
3.9	Koronisia: Turkish gun tower.	155
3.10	Castle of Arta: View from the southwest.	158
3.11	Castle of Arta: Main gate.	161
3.12	Castle of Arta: The double walls west of the main gate.	161
3.13	Castle of Arta: Inner gate to the citadel.	162
3.14	Castle of Arta: North wall and postern.	163
3.15	Castle of Arta: Detail of postern gate.	163
3.16	Castle of Arta: View to the east from the main gate.	164
3.17	Castle of Arta: Original walls of ancient Ambracia.	165
3.18	Castle of Arta: Southwest multangular bastion.	166
3.19	Limnaia: South wall and tower.	168
3.20	Limnaia: Southwest round tower.	170
3.21	Limnaia: Postern Gate.	171
3.22	Limnaia: Eastern long wall.	171
3.23	Limnaia: Arched postern gate.	172
3.24	Vonitsa: Overall view of the castle from the east.	174
3.25	Vonitsa: Outer gate with flanking tower.	177

Figures

3.26	Vonitsa: Inner face of the outer gate.	178
3.27	Vonitsa: Half-round towers of the second line of defence.	178
3.28	Vonitsa: Artillery bastion of the third line of defence.	179
3.29	Vonitsa: Interior of a tower of the second line of defence.	180
3.30	Vonitsa: Second gate and the artillery bastion of the third line.	181
3.31	Vonitsa: Exterior of the Venetian postern gate.	182
3.32	Vonitsa: Arched gunport covering the northern postern gate.	183
3.33	Vonitsa: Southern façade of Turkish barracks.	184
3.34	Vonitsa: Wall and embrasures of the Turkish citadel.	184
3.35	Vonitsa: Lower tower of the southwest town wall.	185
3.36	Vonitsa: Gate in southwest town wall.	186
4.1	Castle of Riniasa: Overall view from the north.	193
4.2	Castle of Riniasa: The approach to the main gate.	196
4.3	Castle of Riniasa: The remains of the northern tower.	196
4.4	Castle of Riniasa: Lower bailey and the second terrace wall.	197
4.5	Kiafas Castle: The blocked northwest gate.	200
4.6	Kiafas Castle: Exterior of southeast gate.	201
4.7	Kiafas Castle: Interior of southeast gate.	201
4.8	Kiafas Castle: Gate in interior crosswall.	202
4.9	Kiafas Castle: The rampart overlooking Kiafas village.	203
4.10	Kiafas Castle: The southwest corridor and casemates.	204
4.11	Kiafas Castle: Northwestern corner tower.	205
4.12	Parga Castle: Entrance corridor and outer gate.	209
4.13	Parga Castle: The Venetian northeast defences.	211
4.14	Parga Castle: The exterior of the main gate.	212
4.15	Parga Castle: Southern round tower.	213
4.16	Parga Castle: Southern square tower.	214
4.17	Parga Castle: Entrance to Ali Pasha's citadel.	214
4.18	Parga Castle: Plaque above the citadel entrance.	215
4.19	Parga Castle: Tunnel vaulted corridor within the rampart.	216
4.20	Parga Castle: Ali Pasha's citadel from the north.	217

Figures

4.21	Parga Castle: Ali Pasha's bathhouse.	218
4.22	Parga Castle: The west face of Ali Pasha's serai.	219
4.23	Parga Castle: The walled lane inside the outer curtain.	220
4.24	Castle of Anthousa: View of the main block from the east.	223
4.25	Castle of Anthousa: Northwest front and main gate.	224
4.26	Castle of Anthousa: Monumental façade of the main gate.	225
4.27	Castle of Anthousa: Outline of Mihrab in the north courtyard.	226
4.28	Castle of Anthousa: Eastern entrance to the keep.	227
4.29	Castle of Anthousa: The parapet and embrasures of the keep.	228
4.30	Castle of Margariti: Northwest corner of the circuit.	229
4.31	Castle of Margariti: Southern corner of the main circuit.	230
4.32	Castle of Margariti: Southeast face.	232
4.33	Pirgos Ragiou: The Turkish tower from the west.	234
4.34	Pirgos Ragiou: View of the tower and entrance bridge.	236
4.35	Pirgos Ragiou: The tower from the interior of the fort.	237
4.36	Castle of Agios Donatos: The east gate.	239
4.37	Castle of Agios Donatos: North wall of acropolis.	241
4.38	Castle of Agios Donatos: The Hellenistic postern gate.	242
4.39	Castle of Agios Donatos: Exterior of the southwest gate.	243
4.40	Ioannina: Overall view of the southeast acropolis.	245
4.41	Ioannina: Outer face of the main gate of the Kastro.	250
4.42	Ioannina: The blocked Molos gate.	251
4.43	Ioannina: The rear face of the Thomas tower.	252
4.44	Ioannina: The southern flank of the central bastion.	253
4.45	Ioannina: The southwestern round bastion.	254
4.46	Ioannina: The Skala gate.	254
4.47	Ioannina: The south gate to Ali Pasha's citadel.	255
4.48	Ioannina: The casemates of the south wall of the Kastro circuit.	256
4.49	Ioannina: The gate from Ali Pasha's citadel onto the south curtain.	256

Figures

4.50	Ioannina: Arcaded central section of the citadel wall.	257
4.51	Ioannina: The gunports in the northeast bastion of Ali Pasha's citadel.	258
4.52	Ioannina: The façade of the main gate to Ali Pasha's citadel.	259
4.53	Ioannina: Bohemond's tower.	260
4.54	Ioannina: The Fetihe mosque and "Bohemond's wall".	261
4.55	Ioannina: The disused gate of the northeast acropolis.	262
4.56	Ioannina: The arched portico of the madrasah.	263
4.57	Fort Bizani: The eastern fixed battery.	266
4.58	Fort Bizani: The rear face of the western battery.	266
4.59	Fort Bizani: Concrete emplacements on the summit of the hill.	267
4.60	Pente Pigadia Fort: Overall view from the southeast.	269
4.61	Pente Pigadia Fort: View of the eastern arm of the fort.	270
4.62	Pente Pigadia Fort: View of the internal ramps and the southern gun platform.	271

Maps and Plans

1	Northwest Greece	xvi
2	The Development of the Greek State	12
3	Aetolia-Akarnania	17
4	Nafpaktos: Castle and town walls	21
5	Nafpaktos Castle: General plan	34
6	Nafpaktos Castle: Main gate complex	37
7	Castle of Roumeli	45
8	Castle of the Morea	53
9	Mesolonghi: Town walls	65
10	Angelokastro	70
11	Dragomestre	73
12	Aetos Castle	79
13	Barnakas: Castle of Glosses	82
14	Preveza and the Lefkas Channel	89
15	The Fortification of Preveza	91
16	Pantokratoras Fort	95
17	Aktio Fort	100
18	Castle of Santa Maura	108
19	Santa Maura: Interior of northeast defences	113
20	Castle of Grivas	118
21	Fort St. George, Plagia	123
22	Nikopolis: Overall plan	128
23	Nikopolis: The Byzantine walls	132
24	Nikopolis: The west gate	136

Maps and Plans

25	The Gulf of Ambracia	144
26	Castle of Rogoi	147
27	Castle of Arta	160
28	Fortifications of Limnaia	169
29	Vonitsa Town	175
30	Vonitsa Castle	176
31	Epiros	192
32	Thomokastro	194
33	Kiafas Castle	199
34	The Souliot Villages	206
35	Town of Parga	208
36	Parga Castle	210
37	Anthousa: Castle of Ali Pasha	222
38	Margariti	231
39	Pirgos Ragiou	235
40	Paramythia: Castle of Agios Donatos	240
41	Ioannina	247
42	Bizani Forts	265
43	Pente Pigadia	268

Outline maps of Greece as a whole are based on those freely available from the Central Intelligence Agency via the library of the University of Texas at Austin (http://www.lib.utexas.edu/maps/greece.html). Site location maps are derived from NASA World Wind Landsat7 images in the public domain (http://worldwind.arc.nasa.gov/index.html). Additional street level information was obtained from the OpenStreetMap project (http://www.openstreetmap.org. Map data © OpenStreetMap contributors, CC-BY-SA). Site plans are sketch maps prepared by the author. The general layout of each site was derived by walking the circuit recording cardinal points with a hand held GPS receiver. These data provide an approximate representation of the position of towers, gates, etc. but in general the sketch maps should be regarded as schematic guides rather than accurate plans. They are only approximately to scale but are designed to assist the reader in finding the major elements of each site. Where sites were heavily overgrown when visited, further approximations were necessary. North on maps is always true north.

Maps and Plans

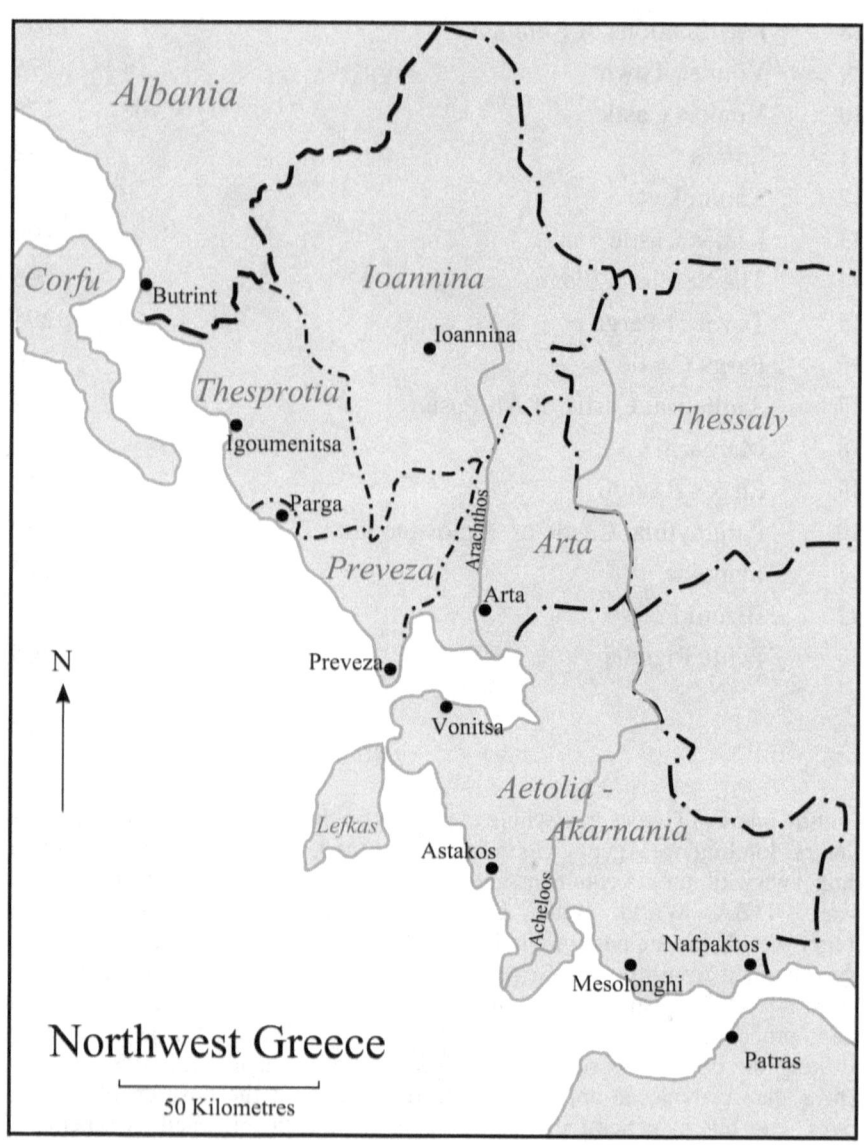

Preface

Northwest Greece has always been relatively isolated from the rest of the Greek mainland and, with the exception of small pockets of intense tourist development on the coast, is still little visited by foreign tourists. Modern guidebooks of necessity concentrate on the few important Classical and Hellenistic sites in the region with only passing reference to mediaeval and later fortifications. This book is intended to redress this imbalance by providing a detailed guide to a selection of the castles and forts of the area dating from the early Byzantine period to the eve of the First World War.

The northwest of Greece consists of the modern districts of Epiros to the north of the Ambracian Gulf and Aetolia-Akarnania to the south. Epiros is sub-divided into the administrative areas of Preveza, Arta, Thesprotia and Ioannina. As its name implies Aetolia-Akarnania is the amalgamation of the two ancient territories of Akarnania to the west of the Acheloos river and Aetolia to the east. The physical boundaries are the Gulf of Corinth to the south, the Ionian Sea to the west, the Pindos Mountains to the east and the border with Albania to the north, a frontier established only in 1912. With the exception of an area now in southern Albania the region corresponds roughly to that of the late Roman province of Epiros Vetus and also to the territory controlled by the Despots of Epiros after 1257. In the mediaeval period these lands were repeatedly attacked. Norman, Italian, Angevin, Serbian, Venetian, Turkish and Albanian invaders have all left their mark on the numerous castles and forts that remain distinctive features in the landscape. The works of these invaders range from the repair of earlier Byzantine circuits to the construction of completely new fortifications; sometimes choosing to build in a previously unused strategic location; sometimes simply re-occupying an ancient site. The Venetians continued to build into the early eighteenth century, the Turks into the twentieth. Ali Pasha was a particularly prolific builder being responsible for a host of new

Preface

forts between 1800 and 1820. Even the British, French and Russians made contributions to the military architecture of the region at various times in the 19C.

The book follows the conventional travel guide format of logical itineraries. Each site is described in detail and is placed within its relevant topographical and historical context. Most importantly detailed directions to remote locations are given whenever necessary.

Practical Notes

This book aims to be a practical guide and is organised into a number of logical itineraries that the visitor may follow. Section one describes the mediaeval, Turkish and Venetian sites in Aetolia and Akarnania. Section two deals with the numerous forts built by Ali Pasha around Preveza and Lefkas, the Turko-Venetian fort of Santa Maura and the major early Byzantine fortifications at Nikopolis. Section three is concerned with the castles and forts to be found around the almost landlocked Gulf of Ambracia. The final section deals with modern Epiros where the range of fortifications to be seen extends to include the only work dating from the brief period of Norman occupation and early 20C field fortifications.

A hire car is the most convenient method of exploration away from major towns. Although the new roads completed in the last decade have dramatically reduced driving times between urban centres, travelling in rural Greece is still hampered by the lack of good maps. One of the best available is the GeoCenter Euromap sheet 'Greece and the Islands' at 1:300000. A good alternative, published in Athens, is the Road Editions series which covers the entire mainland in five sheets at 1:250000. Number three, Epiros, and Number four, Central Greece, cover the routes described in this book. They are sporadically available in UK bookshops but are found everywhere in Greece especially in any shop catering for foreign tourists. However the following caveats apply. On the GeoCenter map passable rural tracks may not appear while the Road Editions maps often show local roads in rural areas that may be little more than footpaths. The Road Editions range shows a larger number of archaeological sites although there are still omissions. The ideal solution for the traveller is to have both maps and compare. However site location maps and detailed directions are given within the text wherever necessary. For more basic practical information it is assumed that the reader will have access to one of the standard travel guides to Greece.

Practical Notes

Variations in the opening hours of archaeological sites can be a problem for the visitor to Greece. Among the sites discussed in this book the castles of the Morea, Nafpaktos, Vonitsa, Santa Maura, Arta, Roumeli and the fort of Pirgos Ragiou are enclosed and have standard opening times. These are published and can be found via alphabetical lists of archaeological sites and monuments at www.culture.gr. Winter opening hours should apply between November and March and are usually 8.30 to 15.00. Summer hours may extend the closing time. Sites are usually closed on Mondays. Times are subject to frequent local variation, the more so following Greece's economic problems. The castle at Arta for example has only been open sporadically in recent years. Only on-the-spot inspection will reveal the situation on any particular day. Fortunately the majority of the sites described here are unenclosed. The town walls of Nafpaktos, Nikopolis, Ioannina, Preveza and Mesolonghi can be inspected at any time. The Byzantine castles of Dragomestre, Barnakas, Aetos, Paramythia, Rogoi, and Thomokastro remain abandoned in the landscape. The majority of the forts built by Ali Pasha still stand in relatively good condition and can be freely visited. It should be noted however that many of the sites covered by this book are overgrown and ruinous. The visitor should be aware of the hazards of unprotected drops, hidden cistern entrances underfoot, crumbling walls and snakes. The towns of Nafpaktos, Vonitsa, Parga and Ioannina, amongst others, have good tourist facilities and are ideal centres from which to explore.

Introduction

The early history of the region

There is evidence of human occupation in the area that now forms the northwest of Greece from the Neolithic period onwards. The earliest cities were established by a succession of colonists. Mycenaean colonies were founded in the 14C BC notably at Ephyra near the mouth of the river Acherontas. In the 7C BC Elean colonies were established at Bouchetion, Baties and Elatria to the north of the Gulf of Ambracia and at Pandosia in the Acherontas valley.[1] Corinthian colonies created at the same time included Ambracia, the location of modern Arta, and Anaktoria on the southern shore of the Ambracian Gulf. In the 5C BC the inhabitants of Corfu established a colony at Toroni to the north of Igoumenitsa, while at Nafpaktos on the Gulf of Corinth the Athenians planted a colony of Messenian exiles.

The native tribes of Epiros were the Molossi who occupied the central area around modern Ioannina; the Thesproti who held the valleys of the Acherontas and its tributaries and whose name survives in modern Thesprotia; and the Chaones whose territory now lies in southern Albania. Further south the tribes of Aetolia had created a federal state, or league, in the 4C BC as had the Akarnanians somewhat earlier. Epiros itself was first unified in the 4C BC by the Molossian king, Alexander. In the 3C under Pyrrhus its borders were greatly expanded and with the acquisition of Akarnania extended as far south as the Gulf of Corinth. However after the death of Pyrrhus's successor, Alexander II, in 240 BC, Epiros began to fragment and Akarnania regained its independence. There followed a protracted period of conflict between Epiros and the Aetolians. At the beginning of the 2C BC Epiros became involved in the wars between Rome and Macedon. Eventually the tribes split into two factions with the Molossians supporting Macedon. The final Roman victory at the end of the Third Macedonian War led, in 167 BC, to

Introduction

the sacking of seventy Molossian settlements in retribution. Epiros became part of the Roman province of Macedonia created after the defeat of a Macedonian uprising in 148 BC. Rome had defeated the Aetolians in 189 BC and Aetolia was thereafter a Roman client state. Akarnania also acknowledged the supremacy of Rome around this time. After the defeat of the Achaian League and the sack of Corinth in 146 BC the whole of Greece was divided into the two Roman provinces of Macedonia and Achaia. Both the Aetolian and the Akarnanian Leagues continued as political entities until 31 BC when, with the founding of Nikopolis by Octavian, their territories were forcibly de-populated to provide the first inhabitants of the new city.

A separate province of Epiros with Nikopolis as its capital was created at the beginning of the 2C AD. At the end of the 3C the Emperor Diocletian reformed the borders to create Epiros Vetus in the south and Epiros Nova to the north. Epiros Vetus, old Epiros, included all of modern northwest Greece as far south as the Acheloos River as well as the extreme south of modern Albania. New Epiros lay to the north and occupied southern Illyria, the area now occupied by the greater part of modern Albania. In 330 Constantine dedicated his new capital of Constantinople on the Bosphorus and in 395 the Eastern Empire formally separated from the Western. Over the following centuries the eastern half became the Greek-speaking entity we now call the Byzantine Empire. The Balkans as a whole were subjected to devastation from successive waves of invaders from the 3C onwards. The Goths in the 3C were followed by the Huns in the 4C and the Vandals in the 5C. These invasions led in turn to a general re-fortification of the main cities of the Empire. The prime example in Epiros is the 5C circuit of Nikopolis probably constructed after the Vandal raids of 475. From the 6C onwards the Balkans suffered repeated invasions by Slav tribes. Byzantine political control in most of Epiros was lost by the end of the 7C and not regained until the 9C in the reign of the Emperor Basil I. Further re-fortification may have occurred at this time.

The Norman Invasion

The Normans had been active in southern Europe as mercenaries since the latter part of the 10C. In the 11C, led by the Hauteville family, they carved out a kingdom for themselves in southern Italy ousting the Byzantines completely in 1071 with the fall of Bari after a three-year siege. From this power base Robert Guiscard and his son Bohemond

Introduction

embarked on an ambitious but ultimately unsuccessful campaign to conquer Constantinople itself. In 1081 they crossed the Adriatic, seized a number of ports on the Illyrian coast and occupied Corfu. The following year Bohemond captured Ioannina and made major improvements to its fortifications, elements of which still survive. He advanced east into Thessaly but was defeated at Larissa in 1083. The Byzantines regained their lost territory and the Norman campaigns came to an abrupt end with Guiscard's death in 1085.

The Despotate of Epiros

In 1204 the Byzantine Empire was dealt a devastating blow by the forces of the Fourth Crusade from which it only subsequently partially recovered. The combined Crusader armies of Franks and Venetians conquered and sacked Constantinople and proceeded to divide up the Empire between them. The Venetians' agreement with the Crusaders had given them three eighths of the Empire, famously expressed as the fraction "one quarter and half of one quarter". Epiros was part of this allotment but in practice the Venetians were interested only in its coastal strongholds and ports. In 1205 Michael Comnenus Doukas, an illegitimate member of the Byzantine imperial family, seized the territory. In 1210 he reached an agreement with the Venetians to govern Epiros notionally on their behalf. The independent Byzantine state he created was eventually to become known as the Despotate of Epiros.[2] Only two other fragments of the Empire remained under Byzantine control. These were known as the Empire of Nicaea and the Empire of Trebizond and occupied small territories in Asia Minor.

Michael and his successor on his death in 1215, his half-brother Theodore, pursued a policy of vigorous territorial expansion and by 1230 their new state encompassed Old and New Epiros, Aetolia, Akarnania, Thessaly and much of Macedonia including the city of Thessalonica. Its capital was Arta, with Ioannina, much expanded by an influx of refugees from Constantinople, forming its second city. Theodore's attempt to create a new Byzantine Empire brought him into conflict with the Empire of Nicaea but his grand plan to recover Constantinople came to a halt when he was defeated by the Bulgarians in 1230. Michael II, the exiled son of the first Michael Doukas, used the opportunity to return to Arta and seize his inheritance. It was this Michael and his son, Nikephoros, who were jointly granted the title of Despot for the first time by the Nicaean Emperor John Vatatzes in 1253 during a brief period of peace between the two states. Thessalonica had by then been recovered by the Nicaeans but a far greater loss of Epirot territory occurred four years later when Manfred, son of the Holy Roman Emperor Frederick II, crossed the Adriatic from Italy and seized New Epiros and Corfu. Michael mitigated his loss by giving his daughter, Helena, in marriage to Manfred. Her dowry was deemed to be the area already in Manfred's possession. Michael had thus gained a powerful ally and he forged another important alliance by marrying his second daughter, Anna, to William of Villehardouin, Prince of Achaia.[3] In 1259 Michael attempted to recover Thessalonica with the help of his new allies but was disastrously defeated by Nicaean forces at the Battle of Pelagonia. The Nicaeans went on to occupy Arta and Ioannina and Michael was forced to flee to Cephalonia. In 1261 the Nicaeans recovered Constantinople from the Franks and the Byzantine Empire was restored although it now occupied only a fraction of its previous territory. Michael and Nikephoros with support from Manfred managed to recover Arta and Ioannina but they were effectively at war with the Empire until 1264. The threat of an armed invasion that year forced them to sign a treaty strengthened the following year by the marriage of Nikephoros to the Emperor's niece, Anna. With this marriage the legitimacy of the Despotate was established although it too had lost a large part of its original territory.

In 1266 Charles of Anjou defeated Manfred in battle and seized the kingship of Sicily that Manfred had acquired in 1258. The following year the Treaty of Viterbo confirmed his claim to Manfred's possessions in Epiros. Charles was to spend several years consolidating his hold on these territories while planning an ambitious campaign to seize Constantinople. Nikephoros, who had become sole Despot in 1267 on the death of his father, formally allied himself to Charles in 1279 and became his vassal. This was not a successful alliance. Charles launched a major expedition against the Byzantine Empire the following year but his coalition of forces was decisively defeated at Berat in 1281. Another serious blow to his ambitions occurred a year later when he lost control of Sicily following a rebellion known as the Sicilian Vespers. He died in 1285. His son, Charles II, eventually assumed the kingship of Naples in 1289. When the Byzantine Emperor Andronikos II launched another campaign to subdue the Despotate in 1292 Nikephoros was forced to seek new allies. He paid Florent of Hainault, Prince of Achaia, and Richard Orsini of Cephalonia to assist him defeat the Byzantine forces.[4] This led to a link with the Orsini family via marriage between Nikephoros's daughter, Maria, and Richard Orsini's son, John. In 1294

Introduction

Nikephoros renewed his Angevin alliance by marrying his daughter, Thamar, to Philip of Taranto the son of Charles II. Another large part of the Despotate passed to direct Angevin control via Thamar's dowry, which included the castles of Nafpaktos, Vonitsa and Angelokastro.

Nikephoros died two years later. Thamar's marriage contract had stipulated that Nikephoros's son, Thomas, could only inherit the title of Despot as the vassal of Philip.[5] In 1304 his mother, Anna, who had been acting as regent during her son's minority, refused to accept this arrangement and successfully resisted a series of attacks by Charles's forces. Thomas once again made peace with the Byzantine Empire in 1307 and married Anna, daughter of the Emperor Michael IX. However in 1318 Thomas was murdered by his nephew, Nicholas Orsini, who had succeeded his father, John, as Count of Cephalonia the previous year. With the death of Thomas the dynasty founded by Michael Comnenus Doukas came to an end. Over the hundred years of its existence its rulers were forced by necessity to forge alliances that conceded much of its territory but yielded little real security. By the beginning of the 14C the Despotate extended no further north than a line roughly equivalent to the modern frontier between Greece and Albania while to the south most of Akarnania was under Angevin control. The 13C was the great period of fortress building throughout the Despotate. The fortifications at Angelokastro, Dragomestre, Aetos, Barnakas, Vonitsa, Rogoi, Arta, Thomokastro, Parga and Ioannina were all constructed or re-built during this period and many can be attributed directly to Michael I or his son.[6]

After 1318 periods of political stability in the Despotate became increasingly rare and brief. Nicholas Orsini succeeded in holding Arta and married Thomas's widow, Anna. However Ioannina declared allegiance to Constantinople and he could not prevent the Despotate dividing. His regime lasted a mere five years. In 1323 he was killed by his brother, John, who not only seized Arta but also regained control of Ioannina ostensibly as governor on behalf of the Emperor. He in turn was murdered four years later by his wife, also named Anna. Although she held power briefly as regent for her young son Nikephoros, by 1340 the Despotate was again part of the Byzantine Empire. In 1341 civil war broke out on the death of the Emperor Andronikos III. The conflict was to last until 1347 and left the Empire incapable of resisting a new wave of Serbian invaders from the north. By 1348 Epiros and Thessaly had been overrun by the forces of the Serbian ruler, Stephen Dušan. He divided his conquests between his half-brother, Symeon Uroš, who acquired Epiros; and Gregory Preljub, one of his generals, who acquired

Introduction

Thessaly. When both Dušan and Preljub died in 1355 Symeon Uroš abandoned Epiros to pursue his claim to the Serbian crown. The exiled Nikephoros Orsini used the opportunity to seize Thessaly and then recover Epiros. His reign as Nikephoros II lasted only until 1359 when he was killed putting down an Albanian rebellion. Symeon Uroš promptly returned with an army and recovered both Thessaly and Epiros.

Albanian tribes had been establishing themselves throughout the Despotate since the beginning of the Serbian conquest and Symeon's control was nominal in many areas. His solution to the problem was to recognise reality and grant the title of Despot to the two most important Albanian chieftains. Peter Losha became Despot of Arta and Rogoi, and Gjin Boua Spata Despot of Acheloos and Angelokastro. By 1367 Symeon was based in Thessaly and had assigned Ioannina to his son-in-law, Thomas Preljubovič. In 1374 Peter Losha died and Gjin Boua Spata was able to create one united Albanian Despotate centred on Arta, the original capital. The partition of Epiros into an Albanian Despotate in the south and a Serbian Despotate of Ioannina in the north was complete. Thomas Preljubovič survived as Despot in Ioannina until his assassination in 1384. His widow Maria, the daughter of Symeon Uroš, married the Florentine Esau Buondelmonti who was subsequently granted the title of Despot by the Emperor John V.

The final years of the Despotate are dominated by the rise to power of the Tocco family.[7] Beginning in 1399 Carlo Tocco began to attack the Albanian territories of southern Epiros from his base in Lefkas and Vonitsa. By 1408 he had gained possession of all Akarnania. When Esau Buondelmonti died in 1411 the citizens of Ioannina turned to his nephew, Carlo. His appropriation of the title of Despot was confirmed by the Emperor Manuel II in 1415. The following year Carlo and his brother, Leonardo, succeeded in wresting Arta and Rogoi from Albanian control and the territories of the Despotate were briefly re-united. Fifteen years later in 1429 Carlo died. He was succeeded by his nephew, Carlo II, but his hold on the territories of the Despotate was brief. In 1430 Ioannina surrendered to the Turks and Carlo was only able to remain as ruler in Arta as a vassal of the Sultan Murad II. This marked the end of the Despotate as an independent Byzantine state. He was succeeded on his death in 1448 by his son, Leonardo, but by the following year Arta was in Turkish hands. Leonardo hung on to the remnants of the Tocco inheritance for another thirty years. Angelokastro and Barnakas fell to the Turks in 1460. The last mainland possession, Vonitsa, fell in 1479 along with the islands of Lefkas, Cephalonia and Zante. The triumph of the Ottoman Turks was complete.

Introduction

The Venetians and Turks

The fall of Constantinople in 1204 gave the Republic of Venice, at least on paper, a new empire. However Venice was a maritime state with resources too limited to control these extensive new territories. Before this date its overseas interests had consisted only of trading bases in Istria and Dalmatia on the Adriatic coast. As its primary concern was to maintain and extend this network of ports and naval bases essential to its sea-borne trade, it chose to develop only a fraction of its theoretical allocation of three eighths of the Byzantine Empire. It first seized Methoni and Koroni at the southwest tip of the Peloponnese in 1206. This was followed by the purchase of Crete from the Franks and its subsequent development into Venice's first colony.[8] In 1209 the Republic also acquired trading rights throughout Euboea. This island also slowly developed into a Venetian colony.[9] It was to be almost two hundred years before the Republic began to establish a presence in Epiros. In 1386, in response to the growing power of the Ottoman Turks, the Venetians acquired Corfu and the stronghold of Butrinto on the mainland opposite.[10] This gave them complete command of the narrow northern entrance to the Straits of Corfu. Further acquisitions on the mainland followed. Parga to the south became a Venetian protectorate in 1401. Sagiada at the mid-point of the Straits, followed in 1413.[11] To extend their influence in the Gulf of Corinth the Republic purchased the town of Nafpaktos from the Albanian Paul Spata in 1407. In the Peloponnese the Venetians had also acquired Nauplion and Argos in 1388 and later gained Navarino in 1415.

As the Turks progressively dismembered the Byzantine Empire and the Despotate of Epiros it was inevitable that the Venetian Republic and the Ottoman Empire would clash. Constantinople fell to the Turks in 1453 and by 1461 they had conquered all the Peloponnese except for the Venetian coastal strongholds. The First Turco-Venetian War broke out in 1463 and Venice lost control of Euboea and Argos in 1470. Nafpaktos was attacked in 1477 but the Venetians had enclosed the entire town and harbour with new walls and the Turks withdrew after a three-month siege. A peace agreement ending the war was finally concluded in 1479.[12] However in 1499 war broke out again. This was primarily a series of naval battles and blockades. Nafpaktos was forced to surrender to the Turks in 1499; Methoni, Koroni and Navarino fell the following year. To secure the Gulf of Corinth the Turks then constructed the Castle of Roumeli and the Castle of the Morea on either shore at the Rio narrows, effectively transforming the Gulf into a Turkish lake. Despite these losses the Venetians were able to consolidate their hold on the southern Adriatic by gaining control of the islands of Cephalonia, Ithaca and Zante in 1500. The Third Turco-Venetian war broke out in 1537 and when it ended three years later Venice no longer had a single possession in the Peloponnese. Cyprus, acquired only in 1489, fell in 1571. Finally in 1669 Crete was lost, its capital, Candia, falling only after a twenty-one year siege.

In 1683 a Turkish army invaded Hapsburg territory and besieged Vienna, ostensibly in support of Hungarian nationalists rebelling against the Holy Roman Emperor, Leopold I. The Turks were decisively defeated by Leopold's forces with strong support from the Polish King John Sobieski. The following year Venice joined the Austrians, the Papacy and the Poles in a Holy League with the aim of driving the Turks from southeast Europe completely. In July 1684 Venice embarked on a campaign to recover her Greek possessions. Morosini, the Venetian Captain-General, assembled a fleet at Corfu, the Venetian's main external naval base after the fall of Crete, and attacked Lefkas and the coast of the mainland.[13] By the end of the year he had taken the fort of Santa Maura, the key to Lefkas, together with Preveza, Vonitsa and Mesolonghi. Three years later the conquest of the Morea (the Peloponnese) was complete. The Venetians also had control of the Gulf of Corinth and had recovered Nafpaktos. The Austrians meanwhile had ejected the Turks from Hungary, Croatia and Transylvania while the Poles had extended their territory to the southeast. From 1687 onwards the Venetians made repeated, but unsuccessful, attempts to extend their gains beyond the Morea. Although they took Athens in 1687, famously blowing up the Parthenon in the process, they abandoned the town the following year. In 1688 a campaign to recover Euboea, known to the Venetians as Negroponte, collapsed after four months. An attempt to take Chania on Crete in 1692 was also quickly abandoned. Finally, in 1694, they succeeded in seizing the island of Chios only for it to be retaken by the Turks early the following year. These setbacks left the Venetians in a weak bargaining position when a peace agreement was finally negotiated at Karlowitz in 1699. The treaty confirmed Austrian and Polish gains and Venetian possession of the Morea and the Ionian islands, but the Republic was forced to give up its conquests north of the Gulf of Corinth including Nafpaktos, Preveza and Vonitsa. Only Parga and Butrinto remained in Venetian hands on the coast of Epiros.

In 1715 the Turks returned to recover the Morea. Although the Venetians had embarked on a massive programme of re-fortification of their main coastal strongholds they were unable to resist the huge force,

Introduction

reputedly one hundred thousand strong, assembled against them. In only three months the Ottoman army overran the entire peninsula. This time however it was the Turks who were unable to capitalise on their initial success. They moved north in 1716 to attack Corfu but after a short siege they were forced to withdraw by a combination of Venetian counter-attacks and serious damage to their camp and fleet by a providential storm. The following year a new Venetian fleet inflicted two further defeats on the Turks and succeeded in recovering Preveza and Vonitsa. In 1718 a treaty was agreed at Passarowitz. This established Venetian possession of the seven Ionian Islands along with Butrinto, Parga, Preveza and Vonitsa on the mainland, an inventory that was to last until the final days of the Republic in 1797.

The French, Russians and British

For a period of twenty years Napoleon Bonaparte dominated the affairs of Europe and his campaigns affected even the backwater of Epiros. By March 1797 he had seized much of northern Italy and was advancing into Austria. In response the Austrians negotiated an armistice, signing a provisional treaty at Loeben in April, which included secret clauses to partition the Republic of Venice. By May Napoleon had intimidated the Venetians into a bloodless surrender. His troops occupied the city and that summer proceeded to seize the Ionian Islands and Venice's neighbouring possessions on the Greek mainland. In October the Treaty of Campo Formio formally granted Venice to Austria and confirmed French sovereignty over the islands and their mainland dependencies. The French occupation proved to be very brief. Following Bonaparte's invasion of Egypt in 1798 the Turks, in alliance with Russia, declared war on France. A combined Russian and Turkish fleet attacked the Ionian Islands taking Zante, Cephalonia and Lefkas that same year and Corfu in 1799 after a four-month siege. Meanwhile Ali Pasha of Ioannina had seized all the mainland territories in French hands apart from Parga. In 1800 an agreement between Russia and Turkey united the seven Ionian Islands in an autonomous state called the Septinsular Republic and jointly guaranteed its independence. The agreement also ceded the old Venetian mainland dependencies to the Turks. This period led to a Russian addition to the fortifications of the area in the form of two small forts at the southern end of the Lefkas channel. The Septinsular Republic survived until 1807. In June of that year Napoleon gained a decisive victory over the Russians at the Battle of Friedland. The battle

Introduction

took place almost on the shores of the Baltic yet the subsequent Treaty of Tilsit included in its provisions the restoration of the Ionian Islands to the French. The Russian garrisons were evacuated and another short period of French occupation began. On the mainland however only Parga was re-occupied. Here the French built a small fort on an islet in the harbour, their sole contribution to the fortifications of Epiros. This second period of French dominion was again short-lived. A British fleet expelled the French garrisons from Zante, Cephalonia and Ithaca in 1809. Lefkas was taken in 1810. Corfu was finally handed over to the British in June 1814. A British force had also occupied Parga earlier the same year. One year later the British signed the Treaty of Paris with Russia, re-creating the Septinsular Republic as the United States of the Ionian Islands. This was intended to be an autonomous state under British protection but it quickly became a British colony in all but name. It remained so until 1864 when the islands became part of the Greek state. Parga however was ceded back to the Ottoman Empire in 1817. Ottoman power in the area was in the hands of Ali Pasha and he occupied the town in 1819.

Ali Pasha

Ali Pasha first created a power base in Albania and northern Greece in the late 18C in the years preceding the fall of Venice. Usually known as Ali Pasha of Ioannina, or Ali Pasha of Tepelini after his birthplace in Albania, he began his career as a brigand leader before reversing roles and working for the Turkish authorities to suppress brigandage and highway robbery.[14] In 1783 he was granted his first Turkish title, that of Pasha of Trikala. Although he acquired Ioannina in 1786 by a combination of trickery and intimidation, his appropriation of the title of Pasha of Ioannina was ratified by Sultan Abdul Hamid in 1788. Ioannina became the base from which he sought to extend his rule throughout northern Greece. By 1803 he had control of most of Albania, Epiros and Thessaly, while his sons, Veli and Mukhtar, governed the Morea and Nafpaktos. By the end of 1803 Ali had also finally subdued the Souliots and expelled them from their mountain stronghold. Their independence had been one of the few challenges to his authority in Epiros. Ali held his territories as an agent of the Ottoman Sultan, but his allegiance to Constantinople became increasingly notional and by 1807 he was a de facto independent ruler. In 1811 he seized Margariti which until that date had been another semi-autonomous area controlled by its own

Introduction

Ottoman Bey. Finally, in 1819, he occupied Parga, the last of the old Venetian possessions to retain its independence.

Ali Pasha was a prolific builder of fortresses and palaces. He completely re-built the old Byzantine walls of his new capital Ioannina, constructed a new inner citadel and built several palaces for himself and his sons within the town. By 1805 he had completed a fortress with its own serai, or palace, at Kiafas in the centre of Souliot territory. New forts appeared in 1807 overlooking the Lefkas channel as part of Ali's unsuccessful attempts to seize the island. After 1807, when he was consolidating his hold on the area independently of the Sultan, substantial fortifications were built around Preveza as he attempted to transform it into his principal port. These works included four forts, an earthwork rampart and moat around the entire town and an elaborate palace. A new citadel was also added to the castle of Vonitsa. Finally, after he gained possession of Parga in 1819, he constructed a new citadel and serai at the highest point of the castle rock.

Ali's enjoyment of his many palaces lasted only three years after 1819. In 1820 Sultan Mahmud II took action to curtail Ali's independence and bring the territory back under Ottoman control. His forces quickly subdued the main towns of Epiros and surrounded Ioannina in October 1820. The ensuing siege lasted until January 1822. Ali Pasha was killed the following month.

Greek Independence and the Development of the Greek State

The Greek War of Independence began with a series of uprisings in the Peloponnese in March 1821. Although there was no direct political connection between the Ottoman siege of Ioannina from 1820 to 1822 and these uprisings, twenty thousand Turkish troops were tied up in the siege and the Ottoman forces available in the Morea were heavily outnumbered by the revolutionaries. By 1822 Greek forces were in control of most of the Peloponnese and had also taken Athens. In the northwest Mesolonghi and Anatoliko joined the revolution in the summer of 1821. Attempts by the Turks to recover Mesolonghi in November 1822 and again in October 1823 failed, but Greek attempts to move north and seize Arta in 1822 were also unsuccessful. In 1824 the balance of the struggle changed completely when Mahmud II persuaded Mehmet Ali, the ruler of Egypt, still notionally part of the Ottoman Empire, to invade the Peloponnese promising the spoils to Mehmet's son, Ibrahim Pasha. Ibrahim began operations with a naval campaign but early in 1825 he

Introduction

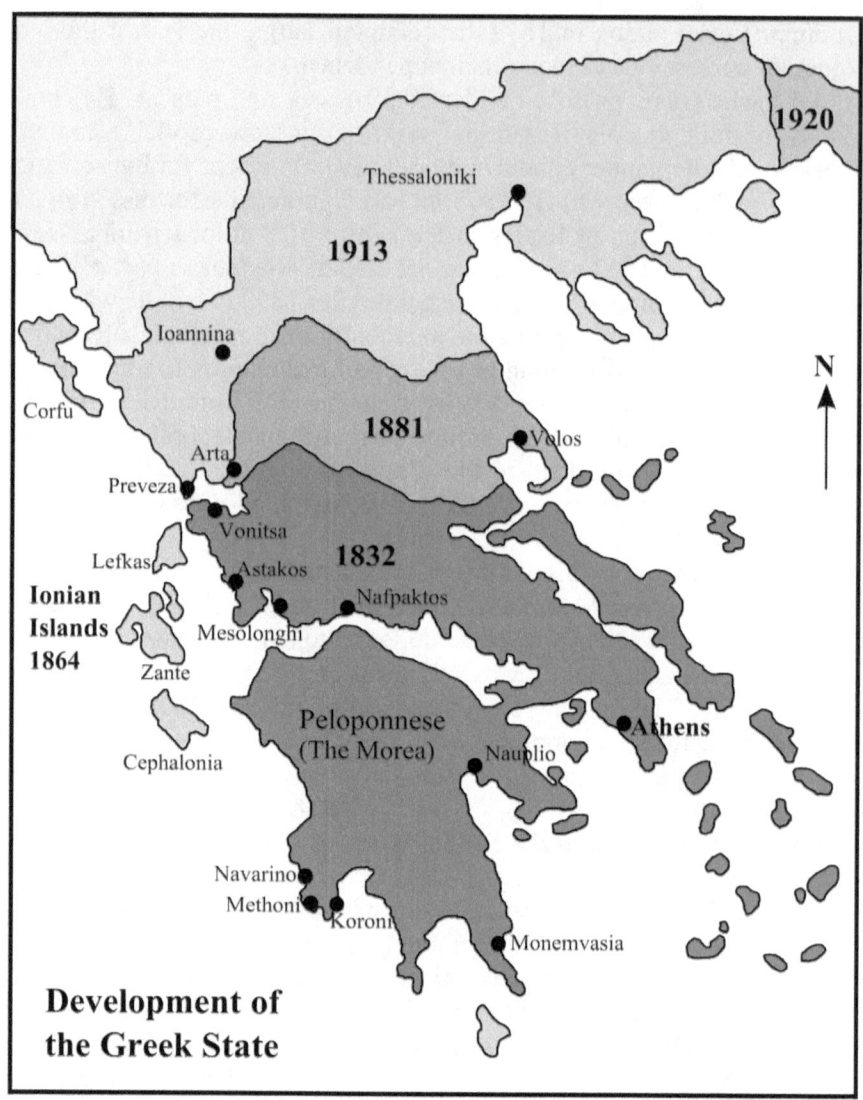

Development of the Greek State

landed troops at Methoni in the southwest of the Peloponnese and by the end of the year had regained control of most of the peninsula except for Nauplion and Monemvasia. Meanwhile the Turkish commander, Reshid Pasha, invested Mesolonghi for the third time in April 1825. The Greeks had re-built the town's walls but early in 1826 Reshid was joined by a force of Ibrahim's Egyptian troops. They entered the town in April after a mass breakout by the Greeks through the siege lines. In response to the Turkish victories the Greeks appointed Sir Richard

Introduction

Church as commander-in-chief of their land forces in April 1827. After his success at Mesolonghi Reshid Pasha had besieged Athens, and in May Church attempted to relieve the garrison that had retreated to the Acropolis. The failure of this attack led to the abandonment of Athens. The Turks were now close to complete suppression of the Greek revolt, but in July 1827 the Treaty of London formalised an agreement between Britain, France and Russia to mediate between the Greeks and Turks and if necessary intervene if an armistice could not be agreed. In October a combined fleet of the three powers confronted the Turkish fleet moored in the bay of Navarino on the southwest coast of the Peloponnese. In the ensuing battle the greater part of the Turkish fleet was destroyed. Despite this defeat Egyptian forces continued to occupy the Morea until a French expeditionary force under General Maison landed near Koroni in August 1828. Ibrahim evacuated the bulk of his troops the following month. Isolated fortress garrisons remained but they quickly surrendered to the French. The Castle of the Morea was the last to fall after a brief bombardment at the end of October. Sir Richard Church had meanwhile established a foothold on the Akarnanian coast at Dragomestre, near modern Astakos, late in 1827. By the end of 1828 he had gained control of the Gulf of Ambracia and taken the town of Vonitsa. In April 1829 he took Limnaia and Nafpaktos and finally in May his forces re-captured Mesolonghi.

The new state of Greece was formally established by the Treaty of Constantinople in 1832. The projected northern border, the Arta-Volos line, ran from the Gulf of Arta, or Ambracia, on the west coast to the Gulf of Volos on the east, although the towns of Arta and Volos themselves remained in Ottoman territory. The precise line of the frontier was established by a combined British and French survey from 1832 to 1835. It bisected the Gulf of Ambracia and passed through the straits of Preveza. The Turks reinforced their new border by building batteries and forts at Preveza and along the northern shore of the Gulf. In 1864 the Ionian Islands were ceded to Greece by Britain. Greece's borders expanded again in 1881 when, as a by-product of the Congress of Berlin, the Ottoman Empire was forced to cede Thessaly and the Arta district of Epiros. The first attempt to recover the remainder of Epiros in 1897, an event known as the Thirty Days War, resulted in a heavy Greek defeat by the Turks, the payment of substantial reparations, but only minor changes to the borders.

Sometime shortly after these events the Turks re-fortified Ioannina and it became their principal stronghold in Epiros. This was the last major work of fortification in northwest Greece. It involved the construc-

Introduction

tion of a ring of detached forts, bunkers and trenches around the town and was known to the Turks as the Yanya Fortified Area. On the 18th October 1912 a Balkan alliance of Bulgaria, Serbia, Montenegro and Greece declared war on the Ottoman Empire. In this First Balkan War the Turks were forced to fight in Thrace against the Bulgarians, against the Serbs in Macedonia, while the Greeks attacked Thessalonica from Thessaly and Ioannina from Arta. Turkish forces in Epiros retreated inside the Yanya Fortified Area. In March 1913, after two unsuccessful assaults, the Greeks broke through the Turkish lines south of Ioannina in an engagement known as the Battle of Bizani. Ioannina surrendered on the morning of the 6th March. The Greeks continued their advance into northern Epiros but in April hostilities came to an end. Greek gains were formally recognised by the Treaty of London in May 1913. This was modified by the Treaty of Bucharest in August following the brief Second Balkan War between Bulgaria and her former allies Greece and Serbia. The Ottoman Empire lost almost all its territory in Europe. Most of Epiros was re-united with the rest of northwest Greece but the decision of the European Powers to create an independent state of Albania denied the Greeks much of the area they had seized northwest of Ioannina. The northern border established in 1913 persists to this day.[15]

Notes

1. The territory of Elis occupied an area in the northwest of the Peloponnese. At its centre is the site of Olympia.
2. The term Despotate was probably first used only in the 19C. See D.M. Nicol, *The Despotate of Epiros*, p. vii.
3. Following the partition of the Byzantine Empire in 1204, Geoffrey de Villehardouin conquered the Peloponnese in 1205 with Guillame de Champlitte and created the Principality of Achaia. William was his second son and the third Prince of Achaia.
4. Cephalonia and Zante fell to the Norman, William II, in 1185 and were given by him to Margaritone of Brindisi, Grand Admiral of Sicily, as a reward for his services. Maio Orsini acquired Cephalonia and Zante by his marriage to Margaritone's daughter in 1194. His son, Maio II, married Anna, sister of Theodore, and established the first link to the Despotate. Richard Orsini was his son.
5. Although the title of Despot passed from father to son on numerous occasions throughout the history of the Despotate it was not an hereditary title and could only legitimately be conferred by a Byzan-

Introduction

tine Emperor. See D.M. Nicol, *The Despotate of Epiros*, p. 56.

6. The Byzantine Kastron was a walled city rather than a castle in the western sense and many of the extensive circuits of the Despotate reflect this distinction. At Parga and Agios Donatos the deserted ruins of the old towns still stand within their fortified circuits whilst at Ioannina the Kastro contains a modern suburb on the site of the earlier settlement.
7. The Tocco family first came to power in 1357 when Robert of Taranto granted Cephalonia and Zante to Leonardo Tocco, one of his principal retainers. In 1362 Leonardo seized Lefkas and Vonitsa. He was married to Maddalena Buondelmonti, the sister of Esau Buondelmonti. Leonardo died in 1375 leaving two infant sons, Carlo and Leonardo.
8. The Republic had first to expel the Genoese from the island and did not gain total control of Crete until 1212. See William Miller, *Latins in the Levant*, p. 48.
9. Miller, *Latins in the Levant*, p77.
10. The Venetians purchased Corfu and Butrinto from the Angevins after the death of Charles III of Anjou. The site of Butrinto is now in modern Albania. It has been extensively investigated by the Butrint Foundation and is a World Heritage site. See A. Crowson, *Venetian Butrint*.
11. Mika Hakkarainen, *Venetian Presence in Thesprotia*, p. 224.
12. Miller, *Latins in the Levant*, pp. 479-481.
13. William Miller, *The Venetian Revival in Greece, Essays on the Latin Orient*, p. 403.
14. Ali's first official post within the Ottoman administration was as *derbendler başbuğu*, chief of police of the mountain passes. See K. E. Fleming, *The Muslim Bonaparte*, p. 41.
15. Greek forces briefly re-occupied northern Epiros in 1940 when they pushed the invading Italians back into Albania. By the end of April 1941 however all of Greece was in German hands.

1

Aetolia and Akarnania

After the fall of the Byzantine Empire to the armies of the Fourth Crusade in 1204, Aetolia and Akarnania became part of the Despotate of Epiros. They remained so for two hundred and fifty years despite frequent changes in political control and the eventual fragmentation of the territory. However by 1460 almost the entire area had been conquered by the Turks. Nafpaktos, purchased by the Republic of Venice in 1407, remained independent for a few more years, finally falling to the forces of Sultan Bayezid II in 1499. The region remained part of the Ottoman Empire until 1829 when it was liberated by Greek forces under the command of Sir Richard Church.

Each period of occupation has left its mark on the surviving castles and fortifications. Venetian and Turkish influence is most evident in the south. Nafpaktos retains its Venetian walls that enclose both the town and the small harbour. A substantial Byzantine castle much modified by both the Venetians and the Turks crowns the hill above the town, the site of an ancient acropolis. Ten kilometres to the west, where the Gulf of Corinth narrows to form a strait less than two kilometres wide, Bayezid II built two forts during his campaign of 1499, the Castle of Roumeli on the north shore and the Castle of the Morea to the south. The latter was subsequently modernised by the Venetians in the period after Morosini's conquest of the Peloponnese in 1687. A further thirty kilometres to the west lies Mesolonghi, first fortified by the Venetians and famous for its role in the Greek Revolution. A little to the northwest of Mesolonghi is Aitoliko, originally Anatoliko, a small town defended in the mediaeval period primarily by its location on an island in the lagoon. Twenty kilometres to the north, Angelokastro stands on a hill above the modern village of the same name overlooking the Acheloos valley. Now much ruined, the castle was of considerable importance during the period of Angevin control and again during the division of the Despotate between the Albanians and the Serbs. Another castle on

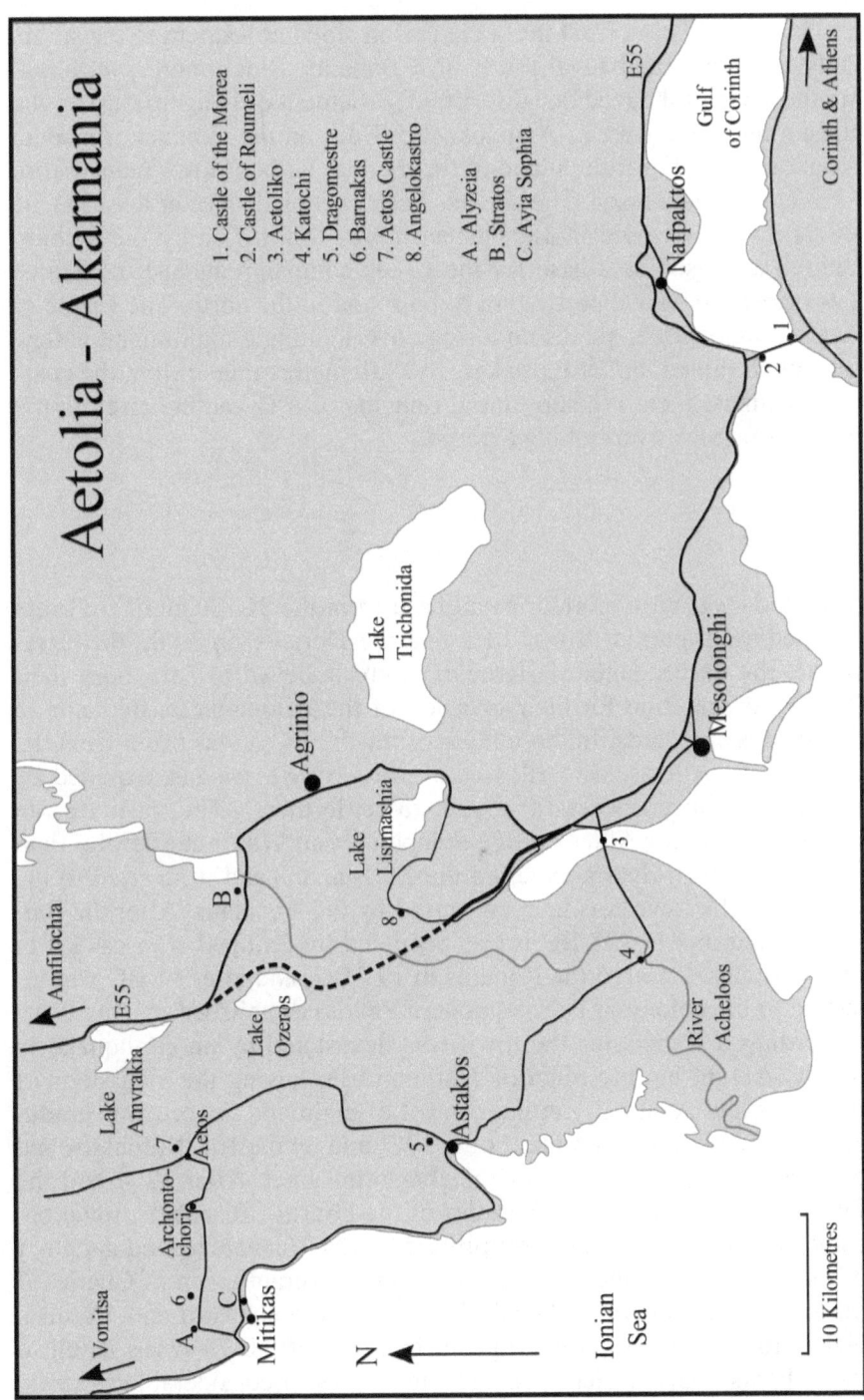

the Acheloos dating from the same period stood at Katochi to the south. Only a solitary mediaeval tower now remains. Much more substantial are the ruins of the mediaeval fortified settlement of Dragomestre on the coast almost due west of Angelokastro. Built on the remains of ancient Astakos it stands a little inland of the modern harbour town named after its ancient predecessor. The site has been occupied since at least the 5C BC and was last used in 1827 when it was re-fortified by Sir Richard Church and used as a base for the Greek campaign against the Turks. Two more mediaeval castles are to be found to the north. The Castle of Aetos, Eagle castle, stands on a ridge overlooking a high inland valley. It is much ruined, but at Barnakas, five kilometres inland from the coast near Mitikas, there are substantial remains of a Byzantine circuit on a precipitous rock overlooking a gorge.

Nafpaktos

Nafpaktos was an important naval base from the 5C BC until well into the mediaeval period. It was here that the Dorians (in myth, the Heraclidae, the descendants of Hercules) were believed to have built their ships in preparation for their invasion of the Peloponnese. Its name in fact means shipyards. In the middle of the 5C BC it was taken from the Locrians by Athens, who allowed a group of Messenians, expelled by Sparta after an unsuccessful revolt, to settle there.[1] The town was an important base for Athens in the Peloponnesian War, but after the final Athenian defeat, Sparta expelled the Messenians and it reverted to the Locrians. The town was later colonised by the Achaians. After the Battle of Chaironia in 338 BC it was occupied by Philip II who gave it to the Aetolians. It fell to the Romans in 191 BC, and after 14 BC was attached to the colony of Patrae (modern Patras) established by Augustus. According to Procopius the town was devastated by an earthquake in the 6C AD during the reign of Justinian.[2] Following the incursions of the Slavs and Avars Byzantine control of mainland Greece was gradually restored in the second half of the 9C, and by the 10C Nafpaktos had become an important port for the Byzantine fleet. After 1204 and the fall of Constantinople to the armies of the Fourth Crusade the town became part of the Despotate of Epiros. In 1294 Thamar, second daughter of the Despot Nikephoros, married Philip of Taranto, son of Charles II of Anjou. Her dowry included Nafpaktos, Angelokastro and Vonitsa. Nafpaktos remained under Angevin control until 1379 when it fell to the Albanian, Gjin Boua Spata. The town was of considerable strategic importance to the Venetians, who called it Lepanto, and in 1407 they purchased it from Paul Spata, nephew of Gjin Spata. In 1429 Patras, which had been under Venetian control for several years after 1408, fell to the forces of Constantine Palaiologos. The majority of the population fled to Nafpaktos on the opposite side of the Gulf of Corinth, which then became the centre for Venetian trade in the area.[3] When Constantinople fell to the Turks in 1453 the Venetians strengthened the defences of Lepanto and in 1477 they successfully resisted a Turkish army who nevertheless ravaged the surrounding country. However in 1499 war with the Turks broke out again. The Venetians suffered a series of naval defeats and they were unable to prevent a Turkish naval blockade. The town, known to the Turks as Inebahti, surrendered later that year.

Lepanto has also given its name to the famous naval battle fought in October 1571 between the Turks and the combined fleets of Spain, Venice and the Papacy under the command of Philip of Spain's half brother, Don Juan of Austria. This bloody engagement, famous as the last major naval battle to involve oared galleys, actually took place in the open waters of the approaches to the Gulf of Patras. The town of Nafpaktos was simply one of the Turks' supply bases, and their fleet assembled offshore before sailing out to meet the Christian forces. The Turks were decisively beaten and never recovered their naval power. The outcome of the battle was of tremendous importance to the western Christian powers as it demonstrated that, for the first time, Ottoman expansion could be halted. Venice however gained nothing from the victory. Lepanto remained in Turkish hands and the Venetians did not regain any of their lost Greek possessions. Another one hundred and sixteen years elapsed before Nafpaktos was recovered by Morosini in 1687. This occupation lasted only until 1699 when Venice was forced to restore the town to Ottoman control as part of the peace of Karlowitz. The Turks were only finally expelled by Greek forces in 1829.

Nafpaktos is built on the south and southeast slopes of a spur reaching down to the sea. As Leake first remarked, its location must have been chosen because of the natural defensive position allied with copious springs and fertile small plains to the east and west.[4] The well preserved town walls are Venetian and date from the first half of the fifteenth century with later Turkish repairs and additions. The circuit is almost complete save for a few short sections that have been demolished. Nafpaktos was as important to the Turks as a naval base as it was to the Venetians and remained so after the defeat of 1571. They continued to maintain the walls and adapted them for the use of heavy artillery. The castle, which stands on the site of the ancient acropolis, retains

Aetolia and Akarnania

many of its original Byzantine features overlain with later Venetian and Turkish work. Nafpaktos still possesses traces of the long period of Ottoman occupation with the remains of mosques, bathhouses and numerous fountains visible within the town and castle.

Town walls and the harbour defences

The Venetians acquired the town in 1407 in order to establish a secure naval base and they surrounded it with a circuit of thick walls reinforced with solid circular towers. Much of this original work is still visible although considerable sections have been modified or rebuilt by the Turks. In general the line of the walls utilises the natural contours of the hill and may follow the course of an earlier ancient circuit. The lower walls extend onto the quays enclosing the harbour and terminate in a pair of squat towers. The harbour is now the hub of Nafpaktos's social life and is surrounded by cafes and bars, but once the area was crowded with warehouses and workshops. Well into the 20C substantial two storeyed buildings stood on the west quay against the walls. The restored sea walls are the thickest of the town's fortifications and appear to include much re-used ancient material in their construction. At some

Figure 1.1 Nafpaktos: Harbour entrance and enclosing walls.

Aetolia and Akarnania

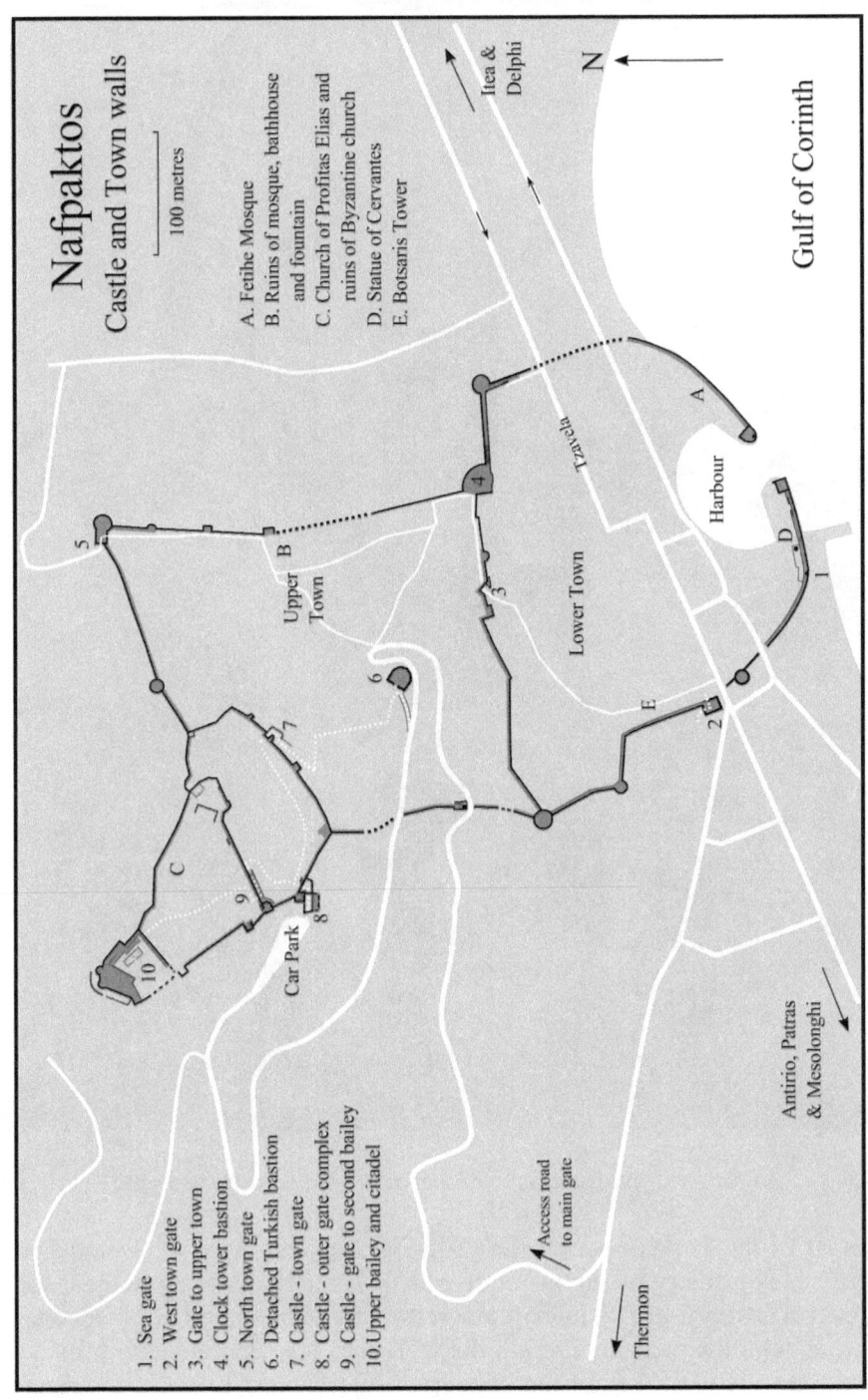

Aetolia and Akarnania

Figure 1.2 Nafpaktos: The partially blocked up sea gate.

point in the Turkish period the walls on the west quay were modified for heavy artillery by the insertion of low level gunports virtually at sea level. These are still visible although they are either partially blocked up or, as with the passage through the wall onto the concrete jetty projecting into the Gulf, have been converted into gateways. In an enclosure built against the sea wall in the southwestern corner of the harbour stands a statue of Cervantes commemorating his role in the Battle of Lepanto when his left hand was permanently damaged by a Turkish bullet. At the far end of this enclosure the original sea gate is now partly walled up. It is best viewed from the shore. A single box shaped machicolation above the gate guards the entrance. A Turkish watchtower has been added to the parapet which retains its notched crenellations. A second statue stands on the west tower at the harbour mouth. The figure represented holding a torch aloft is Giorgos Anemogiannis, killed by the Turks in 1821 after attempting to burn their fleet in the harbour. There is no evidence of artillery modifications on the walls on the east quay. Only the D-shaped tower at the harbour entrance is now crenellated. A square watchtower with a pyramidal roof is built astride its parapet. Since 1909 this has been used to house a navigation beacon. Some twenty metres to the east a flight of steps leads down from the rampart to another small gate opening seawards. In the southeastern corner of the harbour area stands the Fetihe mosque built sometime between 1499 and the death of Bayezid II in 1512. Only the base of the minaret survives but the interior has been restored.

From the quays the walls curve inland enclosing the area of the mediaeval lower town. Beyond the sea gate the western section reverts

Figure 1.3 Nafpaktos: Western harbour defences.

to its original Venetian appearance although much of the parapet is now missing. The line of the wall is broken by a modern street then continues north to a squat solid round tower with the typical Venetian external torus moulding at parapet level. North of this tower the line of the wall is broken again by the main east-west road which passes south of the west town gate housed within a large square Turkish tower. The outer entrance, now obscured by modern buildings, is set in the north flank of the tower protected by a box machicolation in the parapet above. The roof forms a gun platform with splayed artillery embrasures in the north, south and west faces. Old maps indicate that the approach to this entrance was originally across a bridge over a ditch in front of the wall. The passage within the tower makes a right-angled turn to the inner gate in the east face. This can be seen from the lane that runs inside the wall towards the white-painted Botzaris tower (Town plan, E). This heavily restored tower was once part of a fortified compound used by the Turkish governor of the town. It was acquired by the Botzaris family in the 19C and now houses the museum of the Battle of Lepanto.

The lane continues uphill northeastward to the gate in the crosswall between the upper and lower towns. Set at an oblique angle to the line of the walls this gate survives virtually complete. A Turkish fountain is built against the wall to the left of the approach. A square tower flanks

Figure 1.4 Nafpaktos: Blocked up outer entrance of west town gate.

Figure 1.5 Nafpaktos: Gate from the lower to the upper town. Above the gate is a well-preserved box machicolation.

the entrance on the west while a narrow tapering tower on the east projects across the face of the gate and conceals it from below. Another box machicolation at parapet level protects the arched opening which retains its iron studded wooden door. The gate is approximately at the mid-point of the crosswall that runs along the edge of a natural terrace in the hillside. This wall functions as a revetment to the steep slope and its southern face is therefore substantially higher than the northern side where the parapet is often close to ground level. To the west it meets the wall climbing from the west town gate at a large solid round tower. Access to this section of the walls is difficult. Through the gate the lane narrows to a paved path that continues east rising virtually to the level of the parapet. It leads past a half-round tower directly onto the platform of the clock-tower bastion. The clock tower itself is now a landmark for the town but was erected only in 1914 by the Metropolitan of Nafpaktos, Seraphim Domboetis. The bastion is a Turkish structure built directly over the original Venetian round tower that stood at the junction of the crosswall, the east wall of the upper town and the wall climbing the hill from the eastern defences of the lower town. The south face of this heavily battered round tower can still be distinguished from below. The Turks enclosed it in a much larger multangular structure as part of their modernisation of the defences for heavy artillery, although the gun

Figure 1.6 Nafpaktos: The clock tower and the Turkish multangular bastion viewed from the northeast.

Figure 1.7 Nafpaktos: Clock tower, Turkish bastion and the steeply stepped eastern section of the lower town walls.

platform itself was subsequently levelled when the clock tower was erected. They also appear to have heightened the wall to the east as the steep stairway that forms the wallwalk climbing up to the clock bastion seems to be built on top of an earlier Venetian structure. Traces of this can also be seen from below together with the remains of stairs up to the original, much lower, wallwalk. The stairway leads downhill to the round eastern corner tower of the lower town, unmodified since its construction by the Venetians but with the parapet now missing. The wall then turns south to meet the eastern quay. Approximately one hundred metres of this section, including the east town gate, have been demolished. Steps lead down from the wallwalk of the short stub of wall that survives into an alley off the main east-west road (Tzavela).

From the clock tower the eastern wall of the upper town runs north along the flank of the hill. The wall again forms a revetment to the natural slope. A paved path follows the course of the rampart for a short distance and is then interrupted for 100m by houses and gardens. The line of the walls resumes by the ruins of a Turkish complex of religious buildings known as a Külliye (Town plan, B). Built for Amcazade Köprülü Hüseyin Pasha, Grand Vizier of the Ottoman Empire from

1697 to 1702, the main surviving structure is the sunken bathhouse or hamam.[5] A short flight of steps leads down into a courtyard below ground level lined with stone seats. A gated door opens into the domed chambers of the bathhouse itself. The interior is not accessible but its size can be gauged from the tiled domes protruding from the roof. Nearby are the fragmentary remains of the Vezir mosque faced in cloissoné masonry, a Byzantine technique borrowed by the Turks. A few metres to the north a Turkish fountain house, sunk slightly below modern ground level, probably marks the position of the spring that supplied the network of fountains built throughout the upper and lower towns.[6]

North of the Külliye a paved street now runs along the inside of the wall at parapet level. Three solid towers, two square and one multangular, protect the wall in this section. These may pre-date the Venetian fortifications. There are traces of a low outer wall and ditch below the main wall. The surviving section has a parapet provided with square tapering loopholes and is probably Turkish. However the massive circular tower that marks the northeast corner of the town circuit is undoubtedly Venetian 15C work. A relief of the lion of St. Mark is set high up in the wall on the eastern side of the tower. The niche below that would have

Figure 1.8 Nafpaktos: Interior face of the Turkish north town gate with the original Venetian circular tower on the right.

Figure 1.9 Nafpaktos: Lion of St. Mark with the date of 1470 below.

Figure 1.10 Nafpaktos: Exterior view of the Turkish north town gate built against the original Venetian round tower.

housed an inscription is now empty but the date of 1470 can still be discerned below the lion. The western half of the Venetian tower is partly masked by the square Turkish gatehouse built against it to the west. This is the north gate of the town and it appears to be contemporary with the west gate of the lower town described above. The cobbled road makes a right-angled turn through the domed interior of the gatehouse which still bears traces of painted decoration. The parapets of both the gatehouse and the Venetian tower have been largely destroyed. From this point the north wall of the upper town climbs steeply uphill to meet the outer walls of the castle. A single round tower reinforces this section. Its parapet has tall thin merlons pierced by loopholes. A round watchtower has been inserted between two of the merlons.

The west wall of the upper town can be inspected from the access road to the main castle entrance which loops up the hillside cutting through the line of the wall in two places. The road makes the first lower breach by a thin rectangular tower surmounted by a square turret, or watchtower, with a pyramidal roof. A stairway gives access to the surviving wallwalk and to the interior of the turret. The road loops back to the west below an isolated Turkish polygonal artillery bastion built to command the harbour and slopes below. The construction is of alternating bands of red bricks and heavily mortared roughly squared blocks imitating the style of early Byzantine work. The walls support a solid

Figure 1.11 Nafpaktos: The detached Turkish bastion.

Figure 1.12 Nafpaktos: Rectangular tower with pyramid roofed turret in the western wall of the upper town.

gun platform with embrasures positioned to give a one hundred and eighty degree field of fire to the south. Access to the platform is via a ramp at the rear. A path climbs from this point behind the bastion through the trees that now cover the hillside to the well preserved but locked gate between the upper town and the castle (see below). Beyond the detached bastion the road cuts through the wall for a second time before making a final loop to the car park by the main gate of the castle.

The Castle

Standing before the main gate the mediaeval origins of the castle and its subsequent modifications are immediately evident. The original vertical walls and solid square towers that revet the western flank of the hill above the car park show the traces of numerous repairs and modifications. The parapets have probably been rebuilt several times and are now almost certainly entirely Turkish reconstructions. The most obvious addition is the massive Venetian talus which reinforces long sections of the wall. It appears to have been built to stabilise the hillside and provide a degree of earthquake protection.[7] The partial failure of these reinforcements can be seen on the western side of the upper bailey where the foundations have collapsed and the wall now lies at the base of the hill in massive fragments of heavily mortared masonry.

This side of the castle and the exterior of the citadel can be best seen from the dirt track that forks left from the access road 100m before the car park and climbs to the north. Although the castle hill is separated from the mountain beyond by a deep valley on its north side, it narrows to a shallow ravine below the northeastern tip of the upper bailey. This is the only section of the circuit overlooked by higher ground. With the development of field artillery it became the castle's weakest point and there is evidence of successive attempts to improve its defences. The late Turkish citadel that now occupies the northern part of the upper bailey has obliterated the mediaeval works internally but the exterior of the two prominent round towers that originally formed the core of the defences can still be seen from below. A path leads from the dirt track to the base of the towers. From here it is still possible to distinguish the line of the original parapet, now filled in, beneath the Turkish work. It appears to have been in two levels, with arched tapering openings, now blocked up, below an upper wallwalk and crenellated parapet. This arrangement is repeated in the northwest square tower (Castle plan, E), where again the original openings have been blocked up. Intact examples of these features can be seen in two of the towers to the north of the main gate (Castle plan, A, C). Between the west round tower and tower E the Turks constructed a massive artillery emplacement on the flat roof of the citadel as a final attempt to overcome the inherent weakness of the position. Below the round towers and the adjacent section of wall the remains of a lower outwork, designed to protect the base of the main wall, can still be seen. Sections of its crenellated parapet survive. Immediately south of tower E the adjacent wall has clearly been re-built to the west of its original line as it now masks the south flank of the tower

Figure 1.13 Nafpaktos: The massive round towers that formed the original citadel or keep of the mediaeval castle.

Figure 1.14 Nafpaktos Castle: The western defences from the outer courtyard of the main gate complex.

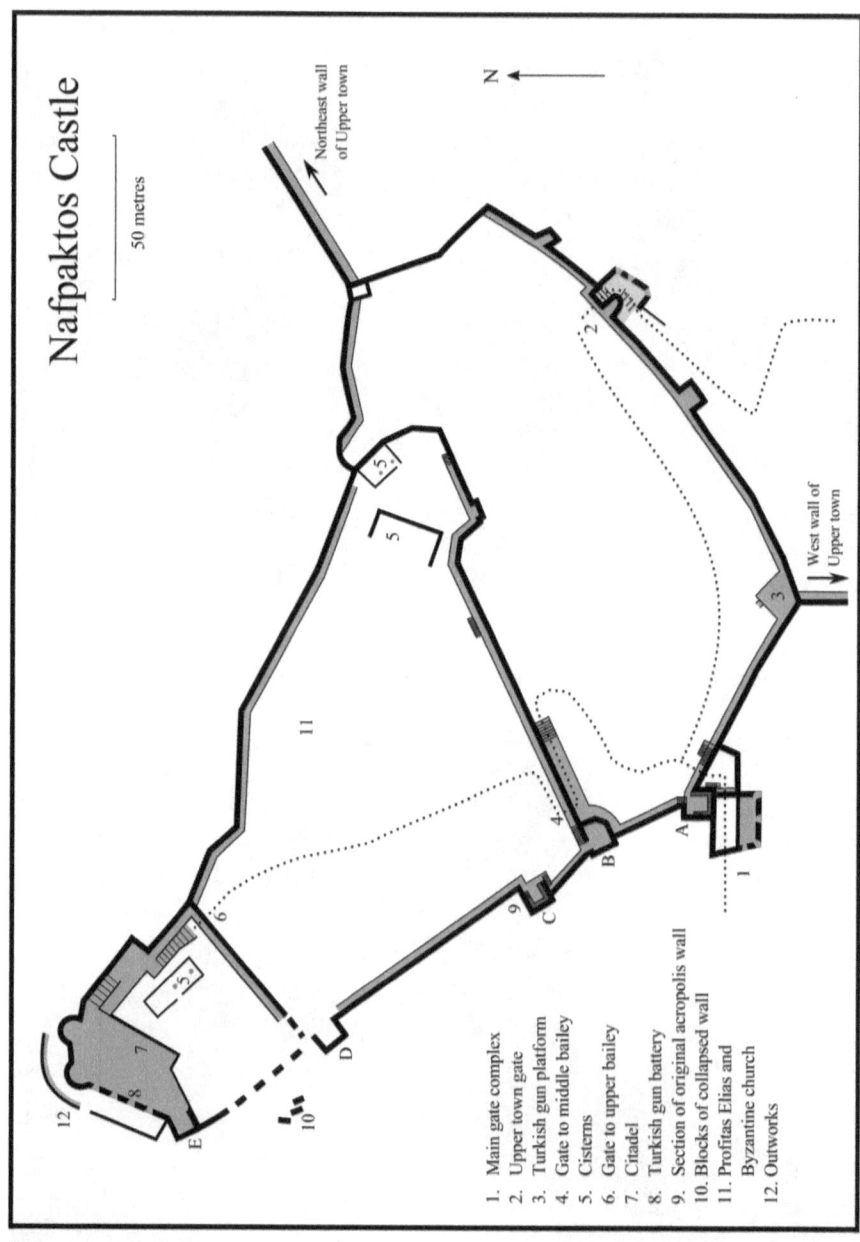

Nafpaktos Castle

1. Main gate complex
2. Upper town gate
3. Turkish gun platform
4. Gate to middle bailey
5. Cisterns
6. Gate to upper bailey
7. Citadel
8. Turkish gun battery
9. Section of original acropolis wall
10. Blocks of collapsed wall
11. Profitas Elias and Byzantine church
12. Outworks

and is not bonded to it. Although reinforced by a massive talus this rebuilding has itself failed and two thirds of the wall as far as tower D have collapsed. Just to the north of tower C it is also possible to see the best preserved section of the early, possibly Hellenistic, acropolis wall.

Aetolia and Akarnania

Figure 1.15 Nafpaktos Castle: Interior of the second gate of the entrance complex with the outer gate beyond.

The main entrance to the castle is through a complex of three gates and two outer courtyards built against the sloping talus of the great square tower standing above the modern car park. The tower projects so boldly from the line of the wall that it is almost freestanding. This small area of the circuit seems to include elements from every period of the castle's existence. The base of the tower incorporates in situ ancient blocks. Its mediaeval vertical walls were subsequently encased in a Venetian talus while the outer courtyards and gates appear to be late Turkish additions. The first gate leads through a thin plain wall into a quadrangular court. The southern half of the enclosure forms a low gun platform with four splayed embrasures facing south and west. The second gate opens through a more substantial wall abutting the tower. Above the gate the parapet is equipped with tapered loopholes facing the interior of the outer gate. A stairway curving around the base of the tower gives access to the walkway over the arched opening. On the south side of the gate an arched and tapered gunport at ground level covers the approach. The third gate is set in the main circuit wall of the outer bailey. Above the gate's flattened outer arch are the stone brackets that supported a box machicolation. The inner arch is triangular and supports the wallwalk above. Access to the parapet is via steps on the

Figure 1.16 Nafpaktos Castle: Interior of the third gate.

Figure 1.17 Nafpaktos Castle: Double parapet of tower A.

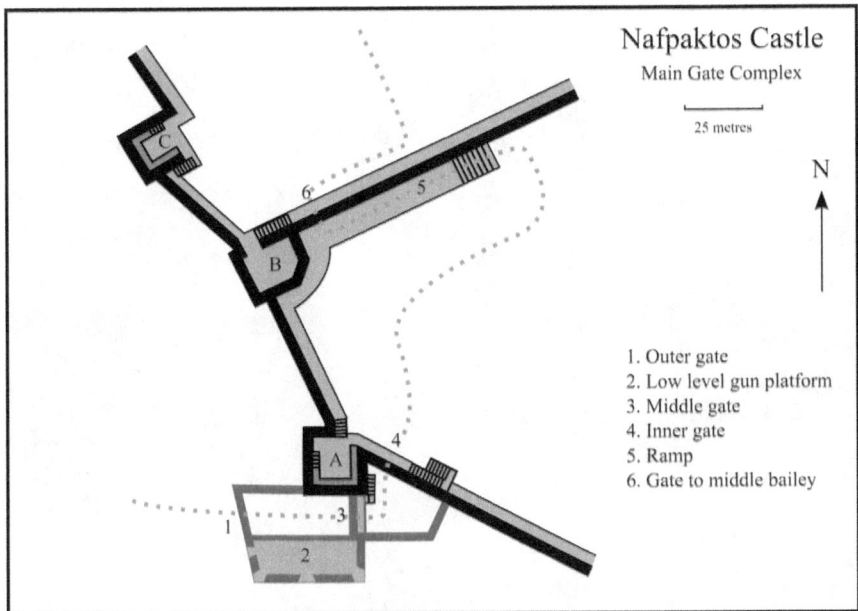

Nafpaktos Castle
Main Gate Complex

25 metres

1. Outer gate
2. Low level gun platform
3. Middle gate
4. Inner gate
5. Ramp
6. Gate to middle bailey

eastern side of the gate. The stepped wallwalk leads in turn to tower A where the intact double parapet can be seen (Fig. 1.17). The upper level consists of a walkway protected by a thin crenellated parapet with small loopholes in each merlon. Below, the three projecting faces of the tower are each pierced by a tapering vaulted gunport. From the tower steps climb to the next section of wallwalk which runs beneath tower B to the top of the ramp leading up to the middle bailey gate.

To the east of the main gate the outer bailey wall runs downhill to a ruined Turkish gun platform built to command the line of the western town wall that meets the castle circuit at this point. The curtain then leads northeast for one hundred metres to the gate from the upper town Again the walls of this section form a revetment to the hillside with the parapet almost at ground level on the inner side. A single square tower provides the only reinforcement. Both wall and tower have been strengthened with a later talus. The approach to the gate from the upper town runs beneath this tower to the rear of a gun platform built across the face of the entrance and provided with three gun embrasures. The gate itself, currently barred and locked, is a plain arch protected by a jog in the line of the wall to the northeast and a narrow, almost triangular, tower to the southwest. The original squared corners of the tower are now covered by a rounded Venetian talus. The joint between the vertical walls and the talus is clearly visible from above. A crudely built

Figure 1.18 Nafpaktos Castle: The upper town gate.

domed sentry box, corbelled out from the wall, has been inserted in the parapet between two merlons on the outer face of the tower. The modifications to this entrance seem to have followed the same phases as the main gate complex above. The solid, narrow mediaeval tower was first reinforced by a Venetian talus at some point in the 15C followed by the later addition of a Turkish artillery platform on a massive terrace built out in front of the gate. To the northeast of the gate the curtain wall is interrupted by a vertical outcrop of rock which has been used to support a small square tower built at a skew to the wall alignment. Twenty metres beyond the tower the wall turns northwest to meet the east town wall at a square tower. To the east there are views downhill of the north wall of the upper town circuit. Finally the curtain, ruinous in this section, runs due west and climbs the hill to meet the wall of the middle

Figure 1.19 Nafpaktos Castle: The upper town gate set between the tower on the left and the jog in the curtain wall on the right.

Figure 1.20 Nafpaktos Castle: Western curtain - view of towers A and B from the parapet of tower C.

bailey. The gate into the middle bailey is approached by a ramp flanked by tower B. The gate's external arch consists of four finely cut ashlared blocks and may be the original opening. The gateway passes beneath the wallwalk but the nearest stairway giving access is some fifty metres to the east. Access to tower B is via a stairway from the wallwalk. The parapet of this tower is largely destroyed. The walkway continues to tower C where another set of steps leads to the platform below the tower's double parapet. This was originally identical in arrangement to tower A. Here the lower vaulted gunports and the upper walkway remain, but the upper parapet has largely disappeared. This tower is built on the foundations of its Hellenistic predecessor. Ancient blocks can be seen in the lower courses of both the inner east face and from below, where both the northern flank and the adjacent stretch of wall stand on ancient foundations (Castle plan, 9).

East of the middle bailey gate the plain wall, built without towers, is well preserved. Its eastern extremity encircles a broad terrace built out

Figure 1.21 Nafpaktos Castle: Gate to middle bailey.

over the slope of the hill. Although this position has the appearance of an artillery platform there are no embrasures in the parapet which is built with simple thin merlons. Both this terrace and another at a higher level to the north contain subterranean water cisterns. The circuit wall then runs northwest towards the upper bailey gate. Near the highest point of the middle bailey stands the church of Prophitas Ilias. This was originally the mosque of Baba Tsaous built in the 17C but converted into an Orthodox church in the 19C. The truncated minaret is still visible. Alongside the church is a Byzantine building in cloissoné masonry tentatively identified as a bathhouse. Foundations of an earlier Byzantine church with the remains of mosaic pavements can also be seen.

The upper bailey is the final redoubt of the fortifications. The enclosure is formed by a crenellated cross-wall and is entered by a simple gate with an ashlared arch on the outer face and a brick arch on the inner. On the northwest side of the bailey the irregularly shaped citadel itself consists of a single massive block, now heavily restored, incorporating and completely masking the pre-existing towers. Although the exterior is built in rough masonry, it has been carefully embellished with brick striations across the full width of the wall and a brick string-course incorporating two dogtooth layers at parapet level. Two brick-arched doors lead into the vaulted interior (not currently accessible).

Figure 1.22 Nafpaktos Castle: The cross wall of the upper bailey.

Aetolia and Akarnania

Figure 1.23 Nafpaktos Castle: the Turkish citadel.

The roof formed one large gun platform, but apart from the splayed embrasures in the parapet, little of the original defensive work survives. The truncated inner faces of the earlier walls protrude slightly above the restored platform and are now protected by clear modern panels. Access for artillery was via the broad ramps from the gate onto the roof. This is all Turkish work and represents the final attempt to overcome the weakness of this section of the circuit where the walls are dominated by higher ground to the north.

Although the general history of the fortifications of Nafpaktos can be described there are difficulties with dating almost every element with any precision. The fragments of Hellenistic work that survive on the western side of the castle indicate that the Byzantine walls were built on the remains of that first circuit which may have lain in ruins since the earthquake in the 6C. Rebuilding probably first occurred in the 10C. Each subsequent re-modelling of the walls of course conceals or obliterates the remains of the preceding phase. Evidence of repairs and reconstruction is evident in many parts of the circuit where sections of wall are not bonded together. The Venetian work includes surprisingly little provision for artillery. By the end of 15C the Venetians were building powerful artillery positions at Nauplion[8] but in Nafpaktos provision for guns seems to have been limited to embrasures in the parapets of the round towers reinforcing the town defences. This would indicate that the majority of the Venetian work was built no later than 1470, the date inscribed on the northeast tower of the town walls. It was left to the Turks after 1499 to bring the fortifications up to date with the addition of new bastions at strategic points. The brief Venetian re-occupation from 1687 to 1699 seems to have added nothing.

The town walls can be explored at any time although access is difficult in sections. The castle can be reached on foot from the harbour area but it is more convenient to drive to the car park by the main gate. The asphalt road to the car park meets the Thermon road some 500m from the west town gate. The castle is open during daylight hours.

Castle of Roumeli, Antirio

Although virtually the whole of the Peloponnese was in Turkish hands by 1461 the Venetians continued to hold their coastal fortresses of Methoni and Koroni in Messenia, Nauplion in the Argolid and Lepanto, their base on the northern shore of the Gulf of Corinth. However in 1499 the Turks crushed the Venetian navy at Sapienza off the southwest coast. This allowed them to blockade Lepanto (Nafpaktos) by sea and land and it fell the same year. Sultan Bayezid II promptly built the two artillery forts known as the Castle of the Morea and the Castle of Roumeli in order to control the entrance to the Gulf of Corinth at the narrows between Rio and Antirio. The original structures were reputedly built in a period of just three months. Despite their command of the channel the forts were not immune to attack and they fell in 1532 to the forces of Andrea Doria, the Genoese Admiral of the Holy Roman Emperor, Charles V. Doria had begun his campaign that year by capturing Koroni from the Turks.[9] He had then sailed on to sack Patras before attacking the Castles of the Morea and Roumeli. The former capitulated but the garrison at Roumeli blew up the fort and themselves.[10] This Turkish setback was short-lived and within a year they had recovered their fortresses. In 1603 the area was attacked by the Knights of Malta who briefly captured Patras and Nafpaktos and caused substantial damage to the Castle of Roumeli.[11] Finally in 1687 Venetian forces under Morosini, having occupied almost the whole of the Peloponnese, took the castles of Morea and Roumeli from the retreating Turks along with Patras and Nafpaktos. Once again the garrison of Roumeli attempted to

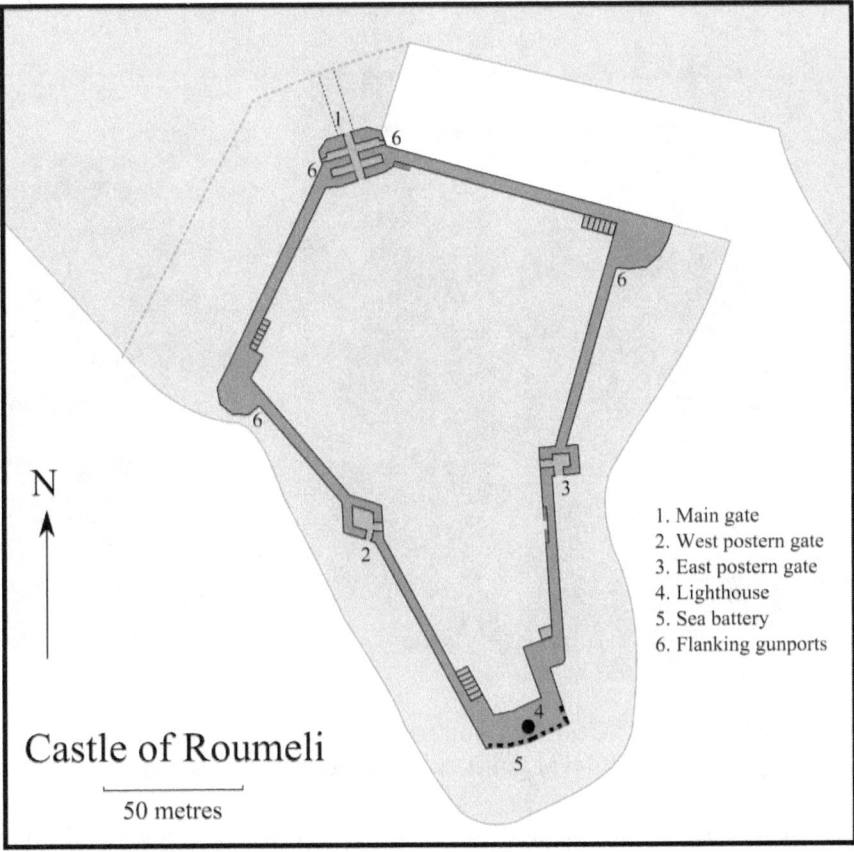

Castle of Roumeli

1. Main gate
2. West postern gate
3. East postern gate
4. Lighthouse
5. Sea battery
6. Flanking gunports

destroy the fort by blowing up the seaward ramparts.[12] The Treaty of Karlowitz in 1699 brought the war between Venice and the Turks to an end. Venetian possession of the Morea was confirmed but at the cost of Turkish retention of their territories north of the Gulf of Corinth. Venice was required to give up Roumeli along with Nafpaktos. Although the treaty stipulated that the castle of Roumeli was to be demolished the Turks ignored this requirement and had refortified the place by 1715.[13] It remained in Turkish hands until 1829.

The fort consists of a single enclosure, roughly kite-shaped in outline, built on a sandy spit projecting into the Gulf and now overshadowed by the massive Rio-Antirio road bridge. The circuit wall is reinforced with irregular bastions and originally was accessible only by a bridge over a moat on its northern side. The western half of the moat has been long filled in to provide loading areas for the vehicle ferries that until recently provided the only means of crossing the Gulf.

Figure 1.24 Castle of Roumeli: North bastion and main gate. The low-level gunport is visible in the west flank.

The surviving eastern section of the moat is now used as a small boat harbour. The sea probably once washed much of the circuit but it is now possible to walk around the foreshore to inspect the exterior of the walls. The northern point of the fort is protected by an irregular hexagonal bastion that functions as the main gatehouse. Its interior consists of a central straight entrance passage into the fort with two vaulted chambers, or casemates, on either side. The outer pair of chambers each has a single ground level gunport in the flank of the bastion designed to enfilade the adjoining curtain. The northeast and northwest angles of the circuit are reinforced by casemated polygonal demi-bastions. Again each bastion is equipped with a single flanking gunport at ground level. South of the west demi-bastion the circuit is reinforced by a single diamond shaped tower forming a triangular projection in the line of the wall. An arched postern gate is built into its southern flank. On the opposite side of the circuit a square bastion reinforces the long east wall. This too has a postern gate in its southern flank. The southern end of the circuit is dominated by the large irregular bastion designed to house the

Aetolia and Akarnania

Figure 1.25 Castle of Roumeli: View of the southwest of the circuit. The west postern gate can be seen in the middle distance. In the background is the western demi-bastion with its single gunport.

Figure 1.26 Castle of Roumeli: View from the southeast. The square bastion in the centre, the east demi-bastion in the background.

Figure 1.27 Castle of Roumeli: The seaward bastion and battery with restored parapet and lighthouse.

fort's main gun batteries commanding the seaway to the south. Vaulted casemates within contained six guns facing south through arched ports. A further two gunports face west and two more east. A second tier of artillery could be mounted on the broad platform above. The parapet, with its narrow embrasures facing south, has been restored. The platform now supports a lighthouse nine metres in height and built in 1880. A keeper's cottage originally stood alongside. Elsewhere around the circuit the parapet is almost completely destroyed save for the section above the main gate.

The interior of the fort is now completely bare. Writing in 1816, towards the end of the period of Turkish occupation, Pouqueville described the fort as being divided into two enclosures and crowded with ruined buildings and temporary huts.[14] A long period of use by the Greek army has obliterated all traces of internal structures. As recently as 2006 the fort was littered with abandoned military vehicles. Two large breaches in the wall had been made to provide access for heavy equipment. This damage has now been repaired, the walls have been consolidated and the casemates within the bastions have been restored. Three ramps supported on arches and two stairways lead up onto the ramparts. Part of the interior face of the gatehouse bastion also stands

Figure 1.28 Castle of Roumeli: The restored casemates of the sea bastion, the lighthouse and artillery ramp.

Figure 1.29 Castle of Roumeli: Interior view - the north bastion with the main gate to the right and the arches supporting the inner part of the northwest bastion to the left.

on arches, as does the inner part of the northwest demi-bastion. The interiors of the two bastions provided with postern gates are accessible.

The castle is usually described as Turkish with subsequent Venetian re-building but structurally there is nothing in the fortifications that can be identified specifically as Venetian. There is no element of the building style at Roumeli that matches any phase of the Castle of the Morea. There is some resemblance between the seaward batteries of the two forts, but the gunports in the face of the bastion at Roumeli are smaller and cruder than their counterparts on the southern shore. The work at Roumeli may be late Turkish in conscious imitation of the Venetian battery opposite. It is probable that during their brief tenure of twelve years the Venetians did little more than patch up the destruction wrought by the fleeing Turks. Certainly the Venetian improvements to the Castle of the Morea had only just begun in 1701 and were not listed as complete until 1714.[15] The continuous narrow string course below the parapet at Roumeli gives an architectural unity to the fort and probably indicates that the surviving structure reflects the re-building that must have occurred during the final period of Turkish occupation after 1700.

The castle can be reached from the main coast road from Nafpaktos, the E55, by following signs for the Antirio ferries. Opening times are the conventional 8.00 to 15.00, closed on Mondays.

Castle of the Morea, Rio

The artillery fortress known as the Castle of the Morea stands on a small promontory on the Peloponnesian shore of the Gulf of Corinth directly opposite the Castle of Roumeli. This complex structure consists of two distinct forts built two hundred years apart. The first is the triangular work with round towers built in 1499 by Bayezid II as the counterpart of the Castle of Roumeli. Its history closely follows that of Roumeli, being attacked by Andrea Doria in 1532 and falling to the Venetians in 1687. Twelve years later the Treaty of Karlowitz between the Holy League and the Ottoman Empire confirmed the Venetian conquest of the Peloponnese but restored Nafpaktos and Roumeli to the Turks. This made the Castle of the Morea of even greater strategic importance and the Venetian response was to embark on a modernisation programme that effectively enclosed the original triangular work in a new bastioned fort with extensive water defences. However the Venetian efforts were in vain. In 1715 the Turks re-conquered the Peloponnese in just three months and the newly extended Castle of the Morea fell after

Figure 1.30 Castle of the Morea: The southwest bastion and the south face of the fort.

only a five-day siege. It remained in Turkish hands until October 30th 1828 when, having refused to capitulate as the other fortresses in the Morea had done following the Battle of Navarino, it succumbed after a three week siege by combined English and French forces. The castle remained in Greek military use and was occupied by German forces during WWII. Its final role as a prison ended in the 1980s since when it has been partially restored and the walls consolidated.

The Turkish fort of 1499 stands on a gravel spit projecting into the Gulf. The main sea batteries were housed in a complex of three round towers at the northern tip of a triangular enclosure reinforced by further round towers in its southern face. The towers all project boldly from the trace of the walls providing virtually complete flanking cover. The fort was separated from the mainland by a moat running across the spit. When first built the sea must have reached the walls on all sides but by 1700 a plan of the fort drawn for Francesco Grimani, Venetian Proveditore or military commander of the Morea from 1699 to 1701, shows that the spit had advanced some two hundred metres to the north.[16] The same plan shows the moat as a relatively narrow ditch partially silted up. The Venetians modernised the defences between 1708 and 1714 by effectively building a new fort around the walls of the original. The southeast and southwest corners of the circuit were enclosed in new angle bastions. Ravelins within broad water defences were added to the south and west and the extension of the spit to the north was enclosed within massive walls with a new battery at the seaward end. The extent of the Venetian works can be best appreciated from the road that runs around the outside of the site fence. The southern bastions and ravelin were designed to completely mask the south face of the Turkish fort. While the parapet of the southeast bastion is now almost entirely destroyed, over half of the embrasures in the parapet of the southwest bastion survive. Similarly, although the southern ravelin is much ruined, its western counterpart stands virtually complete, surrounded by water, and with its parapet and gun embrasures intact. The northwest curtain is in a more ruinous state but the low level gun embrasures and gate in the sea battery can still be seen. With the exception of a short section on the west, the 18C water defences remain in place. However all trace of the covered way and sloping glacis that ran around the perimeter of the moat has disappeared.[17]

The fort is now reached by a modern bridge at the extreme eastern end of the moat. The Venetian entrance route, which still exists, first crosses an arched bridge to the western flank of the southern ravelin. It then runs along a terrace to the rear of the ravelin to a second bridge on

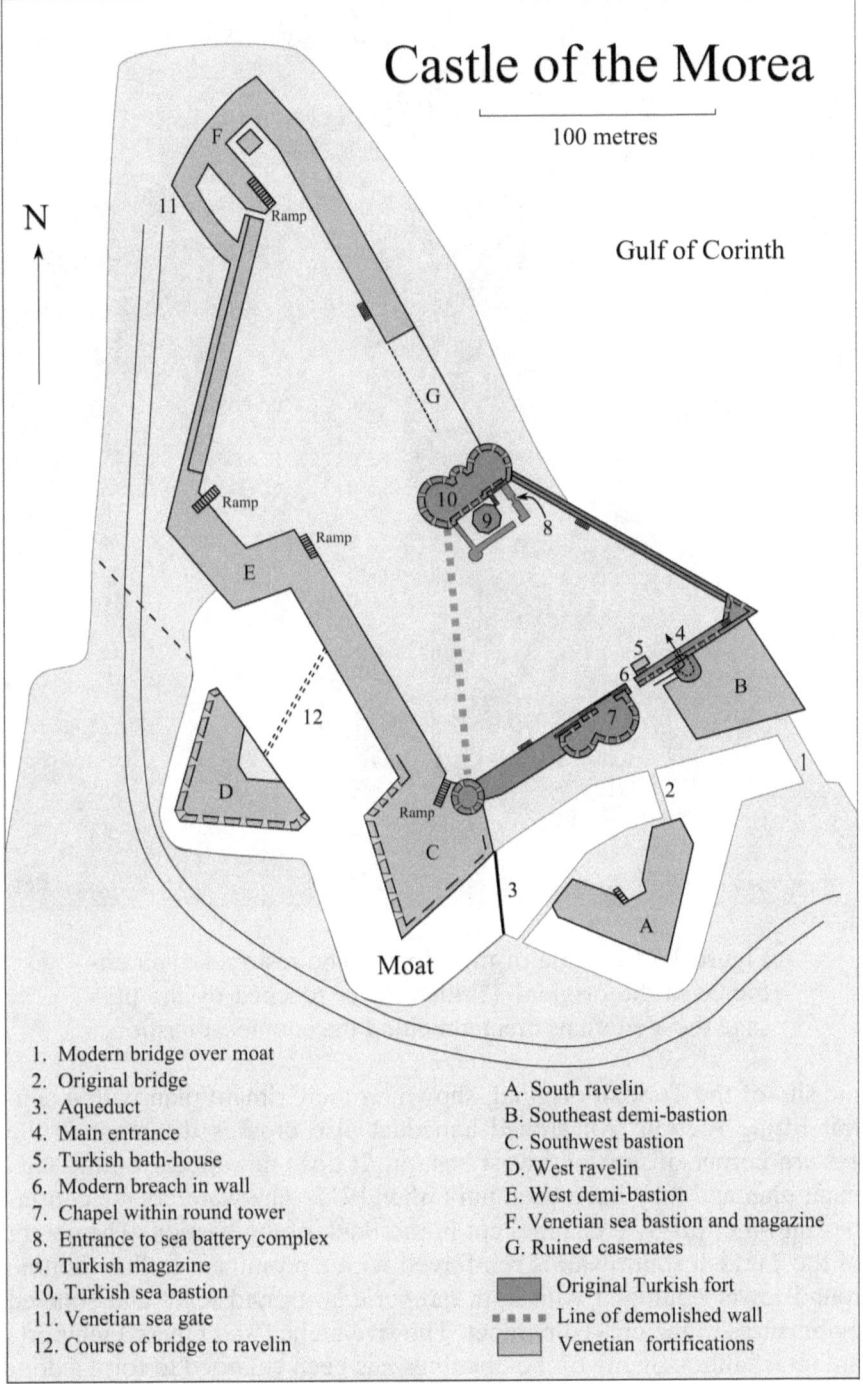

Figure 1.31 Castle of the Morea: The restored main entrance in the original Turkish tower reached by the passage the Venetians created behind the southeast bastion.

the site of the Turkish original, shown on the Grimani plan with a central lifting section. An arched aqueduct also crosses the moat to the eastern corner of the southwest bastion. It does not appear on the Grimani plan and may have been built after 1715. The watercourse continues into the fort by a channel cut in the flank of the bastion. The centre of the Turkish south wall is reinforced with a prominent hollow double round tower equipped with both gunports at ground level and splayed embrasures in the curved parapet. The five arched and tapered gunports are intact although one of the openings has been enlarged to form a door

Figure 1.32 Castle of the Morea: The Turkish double towers. In the foreground the arched bridge leading to the southern ravelin.

giving external access to the church created within the larger eastern tower sometime after 1828. The carefully rounded profile of the towers' parapets is well preserved. Simon Pepper describes the towers of the Turkish fort as "developed examples of smoothed-off, shot deflecting curved surfaces that are only rivalled in my experience by the turn of the century Spanish castle at Salses, or in King Henry VIII's English south coast defences dating from the 1540s".[18] Although a modern breach in the wall to the east of the double tower was used as an entrance until recently, the original Turkish gate has now been restored and brought back into use. It consists of a vaulted L-shaped passage within a projecting half round tower. When the Venetians enclosed this tower within their new southeast bastion they reduced its height and created a corridor at the rear of the bastion to allow continued access to the original gate, presumably for reasons of economy.

Within the interior the Grimani plan shows a range of buildings along each of the three sides of the Turkish fort. No traces of these remain and the west wall of the triangle itself has vanished. It may have been demolished by the Venetians although Leake, writing in 1805, refers ambiguously to a fortress having two enclosures, the interior work

Figure 1.33 Castle of the Morea: Interior of the southern walls and double tower. To the left, the main gate passage. In the foreground the domed Turkish bathhouse.

overlooking the outer.[19] A twin-domed bathhouse built against the inner face of the south wall is the only surviving Turkish structure. Behind the bathhouse are stairs to the wallwalk. The Venetians blocked up the tall crenellations of this section of the wall when the southeast bastion was built. This bastion also partly masks the Turkish triangular corner tower. This is the only tower of the original fort that does not project beyond the line of the walls and its principal purpose seems to have been to command the interior. Its inner face is equipped with an embrasure in the parapet and steeply inclined loopholes for musketry. Steps lead from the south wallwalk to the tower's gun platform. An internal staircase gives access to the eastern wallwalk via an arched doorway from an inner chamber. Before the southern wall was breached its wallwalk provided a continuous line of communication between the southeast and southwest towers. It also provided access to the roof of the central round towers via three independent stairways. The interior face of these towers is now crowned with a belfry built when the church was created within. The roof forms one continuous gun platform with gun embrasures in the parapet placed to provide an all-round field of fire including the interior of the fort. Between the embrasures the

Figure 1.34 Castle of the Morea: The southeast triangular tower with angled loopholes aimed at the base of the tower.

Figure 1.35 Castle of the Morea: The Turkish southwest round tower and ramp to the southwest Venetian bastion.

parapet is pierced by narrow musketry loops. To the west of the double tower the wall widens to form another broad firing platform. Here however little of the parapet remains. The round southwest tower originally projected boldly from the line of the walls although it is now surrounded by later Venetian structures. Its rounded parapet is equipped with six equally spaced gun embrasures that again provide an all-round field of fire. Access to the gun platform was via an internal stair. The tower is now almost entirely enveloped by the Venetian southwest bastion. A stepped ramp gives access to the bastion's platform where the sloping parapet is partially preserved. Arched openings on either side of the ramp appear to open into cisterns. Some confused fragments of masonry on the northern side of the tower are all that remains of the demolished Turkish west wall.

The relatively thin east wall of the fort connects the southeast tower with the Turkish sea battery. Like the double tower to the south, the massive triple towers that form the apex of the triangular circuit are equipped with ground level gunports and embrasures in the parapet. The rear face of the tower complex is flattened to form one side of a quadrangular court built around an octagonal powder magazine. Only the lower courses of the other three walls survive but these show that the enclosure was reinforced with a projecting polygonal tower at its southwest corner. There is a modern breach in the southern wall but the original arched entrance survives on the eastern side. The threshold of the entrance is now below modern ground level. Inside the triple towers massive brick domes support the gun platform above. The walls below the springing of the domes are over five metres thick and are pierced by brick vaulted casemates with stone arched gunport openings at their outer ends. The external arches of these flared ports are variously half round, pointed, or in the case of the smaller central tower, parabolic. With the creation of the larger Venetian circuit to the northwest they ceased to have a function and the gunports in the eastern tower that remained outside the new northeast wall were blocked up. To the east of the powder magazine an L-shaped external stairway leads up to the gun platform through an opening in the parapet. The partial remains of another flight of steps are visible to the west of the magazine. The massive parapet is furnished with alternating embrasures and narrow musketry slits and is another example of ballistic shaping designed to deflect shot from its curved surfaces.

To the north and west of the Turkish fort the Venetian circuit is essentially complete. It has been partially restored although sections remain in ruins and it still bears the marks of its last role as a prison.

Figure 1.36 Castle of the Morea: The triple tower with its curved parapet, sloping embrasures and gunports at ground level.

Figure 1.37 Castle of the Morea: Rear of the triple tower, the octagonal magazine and the remains of the surrounding wall. The entrance to the enclosure is visible to the right.

North of the triple towers a long section of the eastern rampart has been partly destroyed but the ruins reveal the general method of Venetian construction. Both the inner and outer faces of the ramparts are of irregular courses of roughly shaped masonry. The outer face is supported at intervals by internal buttresses. The casemated interior is formed from heavily mortared rubble and brick vaulting springing from ground level. The vaults support a fill of earth forming the terreplein behind the parapet. Beyond the ruined section the northeast ramparts remained in use throughout the twentieth century and the terreplein was covered with a concrete platform now disguised by stone tiles laid during the recent restoration. The brick arched entrances to the casemates have also been restored but the parapet has vanished.

The sea bastion at the northern tip of the circuit is E-shaped in plan with casemates in each arm. The shape seems to indicate that the bastion was built in two phases. The original outer rampart became the central arm of the present structure when an extension with a sea gate was built to the southwest. A corridor was cut through the old rampart to give access to the new enclosure and the gate. The joint between the two sections is marked on the outer face of the bastion by an abrupt change in the height of the semi-circular stringcourse or cordon. This marks the base of the parapet. The cordon is lower on the new section as this was built with a two level parapet with a row of narrow musketry slits below the main artillery embrasures. The few fragments of the upper parapet that survive show that this too was built with a curved shot-deflecting profile. Like its Turkish predecessor the Venetian sea battery was equipped with arched gunports at ground level. The first phase was built with four ports facing northwest towards the entrance to the narrows. When the second phase was added three more gunports were created facing northwest while the new southwest flank was equipped with a further five ports enfilading the long western rampart. All of these later gunports are now walled up. The tunnel vaulted sea gate can still be seen although the outer facing has been lost. These features are hardly visible internally as a modern concrete roof now covers all three arms of the bastion and the western section remains unrestored. However the Venetian powder magazine between the centre and eastern arms of the bastion remains intact. Its thick square walls and brick barrel vault support a solid, pyramidal protective roof.

Apart from the parapet itself, the outer wall of the western rampart from the sea bastion south to the west demi-bastion appears intact from the exterior of the fort. However internally the terreplein and its supporting structures have been demolished leaving only a few courses

Figure 1.38 Castle of the Morea: The Venetian sea battery. The first phase of the work is to the left with its gunports intact. The second phase with its double rampart and walled-up gunports lies to the right of the step in the cordon.

indicating the position of the inner wall. The remains are further confused by the bases of six structures of unknown date and function projecting at right angles to the rampart. The west demi-bastion remains intact although the terreplein is overgrown and the parapet is missing. The masonry parapet was destroyed in the Anglo-French siege of 1828. Nothing remains of the earthwork replacement constructed by French engineers.[20] The broad rampart between the west demi-bastion and the southwest bastion houses twelve casemates. They have been heavily restored and the terreplein is again covered with a concrete platform recently covered by stone tiles. No trace of the parapet survives. From the platform there are good views of the western ravelin standing almost complete within its water defences. A causeway, or bridge, led from the body of the fort to an arched doorway in the wall closing off the rear of the ravelin. The course of the causeway is visible as a line of debris below the surface of the water. The route from the causeway into the fort

Figure 1.39 Castle of the Morea: The Venetian sea-bastion viewed from the pedestrian walkway of the Rio-Antirio bridge.

Figure 1.40 Castle of the Morea: The Venetian powder magazine and the restored arched casemate entrances in the sea bastion.

Figure 1.41 Castle of the Morea: The western ravelin.

is no longer visible. The isolation of the ravelin may account for its excellent state of preservation. The sloping parapet is pierced by tapered musketry slits between widely spaced brick-faced embrasures.

Although built at the same time as its counterpart at Roumeli, the Turkish version of the Castle of the Morea with its curved shot deflecting parapets is a much more sophisticated artillery fortification. The dating of all phases of the fortifications is also much more certain. The Grimani plan drawn around 1700 shows the original triangular Turkish fort much as it stands today. The detailed description of the completed Venetian works given by Augustino Sagredo in November 1714 corresponds closely with the surviving works and an inscription over the sea gate, visible in 1828 but now destroyed, recorded a date of 1713.[21]

The Castle of the Morea is logically part of the group of fortifications that includes Roumeli and Nafpaktos even though it stands on the opposite shore of the Gulf of Corinth in Achaia. Access to the southern shore of the Gulf from Nafpaktos is possible either by the new bridge or by the ferries that continue to cross the narrows. By road the entrance to the castle is easily found by following signs for the Rio ferry. Superb views of the site can be gained from the eastern pedestrian walkway of the new bridge. Access is via a stairway a little to the west of the castle. The site is open every day except Monday from 8.00 to 15.00.

Mesolonghi

Mesolonghi is the modern capital of the nome, or prefecture, of Aetolia-Akarnania. It stands on a promontory that extends south into the shallow waters of the lagoons that form the coastline. About 500m of its walls remain standing. The town is famous throughout Greece for the events of the Greek Revolution and for its connection with Byron who died there in 1824. It emerged from obscurity some time in the 16C when the whole of Greece was in Ottoman hands, developing as a fishing and trading community. In 1684 it was one of the first mainland towns to fall to the Venetians after Morosini's invasion from Corfu and successful siege of Santa Maura.[22] A brief period of Venetian control followed during which the first walls may have been built. The entire area north of the Gulf of Corinth was returned to the Turks after the Treaty of Karlowitz and Mesolonghi was back in their hands by 1700. In 1770 the native Greeks managed to expel the Turks temporarily from the town during the period of Russian interference in Greek affairs known as the Orloff Revolt, but this was quickly reversed.[23]

Mesolonghi and Anatoliko were the first places in northwest Greece to join the revolution in the summer of 1821. The Turks did not attempt to retake the area until November 1822. Blaquire described Mesolonghi's fortifications as they existed at that date as follows. "Its fortifications consisted of nothing more than a low wall without bastions and surrounded by a ditch seven feet wide by four in depth and filled up with rubbish in many places. The parapet which did not rise more than three feet above the counterscarp was formed of loose stones very much out of repair."[24] Nevertheless the Greeks were able to use these primitive defences to resist the Turkish siege and in January 1823 their complete rout of a Turkish assault caused the siege to be abandoned for the winter. A second Ottoman attempt to invest Mesolonghi in October 1823 began with a bombardment of neighbouring Anatoliko. Again in December the siege was abandoned. Byron arrived in the town at the beginning of 1824. By April of the same year he was dead. Although he had contributed to the organisation of the defence of the town his principal achievement was to become a symbol for the Greeks. His heart is reputed to be buried here.

When the Turks returned in force in April 1825 the walls had been rebuilt and the ditch cleared. The fortifications by then consisted of an earth rampart over two kilometres long stretched across the promontory from northwest to southeast. The rampart had an outer stone face, a ditch and, according to Thomas Gordon, a second outer ditch beyond

Aetolia and Akarnania

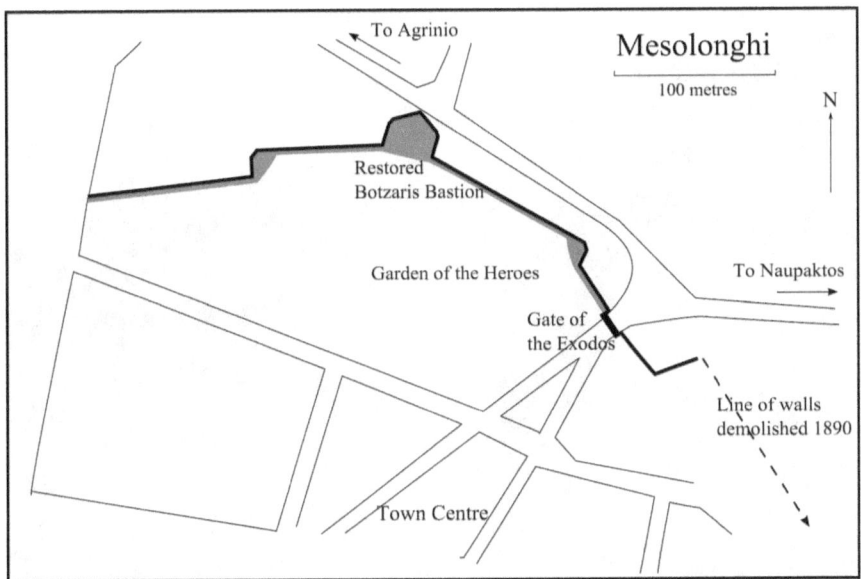

the counterscarp.[25] The walls were reinforced by two bastions in the centre; the Franklin to the west; the Botzaris to the east. A battery on the islet of Marmaro in the lagoon 200m from the shore protected the western end of the ramparts. For the remainder of 1825 these defences allowed the Greek forces to resist the attacks of the Turks under their commander, Reshid Pasha. However towards the end of the year he was joined by Egyptian troops commanded by Ibrahim Pasha. As well as investing the town by land, the combined forces also attacked by sea and by March 1826 they had gained control of the lagoon cutting off the Greeks' supply route. In April the population of the town decided that their only hope was to force a mass breakout through the lines of the besiegers. On the night of the 22nd April breaches were cut through the walls and bridges were built across the ditch to provide an escape route. Nine thousand people forced their way through the Turkish lines. The Turks however had prior intelligence that an escape was being planned and as a precaution had positioned troops on the roads beyond the town. The majority of the escapees were cut down in the ensuing ambush. Fifteen hundred survivors eventually reached Salona, modern Amphissa, days later. The few Greeks who had stayed behind in Mesolonghi fired the magazines when the Turks entered the town. Just three years later Greek forces under the command of Sir Richard Church advanced from the north. The Turks surrendered Mesolonghi on the 17th May 1829 without resistance. One month later Church himself entered the town. In

Figure 1.42 Mesolonghi: The town gate.

Figure 1.43 Mesolonghi: Restored Botzaris Bastion.

1836 a Greek rebellion against the Bavarian led government of King Otho attempted to seize Mesolonghi, but the defences were apparently sufficiently intact to resist the attack.[26] King Otho rebuilt the walls in 1838. In 1890 the construction of the Kryoneri to Agrinio railway line led to the demolition of the entire eastern section to accommodate the infrastructure for the station.[27]

The fortifications visible today represent merely part of the walls rebuilt by King Otho. They probably bear little relation to the defences of the siege which must have resembled hastily dug field works with sections being continually destroyed and rebuilt. By the end of the siege and the exodus the town and its defences were completely ruinous. The restored section consists of the town gate, sometimes known as the Gate of the Sortie, or Gate of the Exodus, a short overgrown section to the east and a 400m long length of wall to the west with a projecting bastion at its centre on the site of the original Botzaris bastion. The walls now appear a mere three to four metres high as all traces of the external ditch have disappeared. All that remains of the Franklin bastion is a low earth mound, surmounted by a single symbolic cannon, standing a little to the southwest of the present western end of the wall. Even the shoreline of 1826 has disappeared as more of the lagoon has been reclaimed and the modern town has expanded. Just within the walls is the Garden of the Heroes containing numerous monuments to the defenders of the sieges including a statue of Byron. His heart is said to be buried beneath it. The main road from Nafpaktos now bypasses the town.

Anatoliko and Katochi

Mediaeval Anatoliko, now the modern town of Aitoliko, is ten kilometres to the north of Mesolonghi and built on a low island in the shallow lagoon. Its first mention in the history of the Despotate of Epiros occurs at the beginning of the 14C when Maria, wife of John Orsini and sister of the Despot Thomas, is recorded owning vineyards in the area.[28] Around 1406 it was attacked and occupied by Carlo Tocco. The Venetians acquired Nafpaktos in 1407 and after a period of dispute concerning the border between the territories of Anatoliko and Nafpaktos, an agreement was reached that confirmed Carlo's possession of Anatoliko's fortified tower while the Venetians retained control of the valuable fisheries of the area.[29] During the Greek Revolution the town's fortunes followed those of Mesolonghi. In 1823 its defences consisted of nothing more than a primitive earthwork battery and in 1826 it fell to

Figure 1.44 Katochi: The mediaeval tower.

the Turks just five weeks before the catastrophe at Mesolonghi. The town was not connected to the mainland until the middle of the 19C when long stone arched bridges to the east and west were built. Its position must always have been one of natural strength as even by sea it was only approachable by small flat-bottomed boats. No traces of the 19C defences remain. The mediaeval tower too has vanished but at Katochi, twelve kilometres away on the west bank of the Acheloos River, a tower that may date from the same period can still be seen. Katochi was in Angevin hands by the end of the 13C following the marriage of

Thamar, second daughter of the Despot Nikephoros, to Philip of Taranto. By 1408 the area had been conquered by Carlo Tocco and he granted control of Katochi to Dimo Boua, his Albanian ally.[30] The tower clearly continued in use throughout the Turkish occupation as its appearance in 1838, just four years after the creation of the Greek state, is described by William Mure in detail. "It was, in fact, the only remnant of the ancient Turkish splendour of the place, and, situated on the crown of the eminence, with the remains of an exterior coat of whitewash, had a striking effect in the general landscape. It had formerly been the pyrgo, or castle, of some Turkish governor or great man, a class of edifice between a tower and a cottage, with a square substruction of stone, beyond which projected two upper stories, composed chiefly of wood and plaster, so as to have something the appearance, at a distance, of the body of a large windmill without sails. The upper portion of its exterior was also relieved by wooden balconies or parapets."[31] The tower stands in the centre of the modern village on a low knoll overlooking the river Acheloos. The present structure is two storeys in height and is much repaired and rebuilt. Whether the tower is the sole surviving structure of a castle is unknown. No trace remains of an enclosure although the surrounding street plan may imply that one once existed. Approaching Katochi from the Acheloos bridge the tower is clearly visible to the right above the village.

Angelokastro

The castle of Angelokastro, twenty kilometres to the north of Aitoliko, was an important feudal stronghold throughout the mediaeval period changing hands many times during the history of the Despotate of Epiros. It is supposedly named after the family of Michael II Comnenus Angelos Doukas, the third ruler of the territory, and from about 1250 the first to be known by the title of Despot.[32] His son, Nikephoros I, succeeded him in 1267 and Angelokastro formed part of the dowry of his daughter, Thamar, on her marriage to Philip of Taranto, son of Charles II of Anjou. Angevin control lasted until 1338 when the Byzantine Emperor Andronikos III regained the greater part of the Despotate. The reunification of Epiros with the rump of the Byzantine Empire lasted only ten years. By 1348 the Serbs under Stephen Dušan had conquered Epiros and Thessaly. Serbian control was briefly interrupted after the death of Stephen Dušan but by the end of 1359 his half-brother, Symeon Uroš, had retaken Epiros. However in 1366 he was forced to

Aetolia and Akarnania

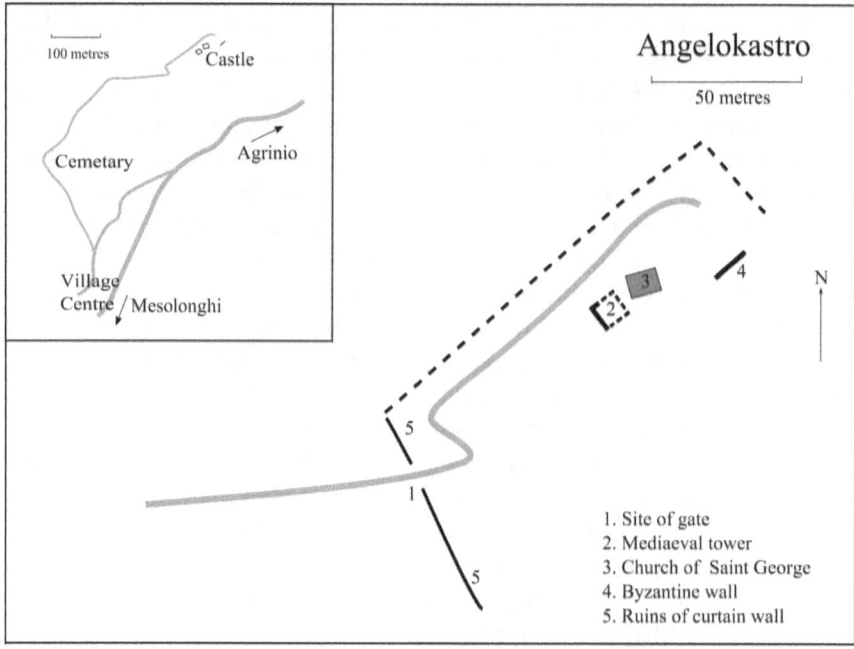

Angelokastro

1. Site of gate
2. Mediaeval tower
3. Church of Saint George
4. Byzantine wall
5. Ruins of curtain wall

recognise the reality of Albanian incursions into southern Epiros when he granted Angelokastro to Gjin Boua Spata with the title of Despot of the district of Acheloos. Spata was killed in 1399 opposing an invasion by Carlo Tocco and Angelokastro passed to his brother, Sgouros Spata. The castle was again attacked unsuccessfully by Carlo in 1402 but by 1408 it was in his hands. It remained a possession of the Tocco family until 1460 when it was one of the last places to fall to the Turks. Thereafter it remained a Turkish administrative centre well into the 16C.

Despite its impressive history the only fragments of the mediaeval castle that survive are the ruins of a large tower, an adjacent stretch of wall and traces of the curtain. They stand on the summit of the steep hill that once formed the acropolis of ancient Konope overlooking the broad plain of the Acheloos to the west and north and the modern village of Angelokastro to the south.[33] Woodhouse describes seeing slight remains of Konope on the plain at the foot of the hill to the north in 1893 but nothing is visible now.[34] His description of the mediaeval structures closely matches the state of the castle today and it has clearly been a complete ruin for over one hundred and twenty years. The exception is the Byzantine church of Agios Georgios standing in the shadow of the tower. This too was ruinous in 1893 but has now been restored. Its lower courses consist entirely of re-used ancient blocks. The asphalt

Figure 1.45 Angelokastro: The tower from the south.

Figure 1.46 Angelokastro: The surviving wall section.

Figure 1.47 Angelokastro: The church of Agios Georgios.

road that leads from the village to the church follows the only practicable route to the summit and cuts through the line of the curtain wall, possibly on the site of the original gate. Although overgrown, the rubble core of this wall survives on either side of the road. The line of the wall to the northwest can also be identified but to the east and south no trace seems to have survived. Only the southwest wall of the tower stands intact. It reaches a height of ten metres but the other sides exist only as foundations. The castle can be found by following signs in the village for Agios Georgios.

Dragomestre and Astakos

Astakos stands at the head of a deep bay on the Akarnanian coast. The bay, which is partially sheltered by the northern Echinades islands at its mouth, seems to have functioned as an anchorage and harbour throughout the mediaeval period and it was probably the west coast port for the inland centres of Aetos and Angelokastro. In fact a harbour may have existed here from as early as the 5C BC.[35] The present town and harbour developed only in the second half of the 19C. All that existed on

Aetolia and Akarnania

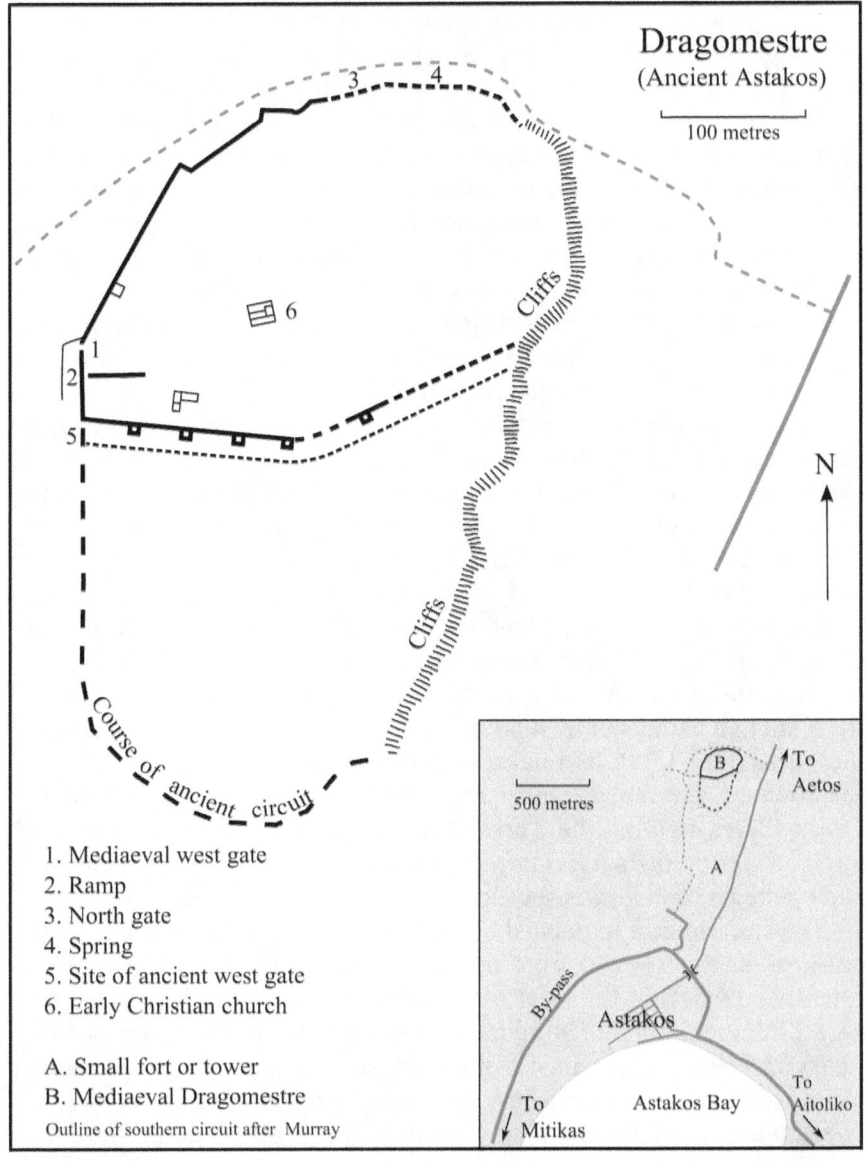

Dragomestre
(Ancient Astakos)

1. Mediaeval west gate
2. Ramp
3. North gate
4. Spring
5. Site of ancient west gate
6. Early Christian church

A. Small fort or tower
B. Mediaeval Dragomestre

Outline of southern circuit after Murray

the shoreline in 1809 when Leake visited the area was a rough mole, or breakwater, and some warehouses.[36] The concrete quays of modern Astakos have brought the present shoreline further south and have obliterated all traces of an earlier harbour. Both the ancient city of Astakos and its mediaeval successor Dragomestre[37] are to be found one and a half kilometres inland on a flat-topped hill on the western side of the valley that runs north from the head of the bay. Although the hill slopes gently to the south and is separated from the mountain to the west only by a low saddle, to the north and east it is surrounded by cliffs, and it forms an obvious defensible position. The valley below provides one of the few relatively large areas of agricultural land in Akarnania. It extends inland a further six kilometres to the north of Dragomestre and until the construction of the modern coast road it was the major route into the interior. The city wall of ancient Astakos encircles the hill and forms a rough oval approximately 500m by 300m. The mediaeval builders of the fortified settlement of Dragomestre re-used the northern half of the ancient circuit by building a crosswall from east to west reducing the defended area by about one half.

Dragomestre is first mentioned in the 1220s as one of the ten bishoprics of the see of Nafpaktos. Its history during the existence of the Despotate closely follows that of Angelokastro and it may date from the same period. It saw successive periods of Angevin, Byzantine, Serbian, Albanian and Italian control before finally falling into Turkish hands around 1460. The long period of Ottoman occupation was briefly interrupted in 1684 when the Venetians gained control of the Akarnanian coast from Santa Maura south to Mesolonghi. The following year Morosini used Dragomestre as the assembly point for his fleet before the Venetian campaign to subdue the Morea.[38] Dragomestre reverted to the Turks after 1700. Its final role in Greek history came in 1827 when Sir Richard Church, recently appointed Commander-in-Chief of the Greek forces fighting the Turks, landed with a force of one thousand men, converted the surviving mediaeval ruins into an entrenched camp and created a base for his subsequent operations in northwest Greece.[39]

The site can be approached either from the south via a track from the outskirts of the town or from the Aetos road to the east. The southern route passes first to the west of a ruined tower, or small fort, standing on a prominent knoll. The remains may be those of the tower seen by Leake in 1809.[40] They consist of a confused mixture of squared ancient blocks and later rough masonry. As there is no direct line of sight between the city and the harbour, a tower in this position would have provided a signalling point both in antiquity and in the mediaeval period. After a further 500m the track passes the southern half of the original city walls of ancient Astakos now very badly preserved. Little is visible beneath the dense cover of scrub vegetation although eleven towers were identified by Murray in this section of the circuit. He also identified the position of the ancient west gate.[41] North of this sector the line of walls running from east to west across the crest of the hill represents

Figure 1.48 Dragomestre: The west tower of the mediaeval crosswall.

the southern face of the mediaeval enclosure. Four of its square reinforcing towers, much ruined, are still visible. The wall and towers are built of roughly cut irregular blocks with tile and brick fragments in the joints and re-used ancient blocks reinforcing the corners. Some 10m south of the mediaeval work the course of a second wall can be traced as a line of massive foundation blocks. They appear to run parallel to the mediaeval wall for its full length and may be all that survives of a cross wall that divided the city of ancient Astakos into two parts. The use of a crosswall dividing the interior space is a common feature of the ancient cities of Akarnania.[42] It is not clear why the mediaeval builders did not re-use these foundations unless the intention was to create a double line of defences at this point. From the western end of the crosswall the mediaeval circuit runs north and is built upon the remnants of the ancient walls. This southwest corner is the best-preserved section of the mediaeval circuit although the ruins are overgrown and confused. A new west gate was constructed in this period some fifty metres north of the crosswall. The approach ramp can still be traced although little else remains. The wall to the south of the gate stands on five or six courses of ancient blocks. Within the circuit a heavy interior wall runs eastward 30m north of the crosswall. This may have formed part of an inner enclosure. Further east again stand the ruins of an early

Figure 1.49 Dragomestre: Southwest section of the mediaeval circuit. Here the re-used ancient wall stands to five courses.

Figure 1.50 Dragomestre: Early Christian church.

Figure 1.51 Dragomestre: View of the circuit above the northern cliffs. The mediaeval wall stands on ancient foundations built on the carefully levelled cliff edge.

Christian church with three aisles and a large central brick-arched apse. This first church must have fallen into disuse at some point as built within its ruined walls is a second simple rectangular church with three arched niches at its eastern end. The northern part of the circuit runs along the top of a line of cliffs above a narrow side valley. The surviving sections, with the mediaeval walls standing on ancient foundations, can be seen from the track below. A second gate stood in the centre of this northern sector and continued in use into the mediaeval period. Access to the gate from below was provided by a ramp cut into the face of the cliff. Only the lower part survives, the upper section now having split away from the rock; the massive blocks lie at the base of the cliff. The gate provided access to a spring below, still visible, which appears to have been the city's main water supply.[43] The cliffs, up to twenty metres high, continue along the full length of the eastern side of the circuit. No trace of walls can now be seen in this area. The temporary fieldworks of Sir Richard Church have also long disappeared.

To approach the site by the southern track, take the bypass northwards from the harbour. Two hundred metres beyond the point where the bypass crosses the Aetos road, a side-road (signpost: Kastro) leads towards a new housing development on the hillside. After 300m a dirt road on the right leads in fifteen minutes on foot to the unenclosed site.

Castle of Aetos

Before the construction of the coast road in the 1960s, the old route north from Astakos ran inland past the site of Dragomestre. It turned east at Vasilopoulo where it crossed a low pass into a major north-south valley that runs north to Bambini and Aetos and eventually gives access to the southern coast of the Ambracian Gulf. A modern road still follows this line. The village of Aetos sits astride the road on the western side of a broad valley where another route to the west leads over a pass to Archontochori and the Mytikas plain. The Castle of Aetos, Eagle castle in Greek, occupies the summit of a steep hill on the opposite side of the valley and must have been sited to control these natural routes through inland Akarnania as well as the agricultural area of the valley itself. Like Dragomestre, Aetos was a bishopric of the see of Nafpaktos in the 1220s. Although the date of the castle's foundation is unknown

Figure 1.52 Aetos Castle: North flanking tower.

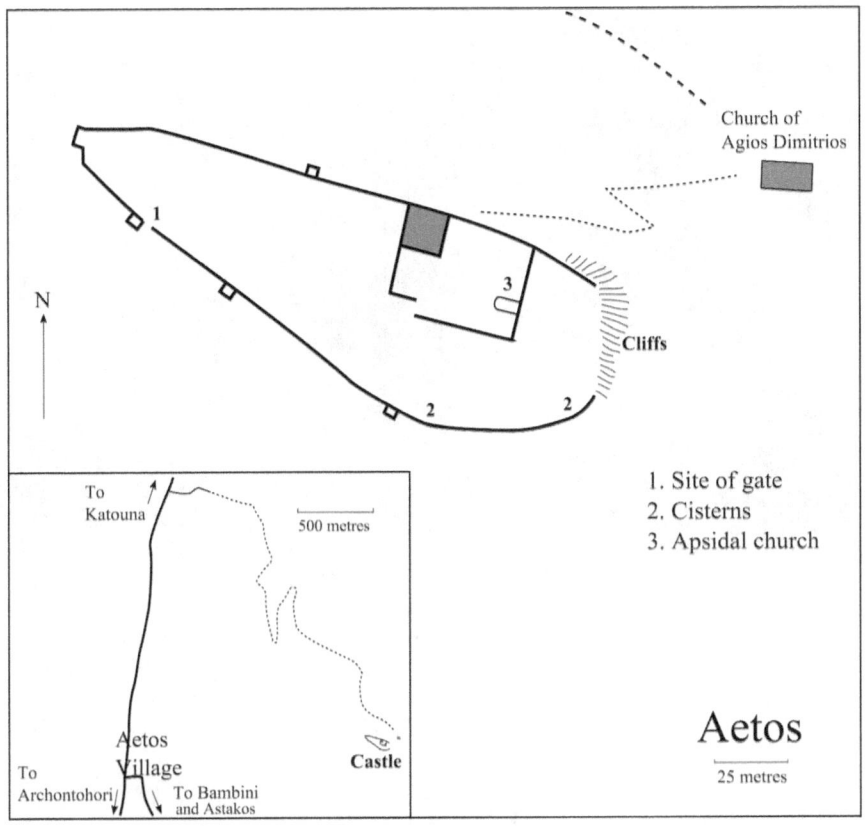

1. Site of gate
2. Cisterns
3. Apsidal church

Aetos

its history mirrors that of Angelokastro and Dragomestre. In 1330, during the period of Angevin control, Philip of Taranto proclaimed John Kabasilas Count of Aetos. Carlo Tocco seized the castle in 1402 and appointed his third son, Menuno, Lord of Aetos in 1416. After the Turkish conquest it disappears into obscurity.

The castle hill stands 40m above the saddle that separates it from the main ridge to the northeast. To the southwest the hill rises precipitously 200m above the main valley floor. Cliffs form the hill's short eastern face. The castle had no ancient predecessor on the site and has an almost Frankish appearance with a layout that corresponds to the conventional elements of outer bailey, inner bailey and keep. The outer curtain revets and encircles the hill and, although much ruined, it can be traced for its full length with the exception of the eastern cliffs where a wall may have been unnecessary. The area enclosed is roughly 200m by 40m. The walls were reinforced with projecting square towers. The best preserved example is the single tower facing north. At the western tip

Figure 1.53 Aetos Castle: The southeast hollow tower.

Figure 1.54 Aetos Castle: The western open tower.

of the hill the north and south walls come together at an open faced tower. A rectangular inner enclosure surrounds the highest part of the hill. A large square tower resembling a keep but now almost completely obscured by trees and scrub vegetation stands in the northwest corner of this enclosure against the outer curtain wall. Against the inner enclosure's eastern wall the foundations of an apsidal church survive. The castle entrance seems to have been situated at the southwestern end of the circuit where there are vestiges of a ramp leading to a gate flanked by another square tower. Two further towers reinforce the southern defences. That to the east is hollow and beyond it a series of cisterns excavated in the side of the hill on the inner face of the curtain wall seems to have provided the castle's water supply.

Approaching Aetos from the direction of Archontohori the castle hill is clearly visible due east on the opposite side of the valley. To reach the site drive north through Aetos village. After 1.5km turn right onto an unsigned tarmac road leading east. This quickly becomes a drivable dirt track that climbs the hillside and leads south down the eastern side of the valley for two kilometres to the church of Agios Dimitrios built on the saddle connecting the castle hill to the main ridge. An indistinct path from the church leads up to the outer walls. There is easy access to the interior through numerous gaps in the circuit.

Castle of Barnakas

The broad plain of Mytikas, thirty kilometres north of Astakos, was dominated in antiquity by the city of Alyzeia which had a harbour on the coast a little to the west of the modern village of Mytikas.[44] Like Astakos, ancient Alyzeia was built some distance inland and the remains of its extensive walls, which may date from as early as the 5C BC, still stand three kilometres from the coast on the northwest edge of the plain. The modern village of Kandila is built over the southwest section of the circuit. The city was probably abandoned after the founding of Nikopolis in 30 BC. Although Alyzeia's inland position must have offered a degree of security the location is not one of natural strength. When the Castle of Barnakas was constructed, possibly as early as the 7C, a new site was chosen two kilometres to the east high above a narrow gorge that enters the plain at this point.[45] Also known as the Castle of Glosses, the fortifications guard the easiest inland route north. Before the construction of the coast road the Mytikas plain was only accessible from the east by a pass leading from Aetos via Archontochori or from

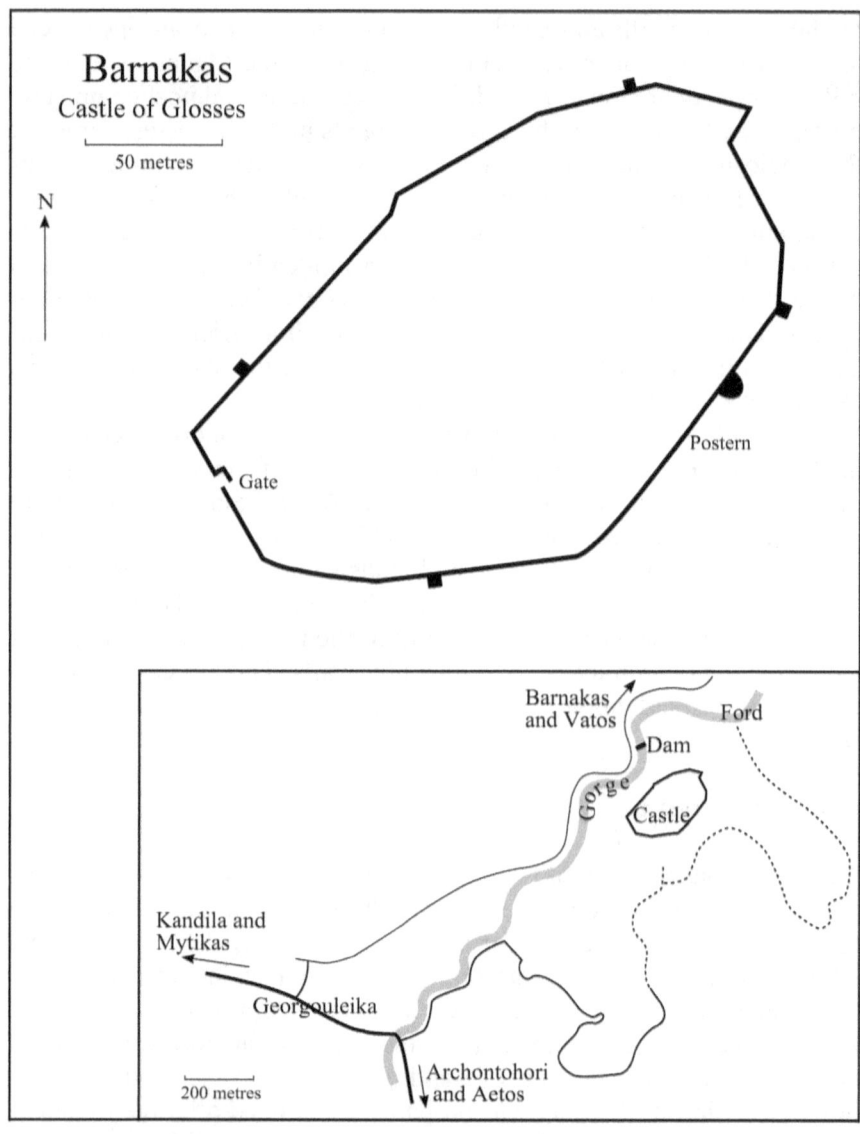

the north by the Glosses pass from Vonitsa via Monastiraki. The early history of the site is completely obscure. It was taken by Carlo Tocco in 1402 and fell to the Turks along with Angelokastro in 1460. The survival of much of the circuit to the present day may indicate that it continued in use throughout the Turkish period.

Barnakas has the most dramatic situation of the mediaeval castles of Akarnania. To the northwest the walls overlooking the gorge are built

Figure 1.55 Barnakas: Southeast wall and postern gate.

Figure 1.56 Barnakas: Northwest walls overlooking the gorge.

on the edge of precipitous cliffs. To the south and east the hill slopes less steeply to the plain. Directly below the crag an ancient dam stands astride the river at the narrowest part of the gorge. Faced with massive blocks laid without the use of mortar it may date from as early as 1300 BC.[46] Until recently the dam completely blocked the gorge and the original route to the north must have run to the south and east of the castle hill rejoining the valley beyond the dam.[47] The castle's position may have been chosen to take advantage of this fact.

The circuit is still largely complete, although it has been quarried for local building, and forms a rough oval some 200m by 120m around the flat-topped hill. The walls are reinforced at irregular intervals by square towers. A single prominent half-round tower survives to the east. A little to the south of the round tower a walled up postern gate can be seen. Its lintel is formed from a single massive block. The main gate seems to have been located in the southwest wall but the remains are now reduced to the foundations. Virtually no traces of the parapet or wallwalk survive. The walls are constructed of mortared rubble with much tile in the joints. Although overgrown in some areas the interior is generally accessible but no structures remain within.

To reach the castle from the main coast road near Mytikas, take the road that runs north to the village of Kandila then east to Georgouleika. Drive through this second village to an obvious bridge over the course of the seasonal torrent that leaves the gorge at this point. On the eastern side of the bridge a narrow side road runs northeast along the bank of the river. After 400m the road narrows further at an abrupt right-angle turn that leads southwest for 100m to the foot of a newly laid tarmac road. This climbs the mountain by a serpentine route to within 300m of the castle. A dirt track then leads past extensive goat pens to the outer walls where a number of breaches allow entry to the interior. The views are extensive and include the entire Mytikas plain and the island of Kalamos immediately offshore. The dam may be reached by a poor road from the centre of Georgouleika.

Notes

1. Pausanias, X.38.5.
2. Procopius, *History of the Wars VIII*, xxv.16-22.
3. Peter Lock, *The Franks in the Aegean*, p. 160.
4. W. M. Leake, *Travels in Northern Greece, Vol. II*, p. 608.
5. ESCUTIS, *Muslim Presence in Epirus and Western Greece*, p. 438

and p. 441. A plan of the hamam can be found in Eleni Kanetaki, *The still existing Ottoman Hamams in the Greek territory*, p. 91.
6. The distribution of these fountains is described by Marcus Milright, *An Introduction to Islamic Archaeology*, p. 91.
7. The earthquake of 1703 provides an example of the destruction that could be caused. This brought down a bastion and cracked the walls on the western side of the castle. See Ambraseys and Finkel, *Material for the Investigation of the Seismicity of the Eastern Mediterranean Region during the period 1690-1710*.
8. Kevin Andrews, *Castles of the Morea*, pp. 94-97.
9. Koroni is the great Venetian castle at the southwest tip of the Peloponnese. The Venetians took the place from the Franks in 1206 and held it until 1500 when it fell to the Turks. Koroni and nearby Methoni were known as the 'oculi capitales communis', the chief eyes of the republic.
10. William Miller, *Latins in the Levant*, p. 505.
11. D. A. Castillo, *The Maltese Cross: a strategic history of Malta*, p. 89.
12. Andrews, *Castles of the Morea*, p. 130.
13. William Miller, *Essays on the Latin Orient*, pp. 417 and 424.
14. Pouqueville, *Travels in Southern Epirus*, p. 56.
15. Andrews, *Castles of the Morea*, pp. 131, 132.
16. Andrews, *Castles of the Morea*, Plate XXX.
17. A description of the state of the fort describing the outer defences was written by a French engineer after the siege of 1828. See Andrews, *Castles of the Morea*, p. 133.
18. Simon Pepper, "Ottoman military architecture in the early gunpowder era: a reassessment," in James D. Tracy, ed., *City Walls: The Urban Enceinte in Global Perspective*, pp. 308-309.
19. W. M. Leake, *Travels in the Morea, Vol. II*, pp. 147-148.
20. The French engineer mentioned in note 17 above describes how the rebuilt earthen parapet was capable of absorbing shot and was therefore safer for the defendants than the masonry original. Andrews, *Castles of the Morea*, p. 134.
21. Andrews, *Castles of the Morea*, pp. 131 and 134.
22. William Miller, *The Venetian Revival in Greece, Essays on the Latin Orient*, p. 404.
23. George Finlay, *The History of Greece under Othoman and Venetian Domination*, p. 311.
24. Edward Blaquire, *The Greek Revolution; its Origin and Progress*, pp. 245-246.

25. Thomas Gordon, *History of the Greek Revolution, Vol. II*, p. 232.
26. George Finlay, *History of the Greek Revolution, Vol. II*, p. 359.
27. The metre gauge railway ran from Agrinio through Mesolonghi and on to the small port of Kryoneri on the coast some twenty-five kilometres west of Nafpaktos. A ferry connected Kryoneri with Patras on the other side of the Gulf providing a connection to the rest of the Greek rail system. The line closed completely in 1975. A European funded project to restore and modernize the route was completed in 2003 but it has never re-opened to traffic.
28. D. M. Nicol, *The Despotate of Epiros*, p. 61.
29. Nicol, *The Despotate of Epiros*, pp. 171-2.
30. Nicol, *The Despotate of Epiros*, p. 172.
31. William Mure, *Journal of a Tour of Greece, Vol. I*, p. 123.
32. The first ruler of the territory that was to become the Despotate was Michael I. Neither he, nor his brother Theodore who succeeded him, used the name of Angelos or acquired the title of Despot. His son, Michael II, seized power around 1236. Michael II and his son, Nikephoros, were subsequently granted the titles of Despot by John Vatatzes, the Byzantine Emperor of Nicaea. See Nicol, *The Despotate of Epiros*, pp. 3-6.
33. For the identification of Angelokastro with ancient Konope and its renaming as Arsinoe in the 3C BC see W. K. Pritchett, *Studies in Ancient Greek Topography, Part. VI*, pp. 136-7.
34. The remains seen in 1892-3 by Woodhouse included a cistern, an unidentified underground chamber, stylobate slabs and fragments of columns. See W. J. Woodhouse, *Aetolia*, pp. 209-213.
35. Thucydides (2.102) describes a Peloponnesian fleet landing at Astakos. Pseudo-Skylax (34) calls Astakos a city with a harbour.
36. W. M. Leake, *Travels in Northern Greece, Vol. IV*, p. 5.
37. Dragomestre is also rendered as Dragomeste, Dragomesto, Tragemesti amongst other spellings.
38. George Finlay, *The History of Greece under Othoman and Venetian Domination*, p. 211.
39. Stanley Lane-Poole, *Sir Richard Church Commander-in-Chief of the Greeks in the War of Independence*, pp. 63-64.
40. Leake's description is as follows: "At the angle of the fortress towards the sea are the remains of a tower, coeval apparently with the ruined church, and built upon a high rock." Leake seems to have over-estimated the extent of the ancient circuit towards the south. Leake, *Travels in Northern Greece, Vol. IV*, p. 6.
41. W. M. Murray, *Coastal Sites of Western Akarnania*, p. 73.

42. The best preserved and most accessible example is that of Stratos, the ancient capital of Akarnania, whose ruins lie astride the main E55 road north of Agrinio.
43. Murray, *Coastal Sites*, p. 71.
44. Murray, *Coastal Sites*, p. 114.
45. One kilometre to the east of Mytikas village the remains of the Byzantine church of Ayia Sophia have been excavated and the site may date to the 7C. Murray speculates that the castle may date to the same period. *Coastal Sites*, p. 129.
46. The dam is an earth embankment faced on its downstream side with a stepped wall of massive stone blocks laid in fourteen courses originally without mortar but with later repairs. Chanson describes it as a stepped spillway, or weir, rather than a dam. The pool, or reservoir, behind the dam is completely silted up. A ruined late 19C mill stands under the cliff at the eastern end of the dam. Murray argued for a construction date in the 4C or 3C BC with a brief period of re-use in the 7C AD. However Knauss has dated the dam to the Mycenaean period around 1300 BC. See: Chanson, *Historical Development of Stepped Cascades*, p. 296; Murray, *Coastal Sites*, p. 105; J. Knauss, "Der Altweibersprung, die ratselhafte alte Talsperre", cited in Jan Queißer, *Entwicklung landschaftsverträglicher Bauweisen für überströmbare Dämme*, pp. 8-10.
47. Photographs taken by Murray around 1980 show the dam wall built hard against the cliff on the western side of the gorge. At some point in the 1980s a new road was built from Georgouleika to the village of Barnakas further up the valley. A concrete ramp was built over the eastern section of the dam to accommodate this road. The winter torrents are such that sections of the road are frequently washed away.

2

Preveza and Lefkas

The coastline around the Preveza peninsula and the Lefkas channel has the greatest concentration of Turko-Venetian fortifications in mainland Greece. Preveza itself was a completely walled city in the early 19C with its earthwork defences augmented by numerous forts on both sides of the entrance to the Ambracian Gulf. The Castle of Santa Maura has guarded the approaches to the island of Lefkas since the 14C and by 1820 four more forts had been built by the various nations competing for control of the area. The extensive remains of Nikopolis, the city founded by Octavian after the naval Battle of Actium in 31 BC, can also be seen immediately to the north of Preveza. This boasts some of the most impressive Byzantine fortifications outside Constantinople as well as considerable remains from the Augustine period.

City of Preveza

Preveza is built on the site of ancient Berenikia, a town founded by Pyrrhus in 290 BC. This settlement must have been abandoned after the foundation of Nikopolis and no trace seems to exist today. The name of Preveza first occurs in 1292 in the Greek version of the Chronicle of the Morea.[1] It was probably settled in the early 13C following the final abandonment of Nikopolis (see below). After the collapse of the Despotate of Epiros the town became Turkish and it remained under Ottoman control until 1684 when the Venetians launched the campaign to regain their Greek territories with the siege of Santa Maura. By the end of that year Lefkas, Mesolonghi and Preveza had all fallen under Venetian control. Although Preveza was ceded back to the Turks by the Treaty of Karlowitz in 1699, the Treaty of Passarowitz in 1718 restored the city to the Republic. It remained in Venetian hands until 1797 when, on the fall of Venice to Napoleon, it passed with the Ionian Islands to the French.

Preveza and Lefkas

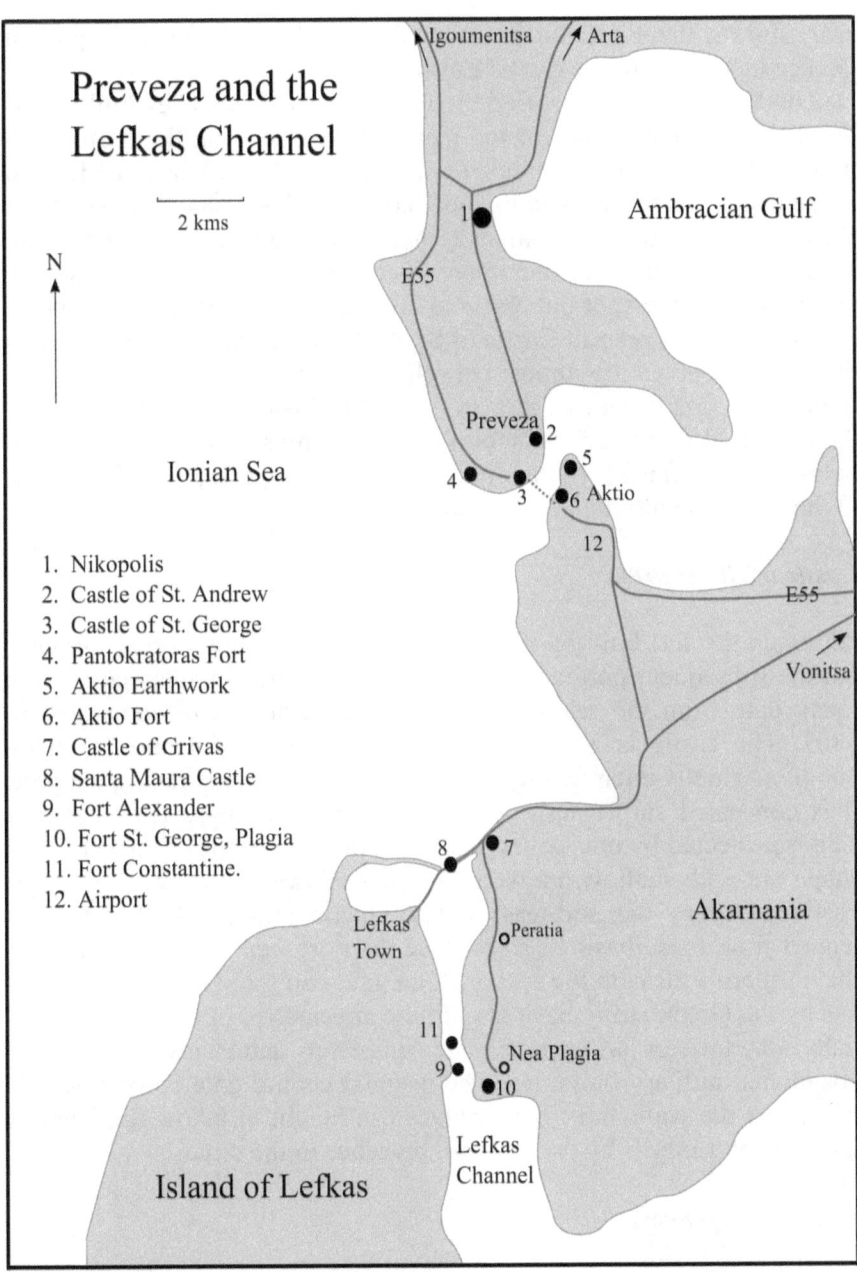

Napoleon's invasion of Egypt the following year caused the Turks to declare war on France and Preveza was taken by Ali Pasha of Ioannina. It remained under Turkish control until 1912 when it fell to the Greek army during the First Balkan War. Preveza became formally part of Greece in 1913 with the rest of Epiros.

The town was first fortified by the Turks in 1478.[2] They built a castle at the southeast point of the peninsula overlooking the narrow entrance channel to the Ambracian Gulf. Known as the Castle of Bouka, its defences were improved by the Venetians after 1684. The Treaty of Karlowitz obliged the Venetians to hand Preveza back to the Turks but before doing so in 1701 they blew up the castle. The Turks did not rebuild on the same spot but chose to erect a new fort 800m to the north on the site of the present Castle of St. Andrew.[3] Today the fortifications that have survived are almost entirely the work of Ali Pasha and were built in the first decade of the 19C as part of his programme to consolidate his hold on the area. Each of the surviving structures is described below but students of military architecture of the period will find a visit to the Fort of Pantokratoras the most satisfying.

Castle of St. Andrew

Although the fort built by the Turks in 1702 must have stood throughout the subsequent period of Venetian control, the remains that survive today date from the rebuilding by Ali Pasha and were completed in 1807. The castle is a quadrangular fortress approximately 250m by 100m, originally encircled by a ditch, with its long side facing the port. It is concealed surprisingly well by modern buildings. The landward side is protected by one central and two corner bastions of conventional shape but with shallow, ineffective flanks. Towards the port polygonal bastions occupy the northeast and southeast corners. Walls once extended from these bastions to enclose the port area. A short section of the northern wall with the remains of a gate still stands. The decades of use by the Greek Army have altered the appearance of the fort substantially. The interior has been levelled completely and is now occupied by abandoned military buildings. The original central gate is long demolished and the walls have been reduced in height to below the level of the parapet. Entry is by two modern breaches in the circuit.

The City Defences

The rebuilt Castle of St. Andrew was just one element in Ali Pasha's extensive programme of fortification. In 1807 he surrounded Preveza with an earthenwork rampart and moat over two kilometres long built with the use of conscripted labour. In March 1809 William Leake

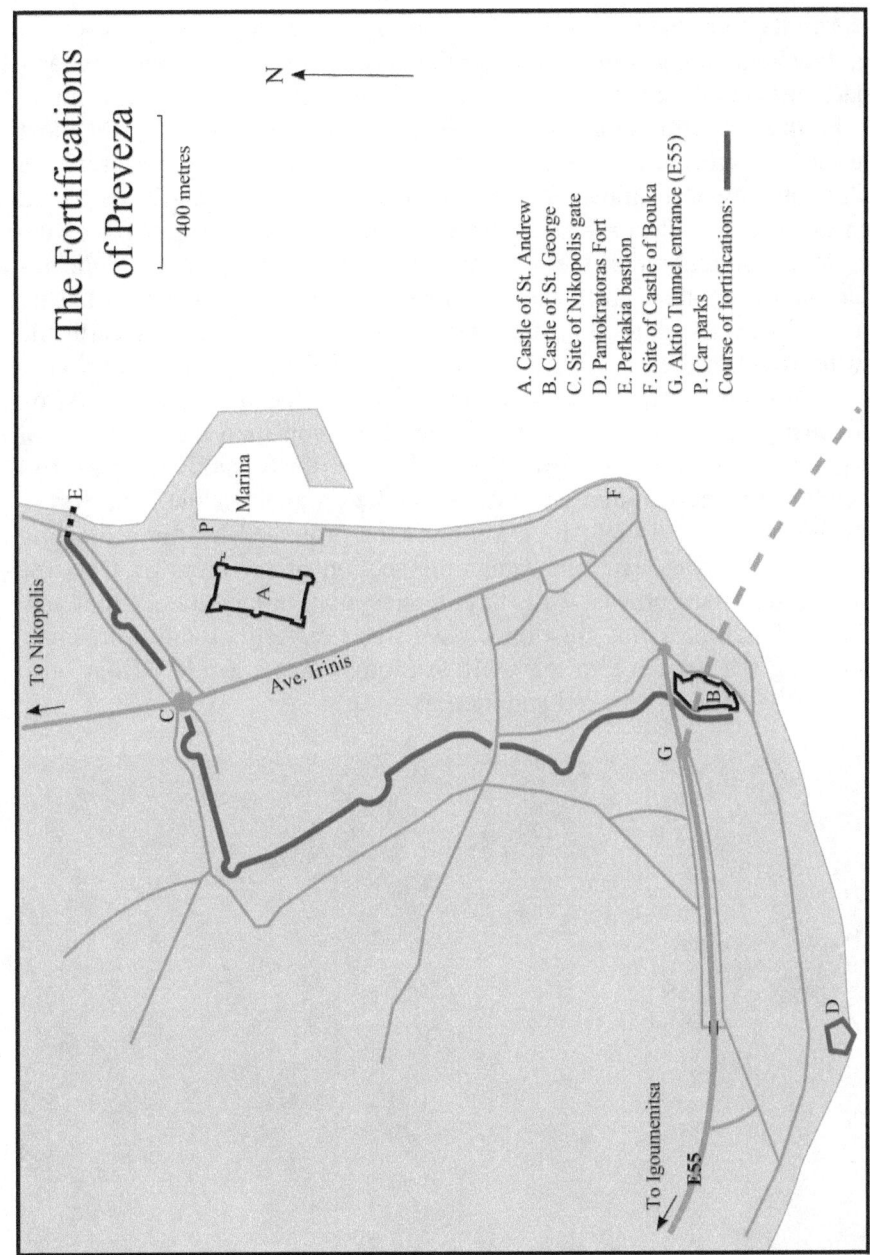

visited the town and described the newly constructed walls as already beginning to crumble.[4] The walls ran from the shore north of the port to another point on the coast to the south of the town. The northeast extremity terminated in a masonry bastion projecting into the sea with embrasures facing south to protect the port. At its southern end the rampart was reinforced with a new fort, known as the Castle of St. George. With the exception of a very short section around this new fort the moat has now been filled in completely. Almost all traces of the rampart have also long since disappeared. Nevertheless its course can still be traced easily and a cycle path occupies much of the western section of the moat. A roundabout at the northern end of Avenue Irinis now indicates the site of the main north gate. However the northeast, or Pefkakia, bastion still exists. Although its interior has been filled in with earth the walls stand to their full height and the gun embrasures are clearly visible. The Castle of St. George, although also used by the Greek Army for many years, has survived in better condition than the Castle of St Andrew. Superficially similar in style, the walls stand to their full height with the original embrasures in the parapet visible. The fort is roughly triangular with the main entrance protected by the projecting northeast bastion. The one remaining section of the moat protects the west side. The southeast walls have an irregular, indented trace that now faces a small park but must once have stood directly on the shore commanding the entrance to the Gulf. Although no longer in military use the fort is currently locked and inaccessible.

Figure 2.1 Castle of St. George.

Figure 2.2 Pefkakia bastion.
View of the gun embrasures from the south.

Figure 2.3 Castle of St. Andrew: Southeast bastion.

Pantokratoras Fort

One kilometre to the west of the Castle of St. George Ali Pasha built a new pentagonal fort in 1807 to command the sea approaches to the Ambracian Gulf from the north. Named the Castle, or Fort, of Pantokratoras after the church that originally stood on the site, it was strengthened and enlarged in the latter part of the 19C with the addition of an elaborate casemated sea battery to the south of the original work.[5] Today the fort still stands, well preserved, on a low headland on the edge of the modern suburb of the same name.

The original fort had a relatively thin and high outer wall enclosing an internal court lined with vaulted barrack blocks on two levels. The flat roofs of these blocks formed the fort's gun platforms. Although the parapets on the seaward sides of the fort are now missing or ruined photographs from the early 20C show a line of gun embrasures along the southeast rampart. The most prominent object on the roof of the fort is now a small modern church built incongruously on a concrete platform above the original vaults.[6]

Figure 2.4 Pantokratoras Fort: General view from the east. The late 19C battery is in the foreground overlooked by the original pentagonal fort with the modern church on its roof.

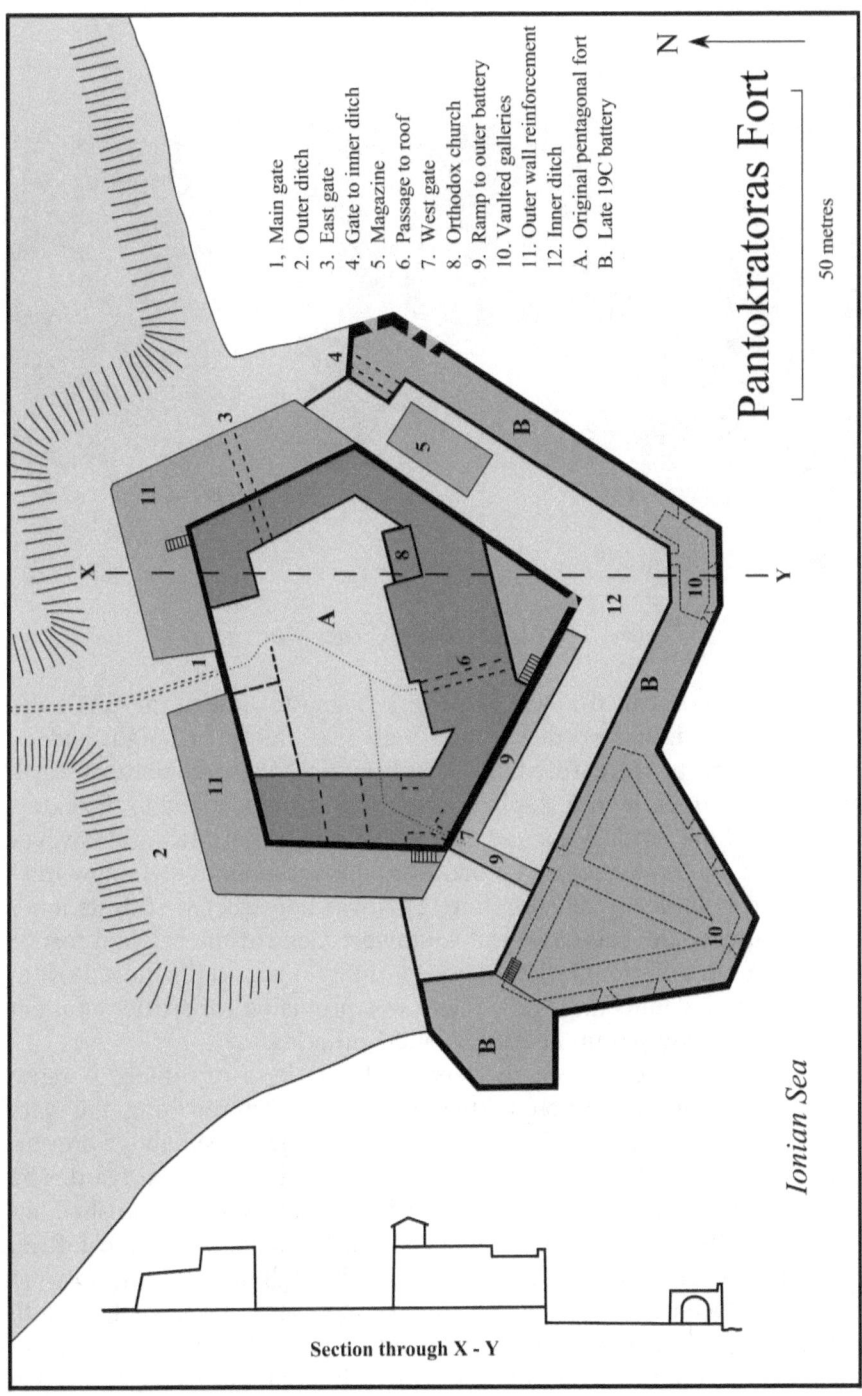

Preveza and Lefkas

Figure 2.5 Pantokratoras Fort: Main gate.

At some point in the late 19C work began to update the fort's defences. The original northern outer wall was raised in height and its arched gunports were filled in. A substantial reinforcement of earth eight metres thick with a sloping masonry scarp was added to the external faces of the north, west and east walls to half their height. However the largest component of this modernisation was a completely new low-level battery built on the shoreline. This was constructed with its inner face parallel to the southeast and southwest faces of the original fort so as to form an additional ditch between the two structures closed off at each end by a connecting wall. There was provision for artillery both at rampart level and within internal vaulted galleries.

The fort is defended on the landward side by a dry ditch. A ramp leads down into the ditch to the main gate. Approaching the gate through the thickened walls, the modifications described above are immediately apparent. The gate leads directly into the inner courtyard. The vaulted structures built against the north wall have largely vanished but are substantially intact on the other sides. Immediately to the left an archway leads to a barrel-vaulted corridor through the east wall to what must have been the original sea-gate before the addition of the south battery. Ahead, a vaulted ramp leads up through the barrack block to roof level. From the west and northeast salient angles steps lead down

Figure 2.6 Pantokratoras Fort: Interior courtyard.

from the original roof to the top of the outer earth platforms. Access to the sea battery is through the ground floor vaults to the right of the courtyard. A door from these vaults through the rear wall of the fort leads to a ramp and bridge across the inner ditch to the outer rampart.

The sea battery is a complex structure designed to give a very wide field of fire to the south. Its main triangular block forms one large gun platform. On the west side of this triangle a six-sided extension, or bastion, flanks the west face of the main pentagonal work. To the east a narrower v-shaped rampart that wraps around the south salient of the original fort provided further artillery positions. It terminates in a pentagonal bastion that flanks the east face of the original fort. This bastion also contains another gate giving access to the shore and the east ditch. With the exception of the three gun embrasures that survive at this eastern end, the parapet has disappeared for almost the full length of the battery. However the internal galleries within the structure are well preserved and accessible. An arched gate almost below the bridge across the ditch gives access to those within the main triangular block. A central tunnel runs through the block to the seaward galleries or casemates. These contain five gunports almost at sea level. The iron frames around the ports are still in position. These would have originally held shutters but today are open to the elements. As a result the galleries are now full of seaweed. The gunports' openings are arched and widely splayed. On either side of the entrance additional galleries run parallel with the ditch. These have rifle slits commanding the ditch and protecting the entrance. A smaller gallery is built within the salient angle of the battery's eastern section. This provides three further gunports on the seaward side and rifle slits covering the ditch on two levels. At the eastern end of the inner ditch stands a heavily vaulted magazine. At various points around the fort modifications in concrete dating from the Second World War can be identified.

Both phases of the fort are built of similar roughly coursed rectangular blocks. The use of the typical Ottoman square stringcourse throughout the fortress gives an impression of architectural unity. The late 19C battery projects into the sea and its lower courses have been built of massive squared blocks in an attempt to resist wave action. The irregular sizes of these blocks and their relatively haphazard placement indicate that they that they have been plundered from some much earlier walls, possibly those of Aktio or Nikopolis.

Figure 2.7 Pantokratoras fort: The central block of the sea battery with gunports. Note the lower courses of massive re-used squared blocks and the square stringcourse at parapet level.

Preveza and Lefkas

Figure 2.8 Pantokratoras Fort: Overall view from the northwest.

The fort is open during daylight hours and access is straightforward. From the E55 Preveza by-pass a turning to the south, signposted to the suburb of Pantokratoras, leads to the old coast road and the fort. The Castle of St. George can be reached from this point by continuing to follow the coast road east towards the centre of Preveza. The fortifications within the town itself are best approached on foot. There is a large, free car park by the harbour close to the Castle of St. Andrew (see map). The Pefkakia bastion is a short walk to the north.

The Aktio forts

The promontory of Aktio or Actium, known as Punta to the Venetians, is a mere 600 metres across the Gulf entrance from Preveza. In order to achieve complete command of the straits Ali Pasha built a further two forts here over a period of fifteen years around the turn of the 18C. However the first structures to appear on the Cape were those of the Sanctuary and Temple of Apollo first built in the 5C BC. After Octavian's naval victory in 31 BC the Sanctuary was enlarged, and captured ships from the battle were displayed in specially constructed buildings. Almost nothing now exists from this era. The remains were heavily

Preveza and Lefkas

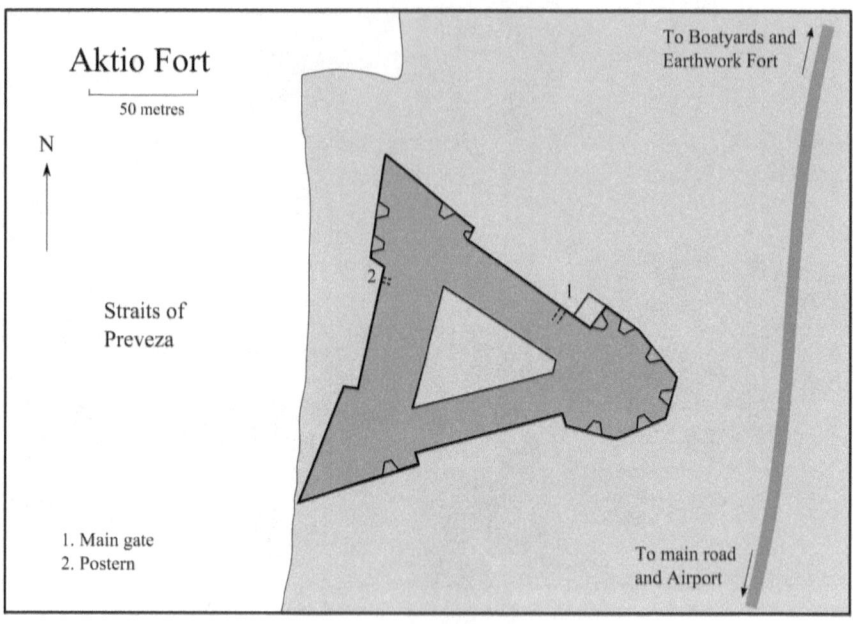

quarried to provide material for the new fortifications and the whole area had been much damaged when Ali Pasha built a large earthwork fort on the site. Erected in the years 1794 to 1795, this fort is pentagonal in outline with a round tower at each angle. It was surrounded by a wet moat fed by a channel cut from the Gulf.

In 1812 Ali completed a new stone fort on the shore directly opposite the Castle of St. George on the Preveza side of the straits. Partially constructed from re-used ancient blocks, its shape is a simple equilateral triangle with walls about 6m high enclosing a small internal courtyard. Except for the southwest bastion the majority of the gun embrasures in the parapet survive. The main gate is in the north face. Two conventional arrowhead bastions occupy the corners on the side facing the channel. However as bastions they are of little use as their flanks are too short to allow room for embrasures covering the face of the work. At the third, landward, apex stands an hexagonal bastion typical of the forts constructed by Ali Pasha's architects. On this bastion the north flank is sufficiently deep to hold one relatively wide embrasure to cover the approach to the gate. After the creation of the Greek state in 1832 the fort remained in use by the Greek army until the early 20C.

The fort stands on the shore by the old ferry terminal. Travelling north on the E55 from the direction of the airport, the old road forks left about 200m before the toll booths for the tunnel. The fort of 1812 is on

Figure 2.9 Aktio Fort: View of the northwest and southwest bastions.

Figure 2.10 Aktio Fort: View from the north.

the left of the road a kilometre further on. It is in a relatively good state of preservation but the interior is overgrown, locked and inaccessible. The road continues to a series of boatyards and marinas that occupy much of the western side of the Aktio promontory. Traces of the walls of the earthwork fort still exist behind the boatyards as low overgrown mounds surrounded by the remains of the moat.

Castle of Santa Maura

Fifteen kilometres southwest of Aktio a long spit of land extends from the northeast tip of the island of Lefkas almost to the shoreline of Akarnania. The spit is bisected by the entrance channel to the Lefkas canal built in 1903 but with predecessors dating back to the 7C BC.[7] On the mainland side of the entrance stands the impressive Castle of Santa Maura defending the fordable approaches to the island across the shallow lagoon south of the spit. Possession of the castle has always been the key to the island and a fort first stood on this site at the beginning of the 14C. However the core of the present structure is Turkish, dating from the late 15C, but with extensive Venetian modifications of the early 18C and even British influence from the 19C.

Lefkas is one of the seven main Ionian Islands but both geographically and historically it is tied more closely to the mainland of Akarnania. It was part of the Despotate of Epiros until 1295 when it passed to John (Giovanni) Orsini on his marriage to the daughter of the Despot Nikephoros I. Orsini probably built the first small fort here some time after 1300.[8] It may have occupied the northeast corner of the present castle. At around this time the island itself began to be known as Santa Maura. Lefkas and the castle were to remain in the hands of the Orsini family until 1331. After a brief period of Angevin control the island passed to another Italian family, the Tocchi, in 1362. Following the fall of Constantinople in 1453 the Turks gradually conquered all Frankish, Byzantine and Venetian Greece. In 1479 they occupied Lefkas along with Cephalonia, Zante and Ithaca and rebuilt the original castle of the Orsini on a much larger scale. With its large circular towers the new fort resembled the Castle of the Morea, built by Bayezid II in 1499, and may date originally from the same period. The Venetians succeeded in taking Cephalonia and Lefkas from the Turks in 1500 but within three years Lefkas was given back as part of the peace agreement that brought the second Turco-Venetian war to an end. Ottoman control lasted for the next one hundred and eighty years until 1684 when

Figure 2.11 Santa Maura: The circular towers of the original Turkish fort. The Venetian northwest bastion is in the left foreground. The southern outwork is visible in the background.

Venice joined the Holy League and a concerted effort to drive the Turks from southeast Europe began. The Venetian contribution was to be the re-conquest of the Morea. In order to secure the sea routes through the southern Adriatic Morosini began the campaign with the siege of Santa Maura. As well as being a Turkish stronghold the island by this time had become a base for the pirates known as the Barbary corsairs. After a siege of just sixteen days the castle surrendered and Lefkas finally joined the other Ionian Islands under Venetian control. Morosini went on to subdue the entire Peloponnese over the next three years. The Venetians set about a complete modernisation of the castle's defences, constructing a new land front to the east with an elaborate system of outworks facing the mainland.

However a mere thirty years later in 1715 the Turks returned in force and in just three months overran all the Venetian possessions in the

Figure 2.12 Santa Maura: View of the Venetian east front across the moat from the north outwork. The ruined piers of the bridge to the east gate are visible in the background.

Morea. They then turned their attention to the Ionian Islands. In order to concentrate their limited defensive resources the Venetians abandoned Santa Maura, partially demolished the fortifications and transferred the guns and garrison to Corfu. They had engaged a skilled professional soldier, Count Matthias von der Schulenburg, to organise the defence of the island. He spent the winter of 1715-1716 supervising improvements to Corfu's fortifications and when the Turks attacked and besieged the island in the summer of 1716 they were defeated after only forty-eight days. Schulenburg then re-occupied Santa Maura and organised the repair of the previous year's demolition work. Two years later, in 1718, the peace treaty drawn up at Passarowitz confirmed Venetian possession of Santa Maura along with Preveza and Vonitsa. It remained in their hands until the closing years of the eighteenth century.

In 1797 Venice fell to Napoleon. He promptly annexed the Ionian Islands realizing their strategic importance to the control of the Adriatic. The French occupied Lefkas in July of that year. The occupation was legitimised in October when the territories of the Republic of Venice were formally partitioned between France and Austria by the Treaty of Campo Formio. The following year Napoleon invaded Egypt, then still part of the Ottoman Empire. The Turks established an alliance with Russia and declared war on France in September 1798. A combined Russian and Turkish fleet attacked the Ionian Islands and by November 1798 had taken control of Santa Maura. Ali Pasha had also taken Preveza from the French by this time, but the Russian presence prevented him extending control to Lefkas. In March 1800 Russia and Turkey created the Septinsular Republic, jointly guaranteeing the territorial integrity of the seven Ionian Islands. However in 1801 both countries evacuated their garrisons. The political chaos that ensued in the islands resulted in the dispatch of a Russian fleet in August 1802. A period of effective Russian control began and this was to last until 1807. The Russians built two small forts at the southern end of the Lefkas channel during this period (see below). In 1806 war broke out between Russia and Turkey. Ali Pasha prepared to besiege Lefkas in 1807 with French assistance but the Russian garrison successfully defended the island. Yet by September 1807 the French were once again in control of the islands. In June Napoleon had defeated the Russians at the Battle of Friedland. The peace agreement known as the Treaty of Tilsit ceded the Ionian Islands back to the French who proceeded to re-occupy them. This second occupation was to be almost as brief as the first. In September 1809 Britain sent a fleet from Sicily under Brigadier Oswald. By October he had taken Zante, Cephalonia and Ithaca. Lefkas fell in the spring of 1810 to a force that included Major (later Sir Richard) Church. The French did not surrender Corfu until June 1814, two months after the abdication of Napoleon. The following year the Treaty of Paris established a British Protectorate of the Ionian Islands. They became British colonies in all but name and were to remain so until 1864 when they became part of the Greek state. The Castle of Santa Maura was occupied by a British garrison throughout this period and saw its third and final period of modernisation with the building of new facilities for the garrison. After 1864 the castle was a stronghold of the Greek army and, along with the castle of Aktio, was used as a base in the First Balkan War. In 1922, after Greece's disastrous defeat in Asia Minor, the castle was used to house refugees. It was eventually abandoned and in 1938 most of the internal buildings were demolished and their materials sold.

Originally the castle was completely surrounded by water with a wide moat separating it from the mainland. Access to Lefkas island other than by boat was only possible through the fortifications. A wooden bridge led across the moat to the eastern gate. The stone piers

Preveza and Lefkas

Figure 2.13 Santa Maura: The original Turkish west gate.

of this bridge survive. From the western gate another bridge crossed the west moat to Lefkas itself. Today the modern road from the mainland to Lefkas is carried on a causeway that blocks the southern end of the east moat. It then runs beneath the walls to the floating bridge across the Lefkas Ship Canal. Except on the east front, the exterior of much of the original Turkish castle with its projecting round towers and thin walls is still visible. Externally the Venetians merely added two low level bastions, or outworks, to the northwest and southeast. However internally they dramatically increased the thickness of the walls at the most vulnerable parts of the circuit. To the east they completely rebuilt the inadequate Turkish defences burying the original walls within a new bastioned front and constructing new outworks beyond the moat. Today

Figure 2.14 Santa Maura: Remains of two-storeyed barrack blocks.

the interior of the castle is empty save for the forlorn roofless buildings scattered about the northern half of the site. These are probably the remains of Venetian military installations from the early 18C and the new facilities erected by the British for their garrison in the 19C. During the Ottoman occupation however the interior of the castle contained a densely packed Turkish town complete with mosques. Early maps show an inner citadel in the northeast quadrant of the castle and a dense network of lanes and buildings in the remainder.[9] After the Venetian conquest in 1684 the Turkish settlement was transferred to the site of the present Lefkas town. The interior buildings and inner citadel were levelled and the castle became a purely military site thereafter.

Entrance to the castle is now via the west gate. Originally the approach to this gate was from a bridge over the moat. The modern canal was cut a little to the west and most of this moat is now buried beneath the wide foreshore that lies between the castle and the canal. However recently part of this foreshore has been excavated to reveal a short section of the original moat together with an arched bridge and a causeway leading to the outer gate. This arrangement must date from the last periods of occupation. The simple iron gate leads past the curve of the large western Turkish tower into the Venetian northwest bastion. The interior of this Turkish round tower contained a vaulted chamber housing guns designed to fire through ports, still visible, almost at sea level. One of

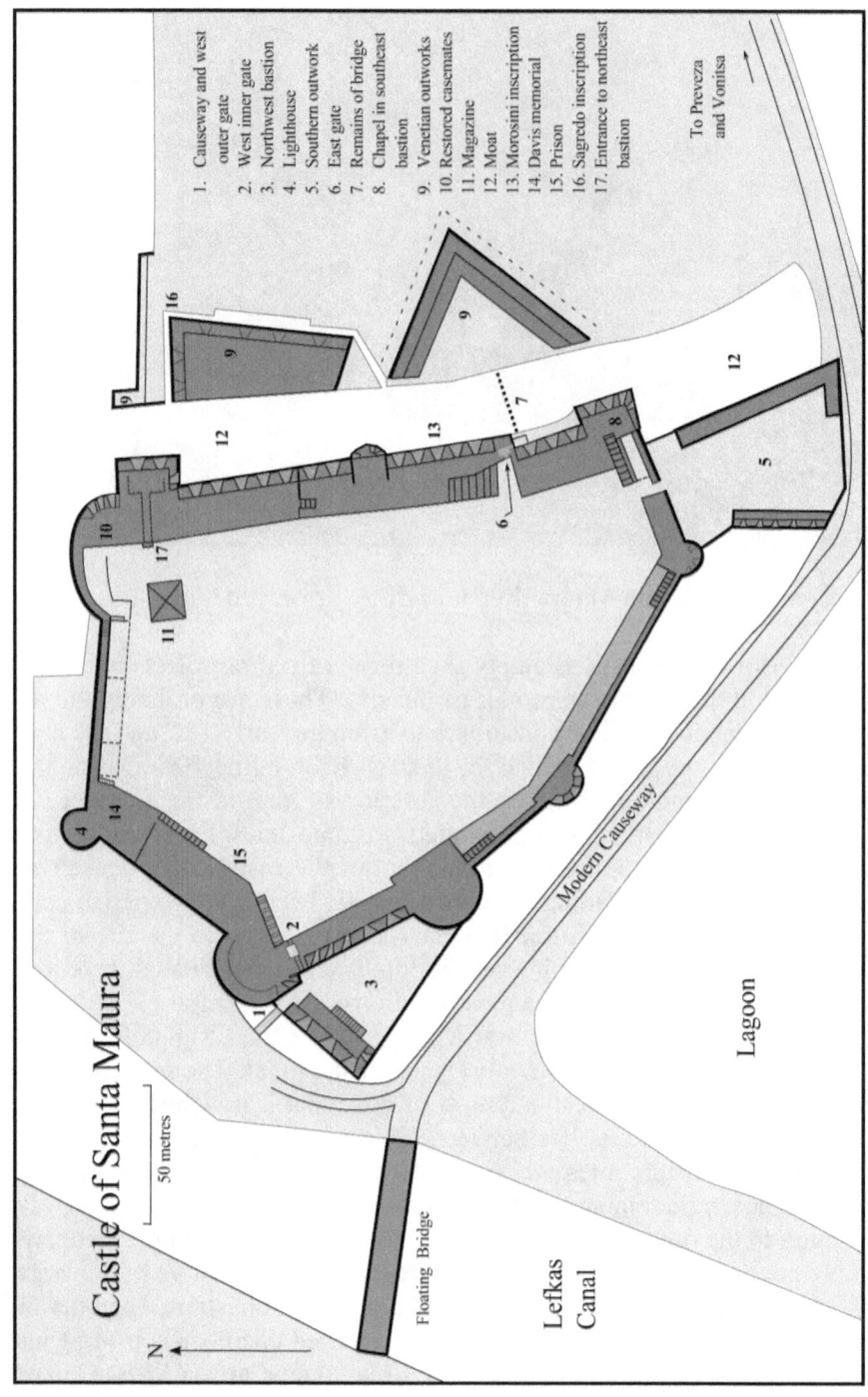

Figure 2.15: Santa Maura: Approach to the west gate.

these ports, made redundant by the building of the Venetian bastion, is visible on the left immediately inside the gate. Once through the gate it is clear that the Venetian bastion is not a solid structure but simply a terrepleined rampart for three guns facing the channel, connected by a screen wall to the round tower to the south. Entry to the main body of the castle is through the original Turkish gate. The entrance passage leads into a small court created when the Venetians thickened this section of wall. Musketry loopholes command the court from above. A second arched gate leads from the court into the interior of the fort. To the left of the entrance a ramp leads up onto the ramparts. In this section of the circuit, from the lighthouse to the southern end of the northwest bastion, the Venetians substantially widened the original thin Turkish walls. The new 20-metre wide gun platform they created completely enclosed the inner faces of the three round towers and provided new batteries to cover the approaches from the island. The parapet was remodelled with deep gun embrasures of brick. These now survive intact only on the section of wall to the south of the gate. At the northern end of this broad platform stand two monuments to the period of British occupation. The most conspicuous is the lighthouse and keeper's cottage built in 1861 no doubt as a guide to the entrance to the canal the British

Figure 2.16 Santa Maura: Venetian brick-built parapet with firing steps between the artillery embrasures.

created across the lagoon to Lefkas town. (The deep ship canal through the full length of the lagoon was not excavated until 1903). Nearby stands a memorial in the form of a marble tomb erected in 1815. The dedication, in Greek, Italian and English, is to the memory of Major General Henry Davis who died in Santa Maura in 1813.[10]

From the lighthouse a wallwalk at parapet level leads towards the northeast bastion. The Venetians chose not to reinforce this section of the circuit, presumably for reasons of economy, building instead a range of buildings against the thin wall. An open semi-circular tower occupies the northeast corner of the castle. This has an infantry parapet above a lower gun platform with six arched gunports. When the Venetians rebuilt the eastern defences the new rampart filled in half of this open tower. In order to continue using the gunports facing the moat two vaulted casemates were built running west to east through the rampart (see Figures 2.17 and 2.18). These casemates are one of the few parts of the castle to have been restored. Close by stands a Venetian magazine. With its pyramid roof, thick walls and heavily vaulted interior this is the only building within the circuit still intact. The new rampart extends the full length of the eastern front of the castle. Its gun embrasures are

Figure 2.17 Santa Maura: The restored northeast casemates.

Figure 2.18 Santa Maura: Gunports of the northeast casemates.

Figure 2.19 Santa Maura: The Venetian eastern defences viewed from the parapet of the southeast bastion. The east gate and the remains of the bridge are in the foreground. The northeast bastion is in the far background beyond the central multangular tower.

well preserved. New square bastions were built at each end to provide flanking fire down the length of the moat. Both bastions were equipped with embrasures in the parapet and internal chambers with flanking gunports. Access to the interior of the northeast bastion is via an arched and gated entrance just a few metres to the south of the restored casemates. The gate leads via a long barrel-vaulted tunnel through the thickness of the rampart to the large casemate within. This has a single gunport in both the north and south faces and a round smoke vent in the

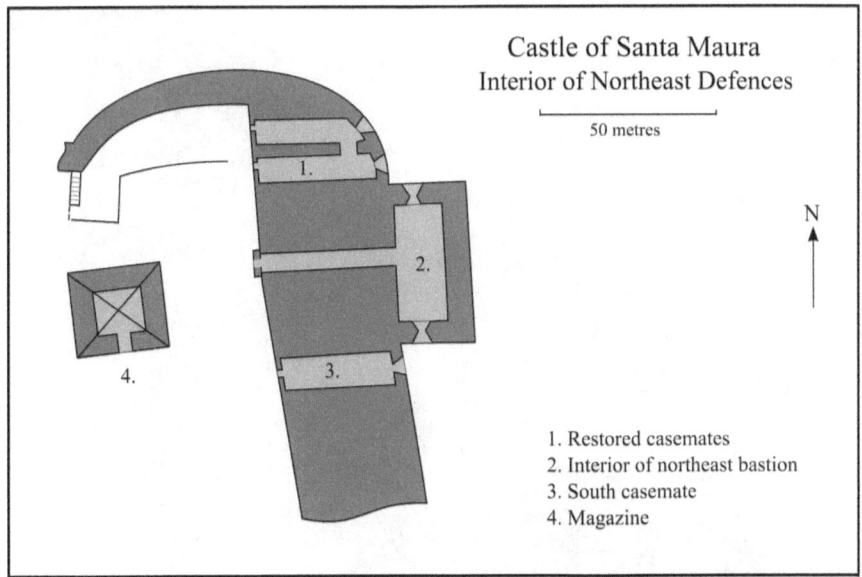

roof. Yet another casemate, twenty metres to the south, provides a further gunport facing east. A multangular tower at the midpoint of the rampart projects into the moat and provides additional flanking protection. Fifty metres to the south of this tower stands the east entrance to the castle and the remains of the bridge over the moat. The Venetians incorporated the Turkish entrance complex into their new rampart by simply leaving a narrow corridor through the terreplein to the original inner gate. This gives access to a chamber within the thickness of the wall and an outer gate at right angles to the first. A further right angle turn leads between two stone pillars. These supported the drawbridge that formed the first section of the bridge. Between the gate and the multangular tower to the north are two stone plaques set high up on the outer wall and visible only from the opposite side of the moat. The larger of the two commemorates Morosini's capture of the castle in 1684. Below it a smaller plaque records the repair of the wall by Aloisio Marino in 1770 following a severe earthquake the previous year.[11]

The Venetian improvements at the southern end of the castle involved increasing the thickness of the short south wall and building a new outwork beyond it. This extension provided two new artillery batteries facing west and east joined by a screen wall at the south. Originally the outwork was separated from the main fort by a further wet ditch. Thin screen-walls carried on arches across the ditch connected the northern ends of the batteries to the main body of the castle. Access

Figure 2.20 Santa Maura: The Turkish east gate.

to the outwork was through a new gate in the centre of the south wall with a bridge across the wet ditch. The western battery provided flanking fire down the length of the southwest walls. Its cannon remain in situ. The eastern battery swept the right flank of the approaches from the mainland. At some point the gate was demolished and the moat filled in. A breach in the wall now leads into the outwork which is heavily overgrown. The new Venetian south wall had a wide terrreplein

Figure 2.21 Santa Maura: Walled corridor leading to the entrance of the chapel in the southeast bastion. The springing of the demolished vault is just visible at the base of the right hand wall.

above internal longitudinal tunnel vaults on either side of the gate passage. To the west of this vanished gate the collapsed vault is still visible. To the east the tunnel led through the wall to the casemate within the southeast bastion. This arrangement mirrored that of the northeast bastion discussed above. The gunport in the bastions's north face commanded the exit from the east gate. The casemate has now been converted into a chapel and the vaulted tunnel leading to the entrance has been completely removed leaving a walled corridor open to the sky. The gunports and overhead smoke vent serve to light the chapel. The original Turkish round tower here was demolished in the construction of the southeast bastion. However the southwest round tower survives. From this point the Turkish wall run runs northwest to complete the circuit. This relatively thin section of the walls has an infantry parapet with narrow musketry slits above a lower platform equipped with a second row of slits for small arms fire.

To protect the walls of their new east front from direct fire the Venetians constructed a range of outworks on the mainland side of the

Figure 2.22 Santa Maura: View across the moat to the southeast bastion (centre) with the southern outwork on the left.

Figure 2.23 Santa Maura: Venetian outwork on the mainland side of the moat. View of the east face and silted up wet ditch. The inscription to Augustino Sagredo is on the far corner of the work.

moat. Although they are currently overgrown and difficult to access they can be approached and partially explored from the beach to the east. The most northerly of these works consists of a simple low level infantry parapet facing north out to sea with a short flanking projection at its west end. Immediately to the south a large quadrangular gun platform protects the base of the walls on the opposite side of the moat. The work is surrounded by a wet ditch and is equipped with a thick parapet and artillery embrasures on its north and east fronts. At the northeast corner an inscription, curiously carved around both faces of a cornerstone, records the construction of the work by Augustino Sagredo in 1713. It is possible to walk around this structure to the northern tip of the south outwork, a V-shaped redan that protected the bridge and masked the southern half of the east front. This position provides the best view of the great battered walls across the moat. It is also the only place from which the Morosini and Marino inscriptions can be seen.

The interior of the castle is periodically cleared of vegetation and some work to consolidate the walls is now being undertaken. This complex fortification rewards an extended visit. Access is straightforward. Normal opening hours are 8.30 to 15.00.

Castle of Grivas

In 1806 war broke out between Russia and Turkey. As part of his campaign to wrest Lefkas from Russian control Ali Pasha built two forts on the coast of Akarnania in the period 1806-1807, one at each end of the Lefkas channel.[12] The northern fort, constructed with French assistance, is known as the Castle of Grivas. It stands on a small rocky hill overlooking the lagoon one and a half kilometres from the Castle of Santa Maura. The Treaty of Tilsit, signed in September 1807, ended Ali's hopes of French help in his plans for territorial expansion. After 1810 and the British annexation of Lefkas the castle lost what little strategic importance it possessed. Ali later assigned the fort to the Grivas family, leaders of local militia used by the Ottomans to maintain control in the area. It became known as the Castle of Grivas thereafter. The fort is rectangular, approximately 60m by 30m, with two projecting multangular corner towers to the north and a single large tower to the south. A further square tower projecting from the southeast corner houses the gate complex. The outer gate leads into a ground floor chamber. An arch in the adjacent corner leads via a vaulted corridor and a final ramp into the interior. This consists of a narrow courtyard giving access to vaulted

Preveza and Lefkas

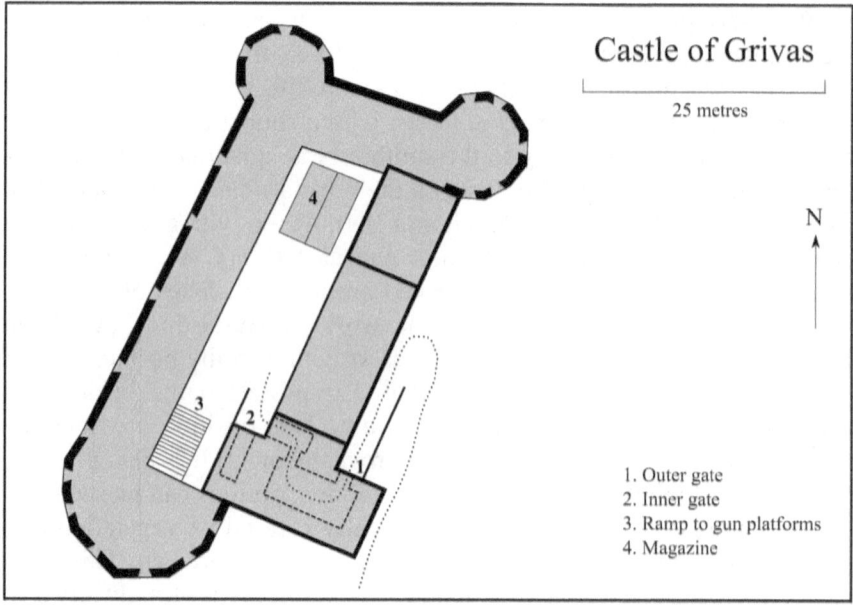

Castle of Grivas

25 metres

N

1. Outer gate
2. Inner gate
3. Ramp to gun platforms
4. Magazine

Figure 2.24 Castle of Grivas: The northwest tower.

Figure 2.25 Castle of Grivas: Entrance ramp and gatetower.

chambers in the thickness of the walls that provided storerooms and barracks. The northern end of the court is filled by a substantial powder magazine. The external walls of the fort are built of rough rubble masonry covered with a thick layer of mortar. Dressed stone is used around the entrance gate and on the corners of the towers. The west and north walls together with the three multangular towers form one large level gun platform approximately eight metres thick that commands the

Figure 2.26 Castle of Grivas: The interior and the central magazine.

Figure 2.27 Castle of Grivas: Overall view from the east.

entire coastline and Santa Maura itself. Access is via a broad ramp from the courtyard to the south tower. The semi-ruined gun embrasures are still visible in the broad parapet above the typical Turkish square string-course. The eastern side of the fort has a higher profile than this main

Figure2.28 Castle of Grivas: The northeast tower and east front.

gun platform. The gate tower has a badly ruined upper storey and there is a further upper storey at the northern end of the range overlooking the northeast multangular tower. These features may represent an earlier attempt by Ali Pasha to build a fort on the site in 1799. Although conspicuous and superficially imposing, from a military point of view the

Castle of Grivas must always have been an anachronism. Indeed viewed from the main road the walls look almost mediaeval. Although built to threaten the castle of Santa Maura, which was certainly within range of the cannon of the period, the high walls and conspicuous position must have made the fort the easier artillery target. The Venetian works at Santa Maura with their low massive walls and protecting outworks would have always been the more formidable fortification despite dating from one hundred years earlier. Today the castle remains in relatively good condition and is open during daylight hours. The main road passes directly beneath the walls and access is from the side road to Peratia and Plagia.

Fort Saint George, Plagia

About seven kilometres south of the Castle of Grivas stands the second of the forts constructed by Ali Pasha between 1806 and 1807 in an attempt to gain command the Lefkas channel. Built with French assistance, it stands on the summit of the hill of Saint George, a site that has been of strategic importance since the 5C BC. The fort is built within the original acropolis of an ancient fortification circuit. From this acropolis walls ran southwest and northwest to the shoreline to enclose a large section of the hillside.[13] Fragments of the acropolis wall can be seen to the left of the path to the main gate. The fort was planned on a considerably larger scale than the Castle of Grivas and by September 1807, when the Treaty of Tilsit was signed and work stopped, it was still incomplete. Although it was used intermittently after this date it was never completely finished.[14]

In plan the fort is a simple rhomboid with a large solid tower, or bastion, at each corner. The east, north and south towers are, unusually, round. The multangular west tower is more typical of Ali Pasha's fortifications with six external faces. The entrance to the fort is set in a wide jog in the northeast wall placed so that the adjacent eastern round tower protects the approach, although the gate itself is covered only by extremely narrow musket slits. The finely arched outer gate leads into a vaulted chamber. Musketry slits in the end wall of the chamber, accessible from an adjacent casemate, cover the entrance. A second arched gate at right angles to the first gives access to the interior. Once inside the fort its unfinished state becomes apparent. Although the builders managed to construct the basic circuit, the rampart of the long southwest wall appears never to have been completed and a section has

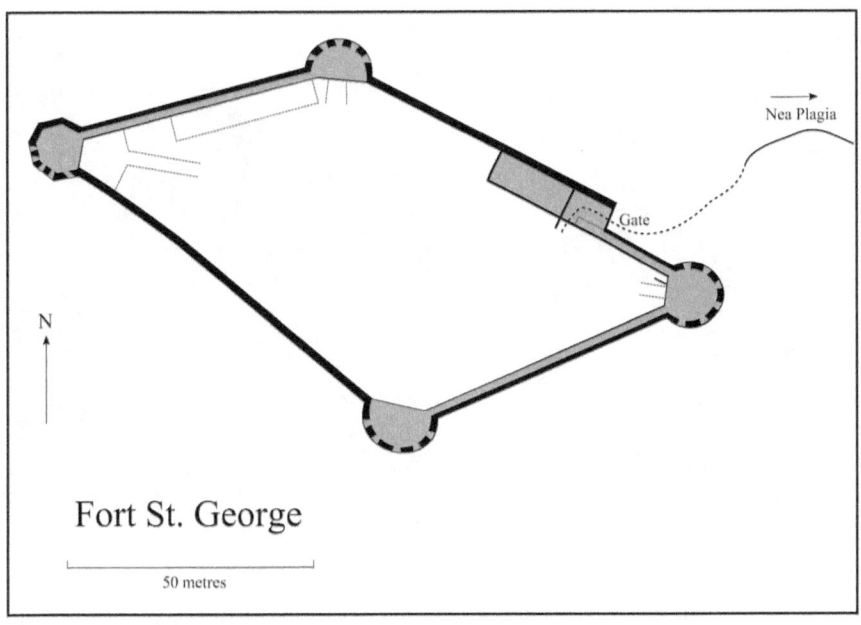

Figure 2.29 Fort St. George: View of the fort on the skyline from the Lefkas shore.

Preveza and Lefkas

Figure 2.30 Fort St. George: The east tower. Note the extremely narrow musket slits designed to cover the face of the gate.

Figure 2.31 Fort St. George: The unfinished southwest rampart.

collapsed. The incomplete foundations for casemated barrack accommodation or storerooms can be traced along the northern walls. Only the short section encompassing the entrance seems to have been finished. Artillery embrasures are provided in the projecting corner towers. A long masonry ramp leads up to the gun platform of the west multangular tower. The embrasures here are appreciably narrower than those of the round towers. The surviving parapets of the north and southeast walls are pierced with musketry slits. Similar slits provide the only flanking arrangements on the round towers. Although imposing from a distance St. George, with its thin walls and cramped bastions, would have been a weak artillery fort even if completed.

Today the fort stands neglected but with most of its structure intact. To reach the site take the road to Plagia from the Castle of Grivas. Note that on some maps Plagia continues to be shown at the location of old Plagia, an inland village abandoned in the 1950s following earthquake damage. St George stands above Nea Plagia, the modern replacement, built near the coast some three kilometres due south of Peratia. Drive through the new village. The road winds uphill almost to the gate of the fort, now abandoned and unenclosed.

Forts Constantine and Alexander

During the period 1803 to 1807 the Russians built two gun batteries at the southern end of the Lefkas channel on small islands within the lagoon itself. The northern battery, the grandly named Fort Constantine, lies on the western side of the channel approximately two kilometres north of Fort St. George. It is a simple square gun platform, hardly 15 metres across, attached to a low landing area. One kilometre further south, on an island to the east of the main channel, stands the larger Fort Alexander. This consists of a circular redoubt with a projecting caponier. There are low walls to the east, north and south, and a separate magazine block. This is entirely an artillery position, built with a very low profile, difficult to locate and designed to direct fire on shipping approaching from the south. As such it represents the state of military architecture of the time despite its small size. The forts are inaccessible without a boat but both are clearly visible from Fort St. George. Closer views can be obtained from the dirt road that skirts the old saltpans four kilometres south of Lefkas town. To reach this shore, follow the Nidri road south from Lefkas town to the village of Kariotes where an unsigned road leads east to the water's edge before turning north along the

Figure 2.32 The square gun platform of Fort Constantine.

Figure 2.33 Fort Alexander: View from the Lefkas shore.

bank that separates the saltpans from the channel. About one and a half kilometres from the main road Fort Alexander is visible one hundred metres away on its island on the other side of the dredged channel of the ship canal. Fort Constantine can be seen to the north.

Nikopolis

Nikopolis, or Victory City, occupies the greater part of the isthmus of the Preveza peninsula between the Mazoma lagoon to the east and the Ionian Sea to the west. It was founded by Octavian after his victory over Mark Antony and Cleopatra at the naval Battle of Actium in 31 BC. The city was built on such a massive scale that most of the inhabitants of Aetolia and Akarnania were forcibly moved to populate it. Such social engineering was possible because by that date Greece had been a Roman province for over one hundred years. Today two great fortification circuits are visible. The first belongs to the original Roman city. The second, smaller but very well preserved, is that of its Byzantine successor built some five hundred years later. The remains are scattered over a wide area and new archaeological work is in progress.

The events that followed the assassination of Julius Caesar in 44 BC had left the Roman Empire in the joint control of Octavian in the west and Mark Antony in the east. The alliance between the two men had been strengthened by Antony's marriage to Octavian's sister, but destroyed when Antony discarded his wife in favour of Cleopatra of Egypt. The immediate result was a declaration of war by the Senate on Cleopatra and implicitly on Antony. The final outcome was the defeat of Antony and Cleopatra at Actium. Antony's camp was on Cape Actium to the south of the entrance to the Ambracian Gulf where both his and Cleopatra's fleets were sheltering. Octavian's camp was on the opposite side of the narrows, north of the site of modern-day Preveza. On the morning of the battle Antony's ships came out to meet Octavian's fleet which had been blockading the exit from the Gulf. At the height of the conflict Cleopatra inexplicably ordered her ships, anchored behind the main fleet as rearguard, to hoist sail and escape to the open sea. Antony followed shortly after but the bulk of his fleet was destroyed and burnt. Although it would be another year before both Antony and Cleopatra were dead the events at Actium effectively marked the end of the struggle for mastery of the Roman Empire.

The immense importance of the victory is reflected in the size of the city that Octavian, soon to be Augustus, founded on the site of his camp. Although an artificial creation the city prospered due to its position on the trading route between east and west. Fifty years after its founding Strabo was able to comment on a rapidly increasing population. Thereafter Nikopolis's history follows that of the Eastern Roman Empire as a whole, expanding and then declining with successive barbarian incursions in the 4C and 5C AD. At some point in the early

Preveza and Lefkas

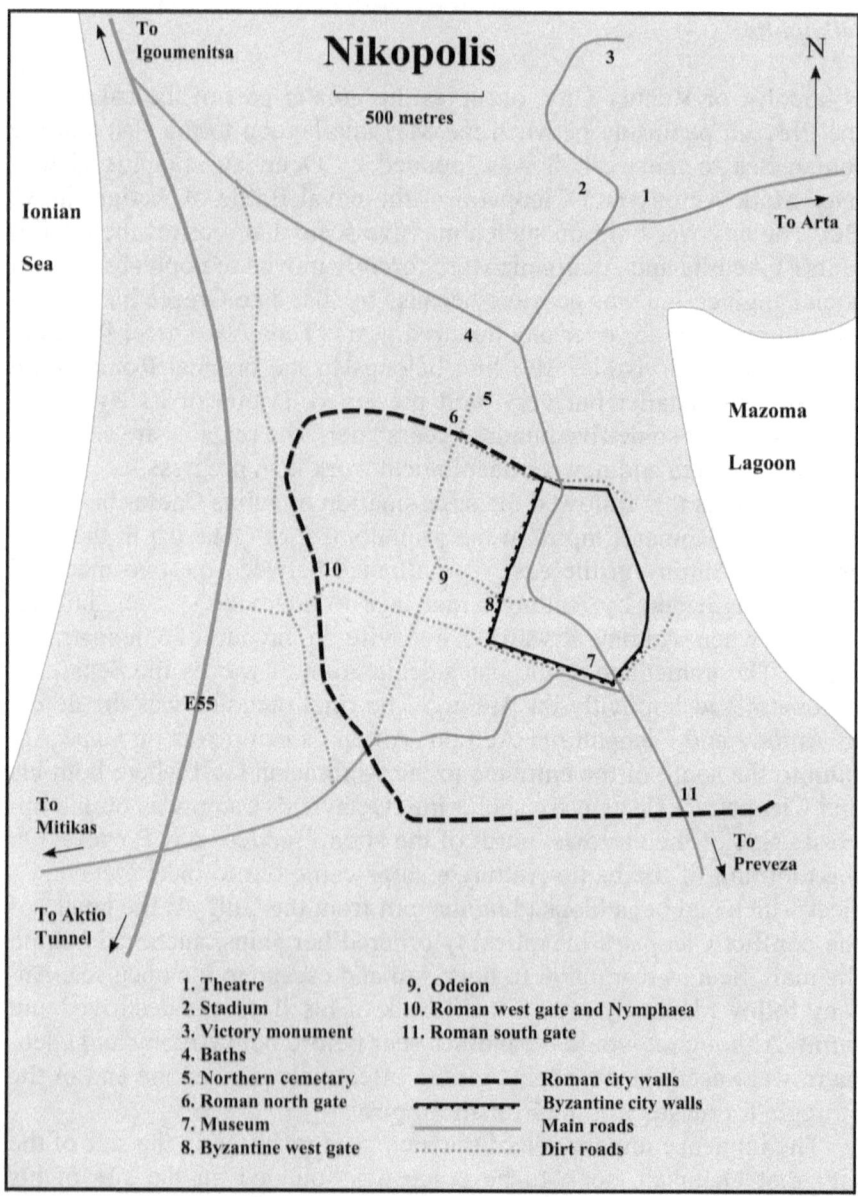

1. Theatre
2. Stadium
3. Victory monument
4. Baths
5. Northern cemetary
6. Roman north gate
7. Museum
8. Byzantine west gate
9. Odeion
10. Roman west gate and Nymphaea
11. Roman south gate

– – – – – Roman city walls
·········· Byzantine city walls
———— Main roads
·········· Dirt roads

Byzantine period, probably the last quarter of the 5C, the original Augustan walls were replaced with a shorter but more easily defended circuit of fortifications. There was then a second period of prosperity in the 6C AD when many of the basilican churches were founded. The final decline and abandonment was in the late 9C or early 10C AD.

Roman Nikopolis

Roman Nikopolis had a circuit of walls over 5km in length. The city had two harbours, one to the west on the Ionian coast and one to the southeast on the Ambracian Gulf at Vathy, an inlet just to the north of Preveza. The western harbour, known as Komaros, was possibly on the site of modern Mytikas. An aqueduct ran for fifty kilometres from the springs of the river Louros to supply fresh water. Beyond the northern gate was an extensive suburb with its own baths. Further north again was a sacred precinct with a theatre, stadium and gymnasium. These were used for the Actian Games which had been transferred from their original site at Cape Actium. The theatre and stadium stand at the foot of the hill where Augustus built his victory monument. Constructed on the spot where his tent had stood during the battle, it consists of a massive podium, originally faced with bronze rams from the bows of captured ships, supporting a stoa above that may have been used to display the spoils of battle. The remains can still be seen a little way above the village of Smyrtoula (now renamed Nikopoli). An inscription across the full width of the podium reveals that the monument was dedicated to Mars and Neptune.[15]

The circuit of the Roman walls forms a rough quadrilateral with sides between 1.5 and 1.25 kilometres in length. The walls have a heavily mortared rubble core originally faced with brick. Except at the main gates they appear to have been built entirely without towers. Although much material has been quarried away and long stretches of the walls are densely covered in vegetation the majority of the circuit can still be traced through the fields. The walls may never have been designed for defence. The absence of towers and the fact that the greater part of the western section incorporated the structure of the main aqueduct indicates that the walls may have been simply part of the political statement that Octavian intended by the foundation of the city.

At the sites of the principal gates the surviving structures have been cleared and consolidated. The south gate led to the southeastern harbour. Today its position is occupied by the main road to the north from Preveza. The D-shaped towers that flanked the gate still stand to a height of three metres. The lower courses of the facing survive and the remainder has been restored in a contrasting modern brick. A long length of the wall to the east has been similarly restored. Immediately outside the walls a large number of tombs and the foundations of masolea have been found. Roman burials were normally located outside the city walls and Nikopolis seems to have had a cemetery area beyond

Figure 2.34 Nikopolis: The restored east tower of the Roman south gate.

Figure 2.35 Nikopolis: The northern Nymphaeum.

Figure 2.36 Nikopolis: The Roman walls and north gate. The rubble and concrete core has lost its brick facing. The foundations of the east tower of the gate are visible in the foreground.

each of the main gates. At the north gate, which led to the suburb and the sacred area, a large section of the walls has been cleared but only the foundations of the towers survive. The cemetery, which was in use from the 1C to the 4C AD, lies on either side of the road beyond the gate. Extensive excavations have revealed graves of every type. The larger structures have been protected with metal roofing.

At the site of the now destroyed west gate stand the Nymphaea or fountains of the nymphs. These massive ruined structures are Roman Nikopolis's best preserved monuments. They stood on either side of the street immediately in front of the gate. They received water from the city's main aqueduct which ran along the length of the west wall from the northwest corner of the circuit. Each Nymphaeum consisted of a water filled open basin in front of marble tiled walls with niches that probably contained statues of the nymphs. Behind this façade was a massive structure that supported the high storage cistern fed by the aqueduct. Through the gate ran the Decumanus Maximus, the main east-west street. It led through the gate to the western harbour at Komaros.

Byzantine Nikopolis

Some five hundred metres north of the Roman south gate the main road from Preveza passes through a gap in the Byzantine walls and enters the interior of the 5C circuit. This occupies the northeast quadrant of the Roman city and was created by building substantial new walls to the west and south. The existing Roman walls on the north and east sides were presumably repaired at the same time. Previously believed to have been built by the Emperor Justinian, it is now thought that the new walls were constructed by one of his predecessors, either Zeno (474-491) or Anastasius (491-518), following the sack of the city by the Vandals in 474 AD.[16] The area enclosed is barely one fifth of the Roman original. This dramatic contraction may reflect a declining population after a century of barbarian attacks or may represent the maximum

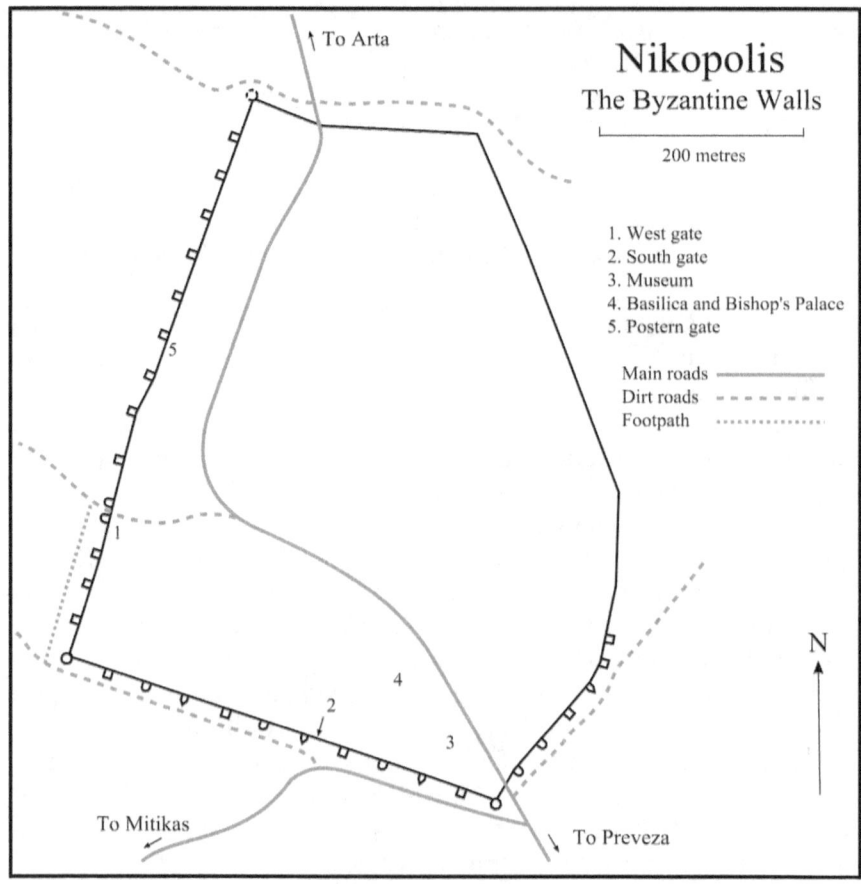

Nikopolis
The Byzantine Walls

200 metres

1. West gate
2. South gate
3. Museum
4. Basilica and Bishop's Palace
5. Postern gate

Main roads
Dirt roads
Footpath

Preveza and Lefkas

area it was possible to defend with the resources available. Curiously the centre of the Roman city, the forum, which lay a little to the south of the ruined odeion, was not included within the reduced circuit.

Approximately two thirds of the circuit has been cleared and can be inspected easily. The south side has a remarkable sequence of twelve towers of varying designs. The southeast corner tower is octagonal. With seven external faces, it projects so boldly from the walls that it is almost freestanding. Moving westwards the towers are alternately square, pentagonal and D-shaped. This sequence is repeated three times and is then followed by a final square tower. The southwest corner is

Figure 2.37 Nikopolis: Ground plans of the five types of tower found along the south walls.

Figure 2.38 Nikopolis: Byzantine south walls.

Figure 2.39 Nikopolis: Restored Byzantine gate in south wall.

protected by another projecting tower, this time of a circular section. The visual impact of this regular succession of towers is enhanced by the appearance of the walls themselves. Above one or more foundation courses of ashlar the walls are constructed of alternating bands of brick and irregular roughly faced stone. The layers of brick are five courses deep and laid with a red mortar. They appear from a distance as three or four continuous strong red bands along the length of the white or grey walls. The brick courses are not simply a decorative facing as they run

Preveza and Lefkas

right through the thickness of the walls. This technique, used earlier in the 5C Theodosian walls of Constantinople, was a feature of Byzantine style, but was also designed to stabilize the walls against potential earthquakes.[17] Near the second pentagonal tower the south wall is pierced by a narrow brick-arched gate recently restored. Its width implies that this must have been designed for pedestrian traffic only and it was presumably intended to provide easy access to the Basilica of Doumetios and the Bishop's Palace just to the north of the walls.

The west side of the circuit is constructed in the same manner as the south wall. Another round tower protects the northwest corner but all twelve intermediate towers have a square ground plan. The outstanding feature here is the monumental west gate. With its massive D-shaped towers this gate is a substantial fortification. It is oddly placed astride the only steep slope on this side of the site. The whole gate complex is therefore stepped with the base of the south tower, gateway and north

Figure 2.40 Nikopolis: the outer face of the Byzantine west gate. Visible in the north tower are two openings for artillery, a single archery slit and numerous small square scaffolding holes. The collapsed outer face of the wall around the gate opening and the exposed internal galleries can be seen clearly.

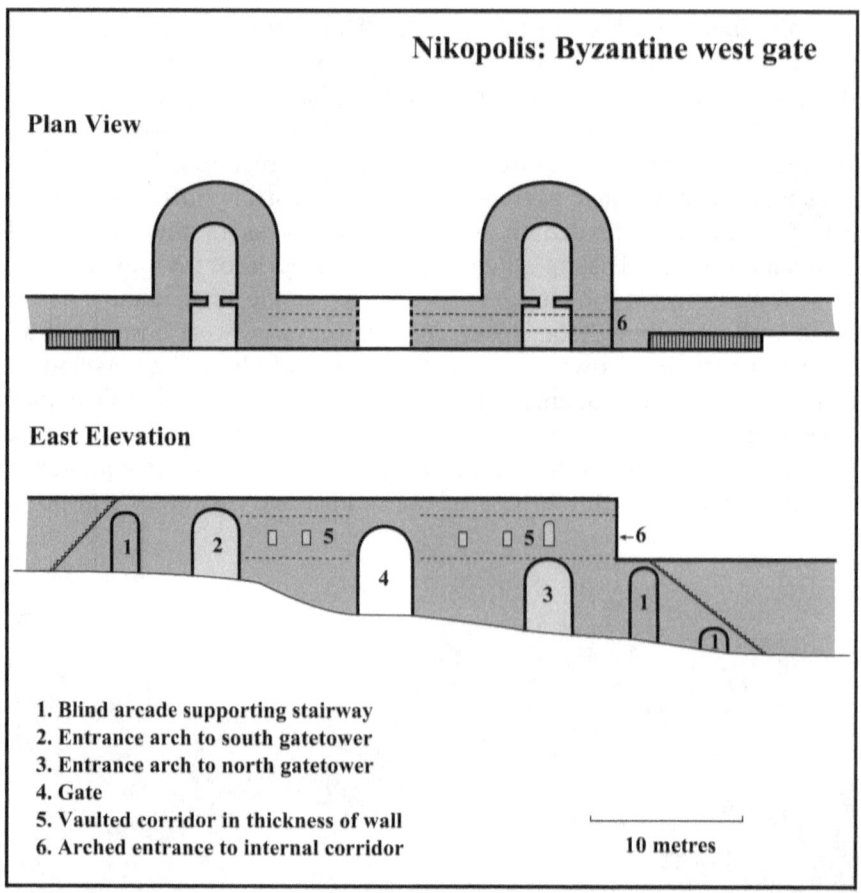

1. Blind arcade supporting stairway
2. Entrance arch to south gatetower
3. Entrance arch to north gatetower
4. Gate
5. Vaulted corridor in thickness of wall
6. Arched entrance to internal corridor

tower each at a different level to accommodate the four metre difference in height between the south and north sections of wall. However the top of the south wall maintains the same level across the gate as far as the north face of the north gatetower. Here it abruptly falls 4m to the level of the north section of wall. At this point an arched doorway leads from the wallwalk into a corridor in the thickness of the wall. This runs across the inner face of the north tower southwards towards the gate arch. There is a similar corridor, or gallery, in the wall south of the gate leading from the upper floor of the south tower. Both galleries appear to have been illuminated by openings in the inner face of the wall. Unfortunately the outer face of the walls on either side of the gate has partially collapsed. This has exposed the galleries but it is no longer possible to discern what part they played in the defensive arrangements of the gate. The gateway was closed by both a door and a portcullis.

Figure 2.41 Nikopolis: Inner face of the west gate showing, to the left and right of the gate, the entrance arches to the towers and the square openings illuminating the internal galleries.

Figure 2.42 Nikopolis: Access to the wallwalk was provided by two opposing stairways on either side of every second tower. The central arch gives access to the ground floor of the tower.

Preveza and Lefkas

Figure 2.43 Nikopolis: Interior of the north tower of the west gate.

The bolt slot and the groove in which the portcullis slid are still visible. According to A. W. Lawrence the portcullis was operated from a winch room situated above the gate where the outer face has collapsed.[18] The two gatetowers were equipped with archery slits on the first floor and larger, slightly splayed openings on the second. These are large enough

Preveza and Lefkas

to have deployed the torsion or tension powered artillery of the period. Access to the gate towers was from the ground floor through tall arched openings and also apparently from the wallwalk via the internal corridor discussed above. Stairs supported on blind arches gave access to the wallwalk on either side of the gate complex. This arrangement of opposing stairways is repeated at every second intermediate tower along the south and west walls with a blind supporting arch on either side of the central opening that gave access to the tower. The regular repetition of three distinctive arches rising almost to the full height of the wall gives a strong architectural rhythm to the fortifications. The towers of the west wall were provided with splayed archery slits in each of their three external faces. Access to the upper timber floors may have been by wooden stairs or from the level of the wallwalk. The walls must have

Figure 2.44 Nikopolis: Postern gate within the stairway-supporting arch.

been provided with parapets but unfortunately all traces have disappeared. The final feature to note in the west wall is a postern gate by the fourth tower to the north of the west gate. This is located within the stairway-supporting arch. It may have been placed here to give access to the nearby Alkison Basilica. Although only half of the lintel survives the relieving arch above has ensured the survival of the wall,

The northern and eastern walls are as yet uncleared except for a short length of the southeast section where a further five towers have been exposed. Presumably a further east gate existed in this uncleared section. A north gate may have stood at the point where the modern road breaches the walls.

Nikopolis is an extensive site and several hours are required to visit all its points of interest. Fortunately only the areas surrounding the Victory monument, the museum and the principal basilicas are enclosed. These have the usual opening hours (8.30 to 15.00). The main Preveza – Arta road passes through the eastern half of the city and then traverses the area of the northern suburb before passing the stadium and the massive ruined theatre. Although the theatre is as yet unexcavated the stadium has been cleared and is approached through the remains of the original eastern entrance tunnel. A network of drivable dirt roads connects the other points of interest around the site and also allows inspection of much of the Roman circuit. The best-preserved Roman monuments are the odeion and the Nymphaea. The odeion, reached from the dirt road that passes through the Byzantine west gate, dates from the founding of the city. It is built of brick and concrete and the seating has been restored. Originally the structure was roofed. The forum, which has not been excavated, lay due south. Beyond the odeion the dirt road forks. To the right a track leads to the Roman north gate. To the left another track leads via a further right turn to the Nymphaea and the site of the Roman west gate.

Notes

1. H. E. Lurier, *Crusaders as Conquerors: The Chronicle of the Morea*, p. 322.
2. N. D. Karabelas, *Το κάστρο της Μπούκας (1478-1701)*, p. 402.
3. The ruins of the destroyed Castle of Bouka survived until the end of the 18C when Ali Pasha re-used the materials in his new fortifications. Karabelas, *Το κάστρο της Μπούκας*, pp. 412-414.
4. Although Ali Pasha had first taken Preveza in 1798 with much

slaughter, his activities thereafter had been partially constrained by the convention of 1800 between Russia and Turkey. Primarily this treaty had established the Septinsular Republic of the Ionian Islands but it had also ceded the old Venetian mainland possessions to the Turks with the proviso that the privileges they had enjoyed from Venice should continue. Nominal control of Preveza was in the hands of a Bey appointed by the Sultan. However in 1806 war broke out between Russia and the Turks and Ali Pasha used the threat of a Russian takeover to re-occupy the town and assert absolute control. His major works of fortification began shortly after with the aim of transforming Preveza into his most important base on the coast. He also built himself a palace, or seraglio, on the site of the old Castle of Bouka. No trace of this structure survives. W. M. Leake, *Travels in Northern Greece, Vol. III*, p. 489.

5. ESCUTIS, *Muslim Presence in Epirus and Western Greece*, p. 414.
6. For much of the 20C the fort was used by the military and as a prison. Several other buildings stood on the roof in addition to the church. These have now all been demolished leaving only their concrete foundation platforms in place.
7. The Corinthians are believed to have colonised Lefkas and the coast of Akarnania in the 7C BC and cut the first navigable canal. The location of this canal and the topography of Lefkas in relation to the mainland of Akarnania has long been the subject of debate. Strabo (10.2.8) describes Lefkas as a peninsula which the Corinthians made into an island by cutting a channel through an isthmus. He locates this isthmus by the ancient town of Nerikos stating that it had become a channel now crossed by a bridge. Remains of a Hellenistic-Roman bridge lie submerged about 3km south of Santa Maura near the Russian Fort Constantine. Recent geological research has identified a raised area at this point, below modern sea level, which probably represents this ancient isthmus. However the nature of the ancient channel through the remainder of the lagoon area and the northern spit remains uncertain. Mediaeval and Venetian maps show the spit pierced only by a narrow moat beneath the western walls of the castle See P. Negris, *Vestiges Antiques Submergés*, pp. 354-360, and S. Brockmüller, A. Vott, S.M. May, and H. Brückner, *Palaeoenvironmental changes of the Lefkada Sound and their archaeological relevance*.
8. Angevin documents of 1300 record Charles II of Naples granting permission to John Orsini to build a fort. See William Miller, *Latins in the Levant*, p. 181.

9. See for example the map by Frederick de Wit, Library of Congress, www.loc.gov/resource/g6812p.ct001460/.
10. Although the monument visible is to Henry Davis there is another well documented but elusive monument somewhere within the castle. During the siege of Santa Maura in 1810 the British forces under Brigadier Oswald, having landed on Lefkas island, fought their way along the spit to the west of the castle. The French had constructed a series of redoubts and trenches across the spit in advance of the castle and a Major Clarke of the 35th Regiment was killed whilst taking one of these defences. Various commentators of the period record that he was buried within the fortress and a marble tomb erected in his honour. See Henry Holland, *Travels in the Ionian Islands, Albania, Thessaly etc.* p. 61.
11. See the Ionian University's project: *Inscriptions of the Ionian Islands*. The Morosini and Marino inscriptions can be viewed online at: http://tab.ionio.gr/culture/activities/projects/epigraphs/index.php (Items 97 and 134 in the index).
12. ESCUTIS, *Muslim Presence in Epirus and Western Greece*, p. 423.
13. The site has been identified as ancient Nerikos or ancient Sollion. Only fragmentary traces of these walls are visible. Immediately offshore lies a sunken breakwater, known as the Mole of the Corinthians, built to protect the entrance to the ancient canal and as a harbour for ancient Lefkas. The remains of the mole lie 1.4 metres below sea level. Its position is marked by the port and starboard (red and green) buoys that indicate the central entrance gap. See W. M. Murray, *Coastal Sites of Western Akarnania*, pp. 224-255.
14. ESCUTIS, *Muslim Presence in Epirus and Western Greece*, p. 423.
15. For the full inscription see W.M. Murray and P.M. Petsas, *Octavian's campsite memorial for the Actian War*, p. 86.
16. J. P. Sodini, *The Transformation of Cities in Late Antiquity within the Provinces of Macedonia and Epirus,* Proceedings of the British Academy Vol. 141, p. 320. However Justinian may well have repaired the walls, see Timothy Gregory, *The early Byzantine Fortifications of Nikopolis in comparative perspective*, Proceedings of the First International Symposium on Nikopolis, p. 261.
17. R. Langenbach, *From Opus Craticium to the Chicago Frame: Earthquake-Resistant Traditional Construction*, International Journal of Architectural Heritage, January 2007, p. 36.
18. A. W. Lawrence, *A Skeletal history of Byzantine Fortification*, pp. 193-194.

3

The Gulf of Ambracia

The Gulf of Ambracia extends eastwards inland from the Preveza narrows for 35 kilometres and has a maximum width from north to south of some 20 kilometres. The northern shore is marshy with substantial lagoons and large areas of reclaimed land. Two major rivers drain into the Gulf from the north and the geography of this shore has altered dramatically over the millenia.[1] In contrast the eastern and southern shores are fringed by hills and the shoreline has changed little. Throughout history the Gulf must have provided an important route into the interior of the mainland. The area is first known from the Corinthian and Elean colonies that were established in the 7C BC and the Gulf is encircled by ancient harbours that served inland cities. To the north the mediaeval Castle of Rogoi stands within an ancient ruined circuit identified as Bouchetion, the port for the Elean colonies of Elatria and Baties.[2] Substantial remains of both the earlier circuit and its mediaeval successor survive. The town of Arta, on the site of the Corinthian colony of Ambracia, has a Byzantine castle built partly on the walls of its ancient predecessor. As well as the original Byzantine work there are also Venetian and Turkish additions to the fortifications. Arta's harbour was at Ambrakos, now known as Phidokastro, near the original mouth of the river Arachthos where traces of the fortifications remain. On the eastern shore of the Gulf is the site of Amphilochian Argos, a town reputedly founded by Alcmaeon after the Trojan war.[3] Ancient Limnaia, situated in the southeast corner of the Gulf above modern Amphilochia, has a fine Hellenistic circuit re-used in the mediaeval period and again in the 19C. To the south of the Gulf the small, modern town of Vonitsa has a large mediaeval castle built on Byzantine foundations with Frankish, Venetian and Turkish additions.

After the creation of the Greek state in 1832 Epiros remained under Turkish control. The new frontier ran through the straits of Preveza. The southern shore of the Gulf was now part of mainland Greece whilst the

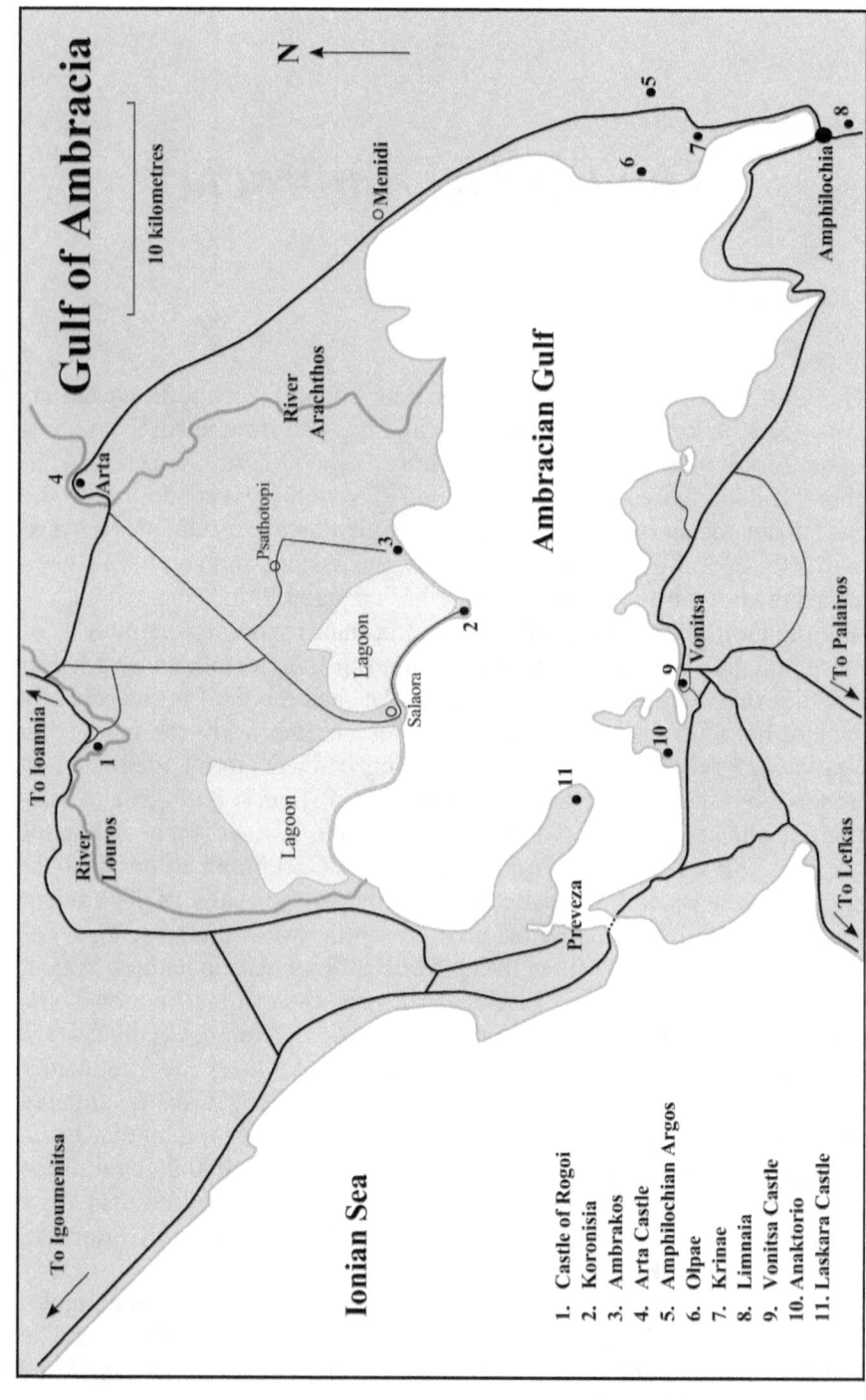

north shore was still part of the ailing Ottoman Empire. To defend this border area the Turks constructed a new series of forts and gun batteries. Examples of these still remain on the Agios Thomas peninsula near Preveza (Laskara Castle) and on the island of Koronisia.

Castle of Rogoi, Ancient Bouchetion

The Castle of Rogoi is clearly visible from the main Preveza - Arta road on a low hill overlooking the Louros River near the village of Nea Kerassous. To the south extends a large area of drained marshland and lagoons separated from open water by a series of sand spit barriers. Approaching from the north the castle is seen as an impressive array of mediaeval towers appearing above the trees of the hillside. The actual remains are considerably more complex than they first appear as much of the mediaeval work stands on earlier foundations and the outer circuit is largely hidden by dense vegetation.

The early 19C topographers of Greece believed that Rogoi stood on the ruins of ancient Charadrus, a site on the coast between Ambrakos and Aktio.[4] However Hammond has identified Rogoi as Bouchetion, one of the Elean colonies established in southern Epiros in the 7C BC, and thought to be the port for the settlements of Elatria and Baties.[5] The site of Elatria has been identified near the deserted village of Palaiorophoros (Oropos on modern maps) ten kilometres to the west of Rogoi. Baties is located on the hill of Kastro Rizovouni about seven kilometres to the north where a circuit of 4C BC walls still stands. Although the hill of Bouchetion lies some distance from the sea, the Louros river was thought to be navigable for the small vessels of the Classical and Hellenistic periods. However today the river takes a long, indirect course north and west from Bouchetion before turning south to meet the Gulf a mere five kilometres to the north of Nikopolis. The total distance is some twenty kilometres. The difficulty of reconciling the site's status as a port with modern topography has now been addressed by the geological work of the Nikopolis project. Jing and Rapp have established that around 2500 BC the coastline of the northwest quadrant of the Gulf lay close to the foothills to the north approximately on the line of the modern road.[6] At this date the hill of Rogoi was an island separated from the mainland by a narrow strait. The Louros entered the bay a little to the east of Rogoi and from there the coastline then probably ran in a southeasterly direction towards Ambrakos. Around 500 AD the shoreline began to move south as the bay silted up, but the river continued to flow south through a developing swampy delta. At some point in the mediaeval period between the 10C and 15C the river was artificially diverted to flow first north, beneath the hill of Rogoi, then west and south along its present route to the sea.[7] This diversion around the outer edge of the bay is reminiscent of the re-routing of the rivers around the Venetian lagoon. It may have been engineered to maintain access to the sea and to allow drainage of the marshes developing to the south.

Although knowledge of the topography of the area is now dramatically improved, the history of the settlements on the hill of Rogoi remains obscure. Bouchetion is thought to have been founded around 700 BC, but the site may not have been fortified until two centuries later. When Epiros was unified under the Molossian king Alexander in the 4C BC Bouchetion, along with the other Elean colonies, was seized and incorporated into the Molossian state. At the beginning of the 3C BC, under Pyrrhus, the territory of Epiros expanded and the period saw much re-fortification. However after the death of Pyrrhus's successor, Alexander II, in 240 BC Epiros began to fragment, and a protracted period of conflict with the Aetolians led to a further period of fortress building. At the beginning of the 2C BC Epiros became involved in the wars between Rome and Macedon. Eventually Epiros split into two factions with the Molossians supporting Macedon. The final Roman victory at the end of the Third Macedonian War led to the sacking of seventy Molossian settlements, including Bouchetion, in 167 BC. However because of its strategic position a settlement continued to exist on the hill until it was abandoned after the founding of Nikopolis.

The refounded settlement, known as the Castle of Rogoi or Rogous, first appears in written sources at the start of the 14C. The French version of the Chronicle of the Morea describes an unsuccessful attack on the castle by an army sent by Charles II of Naples in 1304.[8] John Cantacuzene recounts how he brought about the peaceable recovery of the castle in 1340 from the supporters of Nikephoros II Orsini.[9] The castle must have been in existence at the end of the 13C and may date from the early years of the Despotate after 1205. Another possibility may be a foundation date in the 9C when Epiros was brought back under Byzantine control in the reign of the Emperor Basil I. The site was finally abandoned after the area fell to the Ottoman Turks in 1449. The castle has never been excavated.

The walls of Bouchetion are thought to have developed in three phases.[10] In the first, the relatively flat area on the top of the hill (plan: areas A, B and C) was enclosed by a simple circuit wall with square towers. This presumably formed the acropolis of the settlement. In the

Gulf of Ambracia

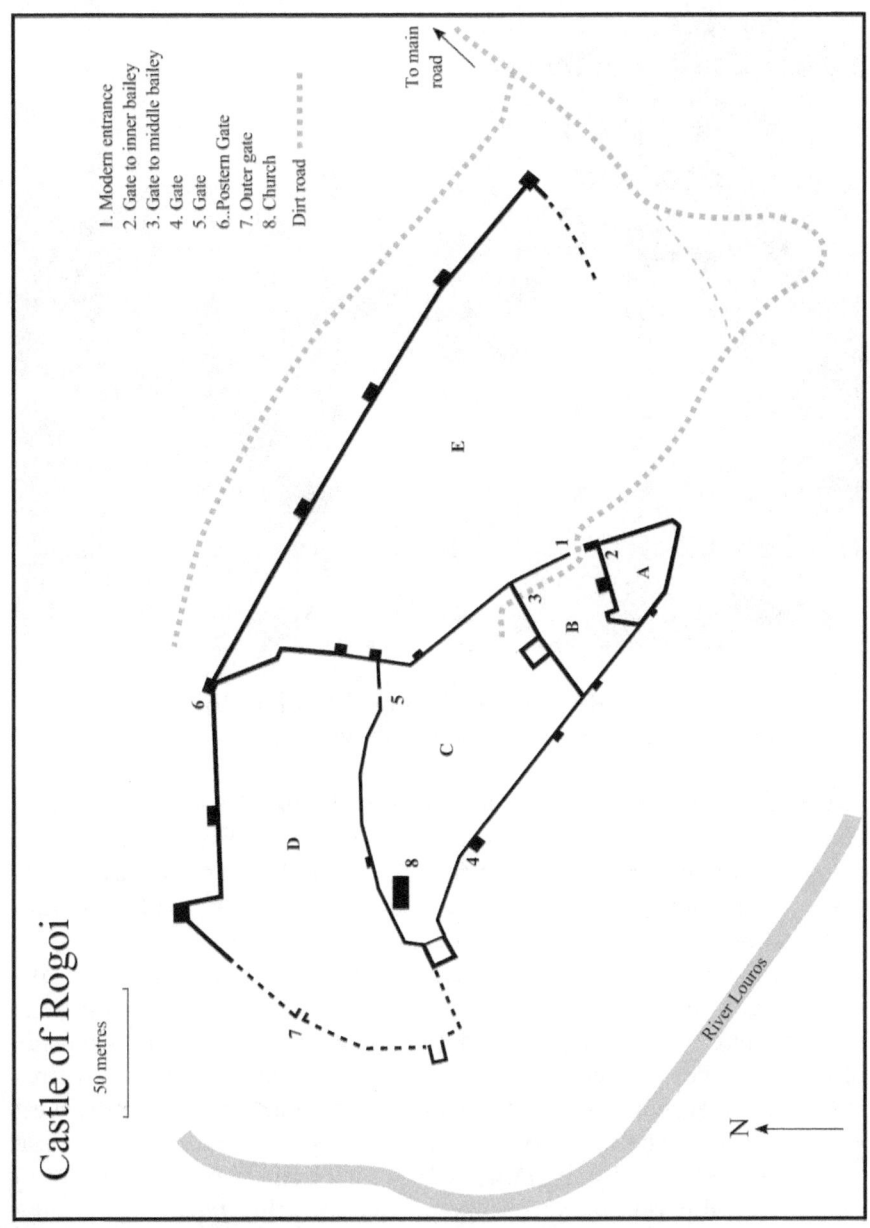

second phase the walls were extended to fortify the northern slope of the hill (plan: area D). Finally a wall was built enclosing the northeastern flank (plan: area E). The first circuit is built almost entirely of quarry-faced ashlar. The later phases consist of polygonal walls with

Figure 3.1 The River Louros below the hill of Rogoi. At this point the river is only two metres above modern sea level.

towers predominantly of ashlar. These walls may have been partially demolished in 167 BC. The castle and town walls of mediaeval Rogoi were built upon the ruins of first two phases of Bouchetion. New crosswalls were constructed within the original acropolis dividing it into three baileys. The town may have occupied areas C and D.

Approaching the castle from the village of Nea Kerassous the dirt road forks at the base of the hill. The road to the right leads on level ground along the length of the long wall that enclosed area E. This side of the hill is heavily overgrown and the wall stands only to two metres but the large corner tower and the three intermediate towers to the west are still visible. The masonry is generally polygonal but with some use of squared blocks. Although this area of the circuit was never rebuilt in the mediaeval period there is still evidence of earlier repair work in the tile fragments to be found in the upper joints of the towers. After 250m the dirt road ends by a massive tower. This is the original corner tower of the wall built to enclose area D. Composed of square dressed blocks, it still stands to a height of eight metres. The tower's corners have been carefully drafted. When first built the tower consisted entirely of fine

Figure 3.2 Castle of Rogoi: The northeast corner tower of the second phase of the original circuit.

isodomic masonry but the upper courses are now irregular with much use of tile infilling where blocks have been replaced. The uppermost courses have been completely rebuilt with rough rubble masonry

Figure 3.3 Castle of Rogoi: Postern gate in the outer circuit wall. Mediaeval stone door jambs appear to have been inserted into an earlier opening.

standing on a thick layer of tile. Immediately to the west of the tower a narrow postern gate leads steeply uphill through the thickness of the wall. At some point, probably in the mediaeval period, the threshold of the gate has been raised and stone jambs have been inserted to narrow the entrance further. The circuit wall continues to follow the foot of the hill westwards, but beyond the next tower it is heavily overgrown, ruinous and difficult to trace. Where the wall turns southwest, Hammond identified a mediaeval outer gate (plan: 7). The large tower at the western-most point of the circuit is also mediaeval and may have been designed as a strongpoint to defend the river. A final short section of wall climbs from this point to the western tower of the acropolis.

Returning to the fork in the dirt road, the left branch leads uphill passing beneath the east wall of the inner bailey (plan: A). Here some ten courses of the original acropolis wall survive surmounted by the rough masonry of the mediaeval rebuilding. Entry is now via a modern breach in the wall of the middle bailey (plan: 1, B). The dividing wall

Gulf of Ambracia

Figure 3.4 Castle of Rogoi: West tower of the outer circuit with the west tower of the acropolis in the background above.

Figure 3.5 Castle of Rogoi: Exterior of east wall and tower of upper bailey.

Figure 3.6 Castle of Rogoi: Centre and west towers of upper bailey.

between the inner and middle baileys is reinforced by three square towers. The centre and west towers are completely mediaeval but the east tower incorporates the remains of a flanking tower of the original acropolis circuit. Entry into the inner bailey is through a simple arched gate (plan: 2). The interior is ruined and overgrown. Another arched gate leads into the outer bailey (plan: 3). The plain dividing wall here is reinforced with a single massive tower, again entirely mediaeval. The walls of the outer bailey (plan: C) survive principally as revetments to the steep hillside. Again they consist of mediaeval repairs upon the original foundations. The exception is the section incorporating a gate from the acropolis to the northern enclosure (plan: 5). This appears to be entirely mediaeval. Unfortunately close examination of the exterior of this wall is impossible as the interior of enclosure D is completely overgrown and inaccessible. A section of the parapet and wallwalk survives on the descending walls forming the east side of enclosure D and can be seen from above. The outer bailey contains the 15C church of the Assumption of the Virgin Mary, the sole surviving structure of the monastery that stood here. The remains of St Luke the Evangelist were supposed to have been secreted here after the Franks of the Fourth Crusade removed them from Constantinople in 1204. They were subsequently moved again for safekeeping when the Turks gained control of

Gulf of Ambracia

Figure 3.7 Castle of Rogoi: Tower of middle bailey.

the area in 1449.[11] At the western end of the outer bailey a large tower projects boldly some eight metres beyond the wall line. The visible superstructure is almost entirely mediaeval rebuilding upon the lower courses of the original tower. However this itself was a replacement for an earlier smaller tower built of the same ashlar masonry as the rest of the acropolis circuit. Thirty metres to the east a gate flanked by another tower provided access to the southern slope of the hill (plan: 4).

Gulf of Ambracia

Figure 3.8 Castle of Rogoi: West tower of the outer bailey. Mediaeval re-building on ancient foundations.

Access to the castle is straightforward as the site is unenclosed and visible from the main Preveza – Arta road. Although precise dating of any aspect of the fortifications is impossible, the distinction between the original walls of Bouchetion and the later mediaeval work of Rogoi is clear and repays detailed examination.

Koronisia

After the success of the Greek revolution the borders of the fledgling state were confirmed by the Treaty of Constantinople in 1832. The actual mapping of the border along the Arta – Volos line was carried out by a combined British and French survey from 1832 to 1835. The new

Figure 3.9 Koronisia: The heavily restored exterior of the late Turkish gun tower. The opening of one of the three gunports can be seen on the right of the main tower.

border passed through the straits of Preveza and crossed the Ambracian Gulf to a point on the eastern shore near Menidi.[12] In order to fortify this new frontier the Turks built a series of gun batteries and forts along the northern shore of the Gulf. The 19C battery constructed at Pantokratoras fort near Preveza was discussed in the previous chapter. Five kilometres east of Preveza on the summit of Mount Tourkovouni at the tip of the Agios Thomas' peninsula a simple circular gun fort, now known as Laskara Castle, was built in 1860 to command the inner narrows of the Gulf. This building is now a ruined shell, but a similar fortified tower constructed around the same time on the island of Koronisia has recently been restored.[13] The fort consists of a two-storey circular tower approximately 13m in diameter with two semicircular turret-like extensions to the east and west. The entrance is on the first floor reached by a stone ramp and wooden bridge. Above the arch of the doorway an inset plaque confirms the year of construction as 1860. The ground floor is provided with narrow rifle slits and has at its centre a circular powder magazine. The upper storey had a wooden floor and was provided with broader splayed rifle slits and three large gunports.

Koronisia was once an island in the Gulf but is now connected to the mainland by sand spits to the east and west. In 1832 the only buildings on the island were a small convent and a chapel. Today the village is a modest beach resort. Access from the mainland is by a modern road along the western spit. The fort lies at the southern end of the island beyond the village.

Ambrakos (Phidokastro)

Ambrakos was the fortified port of Ambracia, the Corinthian colony established in the 7C BC on the site now occupied by the town of Arta. It was built on a marshy islet at the mouth of the River Arachthos. Unlike its counterpart at Bouchetion, the port of the Elean colonies, the references to Ambrakos in early literature describe both its location and the nature of the site. Pseudo-Scylax (33) refers to a fort upon the sea with an enclosed harbour about eighty stadia (15km) from Ambracia. Polybius (4.61.7) describes Ambrakos as standing in a lake, strongly fortified by a wall and outworks and with only one narrow approach.

The site was known to the travellers of the early 19C. When Leake visited the area in 1805 he discovered the ruins of Ambrakos at the eastern side of the shallow bay of Palea-Bukka, named after the old mouth of the River Arachthos.[14] He describes it as, "an island in the lagoon covered with the ruins of a castle built of small stones and mortar mixed with Hellenic work towards the foundations". A much more detailed account comes from a report by Lieutenant Colonel Baker to the Royal Geographical Society in 1837.[15] This describes an irregular quadrangular circuit rising abruptly from the lagoon to form an enclosed basin approximately 150m by 130m with walls standing to a height of 4.5 to 7.5 metres. Two thirds of the height of the walls consisted of large blocks of isodomic masonry. The upper third was built of rougher material referred to as "Roman". The walls were awash on both sides although the water was merely a few centimetres deep. The report notes four towers in the circuit. The entrance to the basin was at the southeast.

The site, now known as Phidokastro, still exists. It stands approximately four kilometres to the northeast of Koronisia but is reachable only by a long track across the reclaimed marshes from the village of Psathotopi. The walls are overgrown and much reduced in height since 1837 but their line is still discernable. It is not clear whether the remains are merely those of a fort built to defend the mouth of the river or if the walls enclosed the port itself. Leake believed that the harbour was an artificial basin excavated near the fortress. Baker however clearly states that the walls formed the basin of the port. Dating the site remains very difficult. If the Periplous of Pseudo-Scylax belongs to the 4C BC then Ambrakos may be contemporary with Bouchetion. The rebuilding of the walls in rough masonry with tile fragments may indicate a period of re-use in the early Byzantine period. Eventually the harbour must have become unusable as the river changed its course and the area silted up. Salaora, or Salagora, some seven kilometres to the west of Phidokastro, is mentioned as a harbour for Arta as early as 1292.[16]

Castle of Arta, Ancient Ambracia

The modern town of Arta possesses a fine 13C Byzantine castle. It bears some similarity to the castle of Rogoi and may have been founded around the same time. Its better state of preservation, at least externally, owes much to its continuous use as a fortification which lasted until 1881 when Arta was finally liberated from the Turks. Rogoi, by contrast, was abandoned after 1453 and is now a ruin. Arta shares another feature with Rogoi in that it is also partly built upon much earlier walls. The Byzantine town of Arta stood on the remains of the city of Ambracia originally founded by Corinthian colonists in 625 BC.[17] The city possessed an acropolis and a wall circuit reputedly five kilometres long. The eastern section of this circuit overlooked the River Arachthos and was incorporated into the east wall of the new castle. Early sources suggest that the Arachthos was navigable as far as Ambracia.[18] However the importance of Ambrakos as a port at the mouth of the river in antiquity implies that navigation upstream must have been limited and may have involved the transhipment of cargoes into smaller vessels. Certainly by 1448, when Cyriac of Ancona describes sailing down the Arachthos in small boats and journeying from Koronisia to Arta "over sea and land by ship and horse", navigation was clearly difficult.[19] Nevertheless in the 6C BC Ambracia was an important centre for trade between Epiros and its mother city of Corinth. It developed into an

Gulf of Ambracia

Figure 3.10 Castle of Arta: View from the southwest. The Turkish clock tower, built in 1875, in the foreground.

independent state with a large territory including all of the plain to the south. It is known to have sent seven ships to participate in the Battle of Salamis against the Persians in 480 BC and its citizens fought alongside Corinth against Corfu. The city was an ally of Sparta in the Peloponnesian war. The city's power was severely curtailed when the territorial wars with neighbouring Argos Amphilochia ended with a crushing defeat at the Battle of Olpae in 426 BC.[20] In the second half of the 4C BC Ambracia was drawn into the Macedonian orbit and saw a further period of greatness when Pyrrhus made it the capital of an expanded Epirot state in 297 BC. After the death of Pyrrhus's successor, Alexander II, in 240 BC Ambracia separated from Epiros and again became an independent state. Towards the end of the 3C BC it become part of the Aetolian league and as a consequence endured a famous siege when war broke out between Rome and the Aetolians.[21] Although the siege was concluded by a truce the city was still stripped of its sculptures and art by the Roman consul Marcus Fulvius Nobilior in 189 BC. This marked the beginning of Ambracia's decline, which became total when Augustus transferred the population to the new city of Nikopolis after 31 BC.

The site may have been re-occupied in the 9C when the Byzantine Empire regained control of Epiros. However the name of Arta appears for the first time in 1082 when Bohemond, the son of Robert Guiscard the Norman Duke of Calabria and Apulia, laid siege to the town.[22] The fact that a siege was necessary indicates that some form of fortifications must have existed at this date. In 1204 Constantinople fell to the combined forces of the Fourth Crusade and the rump of the Byzantine Empire was partitioned between the Venetians and the Franks. Although the coastline of Epiros and the Ionian Islands were assigned to Venice, in practice the Venetians were only interested in the strategic harbour towns and in 1205 Epiros was seized by Michael Comnenus Doukas, a minor, illegitimate, member of the Byzantine imperial family. The state he founded was later to become known as the Despotate of Epiros with Arta as its capital. Michael and his successor, his half-brother Theodore, pursued a policy of territorial expansion and by 1230 the fledgling state controlled almost all of Greece north of the Gulf of Corinth including the city of Thessalonica. The core of the present castle was probably constructed between 1231 and 1267 by Michael II, the first Despot. The Despotate survived for another two hundred years passing from Byzantine rule first to the Orsini family and then, after a period of Albanian control in Arta, to another Italian clan, the Tocchi. However in 1449 Arta fell to the Turks just four years before the final sack of Constantinople. Thereafter its history mirrors that of Preveza. It saw a brief period of Venetian control after 1684 when Morosini invaded the province. The city became Turkish again after the Treaty of Karlowitz in 1699 but was re-taken by the Venetians in 1717. Their influence lasted until 1797 although as an inland town Arta could only have been of importance to the Venetians as an administrative, tax-gathering centre. When Venice finally fell to Napoleon, the Treaty of Campo Formio assigned Arta to France along with Venice's coastal possessions. (The town is specified by name in the treaty). However by 1799 it was in the hands of Ali Pasha and it remained part of the Ottoman Empire until 1881.

There is now little to be seen of ancient Ambracia. With the exception of the section incorporated into the east wall of the castle the city walls have almost completely disappeared. When Leake visited the town in 1804 he was able to trace much of the original circuit and he identified the foundations of the acropolis walls on the hill to the south of the town. Today the only substantial structures that survive are the foundations of a temple of Apollo and a small theatre, both located in the town centre. In contrast the Byzantine castle of Arta stands largely complete, at least externally, on the northeast edge of the modern town.

Gulf of Ambracia

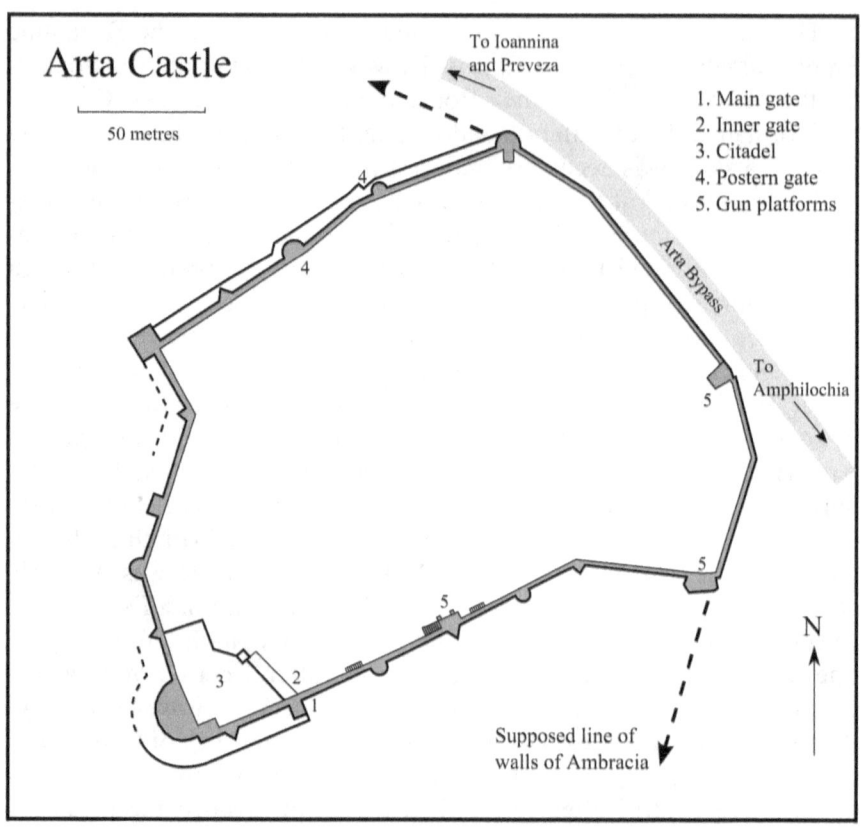

The castle is built on a low hill, only a few metres high, overlooking the river Arachthos. The river now flows almost two hundred metres to the east of the walls but originally the channel probably ran along the line occupied by the modern by-pass. On this side of the fortress a single massive wall, which includes a lengthy section of the city wall of Ambracia, seems to have been thought sufficient protection. To the west, south and north however the defences consisted of an inner wall, up to ten metres high and reinforced by a variety of flanking towers, and an outer wall, four to five metres in height, designed to shield the base of the inner from assault by siege weapons. The inner wall survives complete, the outer for approximately half its original length. The distance between the two walls is just sufficient for the outer wall to enclose the towers, which are variously square, round and triangular. The difference in height allowed each wall to have a clear field of fire from parapet level. The masonry is of heavily mortared rough blocks. The main gate is a simple arched opening in the inner wall placed close to

Gulf of Ambracia

Figure 3.11 Castle of Arta: Outer face of the main gate.

Figure 3.12 Castle of Arta: Double walls west of the gate.

Gulf of Ambracia

Figure 3.13 Castle of Arta: Interior of the main gate with the entrance to the citadel to the right.

the eastern side of an inner enclosure or citadel. The gate may have once been a more complex structure. The line of the outer wall now stops by the square tower to the west of the gate but it probably continued along the full length of the southern defences. The short cross wall that blocks off the gap between the outer wall and the tower is clearly a later insertion as the masonry is not bonded to the tower's outer face. On the left through the entrance a second gateway can be seen in the outer wall of the citadel enclosure. The wall on either side of this inner gate is pierced with loopholes. Its lower courses are of massive re-used blocks with irregular rougher construction above. The citadel is currently closed and inaccessible.

Unfortunately at some point in the 1960s the interior of the castle was landscaped and an incongruous concrete Xenia hotel built in the centre. The hotel buildings are now derelict and much of the periphery is overgrown. As a result there is now little to see within the main body of the walls. However the parapets and wallwalks are largely intact as are the gun platforms and associated ramps added when the castle was adapted for artillery. A conspicuous example of these modifications can be seen fifty metres east of the main gate where a platform and ramp

Gulf of Ambracia

Figure 3.14 Castle of Arta: Rear of round tower in the north wall. The entrance to the postern gate is visible below the wallwalk.

Figure 3.15 Castle of Arta: The entrance to the postern gate tunnel beneath its massive lintel.

have been built behind the triangular tower. A single large gun embrasure has been inserted at the salient angle of the tower. The work may date from as late as the beginning of the 19C during Ali Pasha's brief tenure. The other internal feature of note is the postern gate located in the centre of the northern wall, probably placed to give access to the river. The gate was reached from an opening beneath a massive lintel leading beneath the wallwalk into the interior of a hollow tower (plan: 4). This originally gave access to the narrow corridor formed between the inner and outer walls. Forty metres to the east an arched gateway set in an angle of the outer wall provided the final exit.

The various phases of the castle's construction are best appreciated by walking around the outside of the walls. Proceeding anti-clockwise

Figure 3.16 Castle of Arta: View to the east from the main gate.

Figure 3.17 Castle of Arta: The massive smooth-faced blocks of the original walls of Ambracia surmounted by Turkish artillery embrasures and a WWII concrete gun emplacement.

from the main gate, the south wall is reinforced by four towers alternately half-round and triangular with an irregular rectangular bastion at the southeast corner. Externally at least this section seems purely Byzantine. The defences then run north for 200m following the line of the original walls of Ambracia. Surviving sections of these ancient walls consist of massive rectangular blocks with close fitting joints and finely worked faces. They stand to six courses. In places they rest on courses of smaller cruder blocks that may represent the earliest city wall. The Byzantines restored missing sections of this wall and rebuilt the upper courses in their standard rough masonry but no towers were added. Later the walls were repaired again by the Turks who also inserted wide splayed gun embrasures in the parapet. Examples of these can be seen in the section of wall parallel to the by-pass. The northern side of the circuit has a prominent round tower at the northeast corner, a large square tower to the northwest and three intermediate towers. The double walls here survive for their full length. The postern gate in this face provided the only other entrance to the castle. From the northwest corner tower to the citadel the outer wall is incomplete but its line can still be traced. Here the towers of the main wall are alternately triangular, square and round. The southwest corner of the castle has been subject to much rebuilding. A multangular bastion forming a rough semicircle has been constructed against the west wall at its southern end. This projects some twelve metres from the line of the walls. The parapet, which is defined by a semicircular stringcourse, or cordon, is provided with five large gun embrasures. The south wall immediately adjacent to the bastion has also been rebuilt to provide a further two gun positions but at a level one metre higher. Again a prominent cordon defines the parapet. The distinctive style of these two features may indicate Venetian work. The next section of the wall to the east has a triangular tower and appears to be part of the original Byzantine wall. A single gun embrasure has been inserted at the apex of the tower parapet. Finally, returning once again to the rebuilt square tower to the west of the gate, there is a further change in wall height and again a cordon at parapet level.

Figure 3.18 Castle of Arta: Southwest multangular bastion.

Gulf of Ambracia

Dating the castle is difficult. The remnants of the walls of ancient Ambracia may date from the 4C BC or the reign of Pyrrhus in the 3C BC. The precise date of the castle's main elements is not certain. The alternating tower shapes are a definite Byzantine feature but there is little specific dating evidence. On the third tower to the east of the main gate is a monogram in brick believed to show the initials of Michael Angelos Comnenus Doukas.[23] This has been taken to refer to Michael II (1236-1271). Although Michael I (1205-1215) had the same full name he is known never to have used the family name of Angelos. Each successive change of ruler must have left its mark but the majority of the later work is executed in the same style of masonry. The only section that might be dated on stylistic evidence is the Venetian work at the southwest corner of the circuit. The long period of Turkish occupation had the greatest impact with extensive re-modelling of the wall parapets and the conversion of the existing towers to accommodate artillery.

Access to the castle is straightforward. There are no formal opening hours, the gate is sporadically open during daylight. Parking in the centre of Arta can be difficult and it may be preferable to use the car parks on the by-pass.

Limnaia

The fortifications of ancient Limnaia stand high above the modern town and inland port of Amphilochia forty-six kilometres to the south of Arta at the southeast extremity of the Gulf of Ambracia. A circuit of Hellenistic walls reinforced with square towers forms a rough quadrilateral around the hilltop. Two long walls run down from this enclosure to the site of the original harbour area by the modern quayside. There is evidence of mediaeval repair to the walls of the main circuit, or acropolis, thought to have been re-occupied in the 13C or 14C when it was called Valtos. Further repairs to the fortifications were carried out by Ali Pasha at the beginning of the 19C and the interior also contains the foundations of the settlement he established at that time by forcibly moving the inhabitants of a nearby village.[24] The site remained of strategic importance throughout its history as it commands the pass leading south from the Gulf to Stratos and the interior of Akarnania.

The first mention of Limnaia in the historical record is in the 5C BC when Thucydides (2.80), describing the campaign by Sparta and her allies against Akarnania, calls it an unfortified village. Walls are first thought to have been built around the settlement in the late 4C or early

Figure 3.19 Limnaia: South wall and tower.

3C BC. The site was almost certainly abandoned after the creation of Nikopolis and the forcible transfer of the inhabitants of Aetolia and Akarnania to populate the new city. Evidence of re-occupation in the 14C comes from John Cantacuzene who lists the places remaining loyal to the Byzantine Empire during the attempt to restore Nikephoros II as Despot. This list includes Balton, or Valton, which has been identified with Limnaia.[25] The settlement founded by Ali Pasha was quickly abandoned after his death in 1822. The inhabitants established a new village below on the Gulf at Kervasaras, or Karavasaras, now modern Amphilochia. Limnaia itself remained part of the network of Turkish forts that controlled the area. It functioned as such throughout the struggles of the Greek Revolution until the 7th April 1829 when its Turkish garrison surrendered to Greek forces under the command of Sir Richard Church. This action opened the way south and a Greek division retook Mesolonghi on the 17th May.[26]

Today the site is approached via a modern road that climbs the flank of the hill from the southwest. Where this road crosses the line of the western long wall it doubles back on itself and runs south. Here the surviving lower courses of the long wall are of rough polygonal masonry

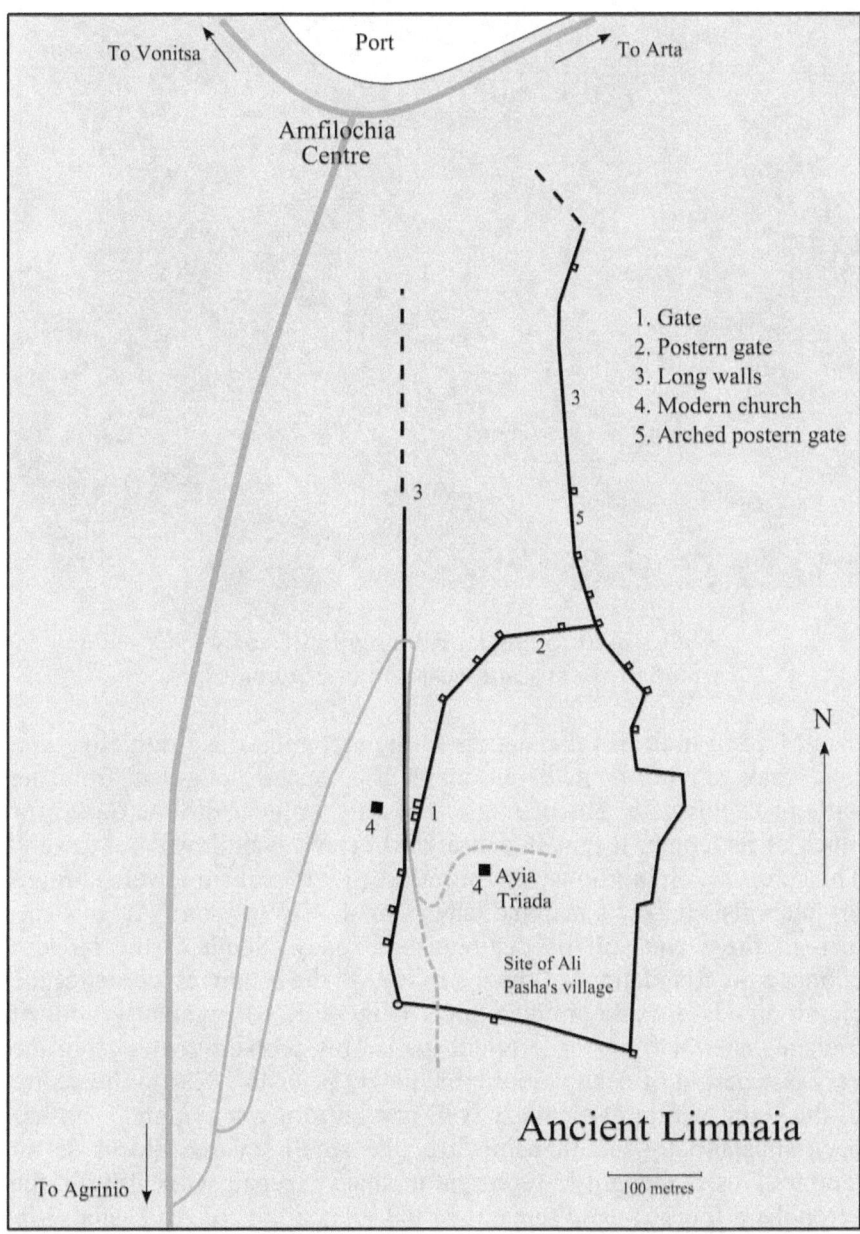

and they now form a revetment supporting the road. The long wall joins the main circuit of the acropolis at an acute angle. The road enters through a breach at this point but a few metres to the north the lower courses of two square gatetowers mark the original entrance. Heuzey's

Gulf of Ambracia

Figure 3.20 Limnaia: Roughly built, early 19C round tower at southwest corner of circuit.

plan of 1860 indicates that access to the acropolis was originally via a long track running immediately inside the western long wall from the harbour to this gate. The course of the long wall can still be traced for much of its length. It runs in a straight line and is built without towers. The acropolis circuit however is reinforced with square towers at regular intervals. Heuzey's map indicates a total of twenty-one. At least sixteen of these can still be distinguished today. South of the modern entrance the foundations of three survive. At the southwest corner of the circuit stands a crude circular tower (Figure 3.20) apparently built of broken material from the original wall. This probably dates from the very last period of occupation immediately prior to 1829. In the centre of the south wall a particularly well-preserved tower (Figure 3.19) has been substantially rebuilt using irregular small squared blocks set in mortar. This is thought to represent mediaeval repair work. Within the acropolis a few scattered remains of the foundations of Ali Pasha's village can be seen among the pine trees that now occupy much of the interior. The only building now standing here is the church of Ayia Triada, the sole survivor of the short-lived village. In the north wall of the acropolis is a second entrance. This is a postern gate giving access to the extensive area between the long walls. Now half buried by

Gulf of Ambracia

Figure 3.21 Limnaia: Postern gate leading from the acropolis to the area between the long walls.

Figure 3.22 Limnaia: View along the length of the eastern long wall.

Gulf of Ambracia

Figure 3.23 Limnaia: Arched postern gate, eastern long wall.

fallen masonry, the massive lintel is still in situ. The eastern long wall is the best preserved section of Limnaia's fortifications. Sections still stand to eight or nine courses. It can be traced for almost its entire length from the northeast corner of the acropolis to the shore. The outer face of the wall is built of carefully cut isodomic or pseudo-isodomic masonry. The inner face however is constructed of polygonal blocks. A rubble fill forms the core between the two faces. Here also is to be found the most remarkable of Limnaia's surviving features; a postern gate with the lintel carved to imitate an arch.

Although the greater part of the surviving walls at Limnaia are Hellenistic and there is little now standing from the mediaeval period, the site has strong connections with the Greek War of Independence and is worth visiting for this reason alone. Much of the hill is heavily overgrown but it is possible to follow the circuit with care. To reach the site, follow the main road south from the centre of Amphilochia for approximately 1200 metres to the southern end of the large modern cemetery to the right of the road. Opposite is the left turn that leads uphill to the church of Ayia Triada within the walls where it is possible to park.

Castle of Vonitsa

From Amphilochia the E55 follows the southern coastline of the Gulf of Ambracia to Vonitsa and then Preveza via the Aktio tunnel. The Byzantine Castle of Vonitsa is built on a conspicuous hill above the town. Approaching from the east its triple line of walls overlooking the harbour can be seen from a considerable distance. In contrast to the fortresses of Rogoi and Arta the Castle of Vonitsa does not stand on the foundations of an earlier settlement. A Corinthian colony known as Anaktoria was established on this coast at the same time as its counterpart at Ambracia but this was located about five kilometres to the east of Vonitsa. Establishing the date of the first castle on the hill is as difficult here as for Arta and Rogoi, and the same speculative range of dates, from the 9C to the 13C, may apply. The town was plundered by the forces of Robert Guiscard in 1081, but whether the castle was already in existence at this date is unknown.[27] Another source actually names Vonitsa as the place of Guiscard's death in 1085, although it is more generally accepted that he died on Cephalonia.[28]

From the mid-13C Vonitsa figures prominently in the history of the Despotate of Epiros. After the disastrous defeat at Pelagonia and the Byzantine Greeks' invasion of Epiros, Michael II fled to Cephalonia, then in the hands of the Orsini family. In 1261 his forces regrouped and he was able to land at Vonitsa and regain Arta and Ioannina. In 1294 the town passed to Philip of Taranto, son of Charles II of Anjou, via his marriage to Thamar, daughter of the Despot Nikephoros. The town was recovered briefly by Thomas, son of Nikephoros, in 1304, but retaken by Philip of Taranto in 1306. It was captured by Byzantine forces in 1314 but by 1323 was again part of a re-united Despotate under John Orsini. In 1331 it fell to Walter of Brienne, the son-in-law of Philip of Taranto, and for the next thirty years it remained under Angevin control until it was seized by Leonardo Tocco in 1362. The Tocco family held Vonitsa for the next one hundred and seventeen years save for a brief

Gulf of Ambracia

Figure 3.24 Vonitsa Castle: Overall view from the east

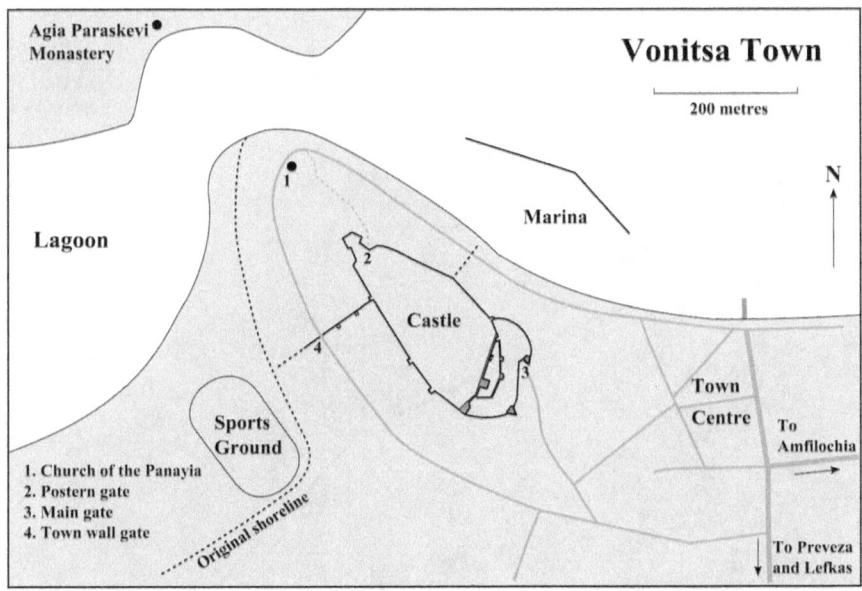

period after 1375 when Leonardo's widow invited the Knights of St. John of Rhodes to take over its defence. It finally fell to the Turks in 1479 sixteen years after their conquest of Constantinople. Turkish rule lasted until 1684 when the town was taken by Morosini's forces. The subsequent Venetian occupation was reversed in 1699 by the Treaty of Karlowitz, and in 1715 the town was again under Turkish control. However by 1717 the Venetian, Andrea Pisani, had retaken Preveza and Vonitsa and the town was formally restored to Venice by the Treaty of Passarowitz in 1718. It remained part of the Venetian empire until 1797 when, along with Venice's other surviving overseas territories, it passed into the hands of Napoleon Bonaparte. The following year the castle was seized by Ali Pasha and it remained in Turkish hands until 1829.

The Castle of Vonitsa occupies a steep-sided hill some forty metres in height. To the north of the hill a narrow strait joins the open bay on the west to a shallow lagoon that runs eastwards for two kilometres. When William Leake visited Vonitsa in 1805 the town retained its Venetian layout of three distinct suburbs known as Recinto, Borgo and Boccale, and the lagoon was used as a harbour. Recinto lay on the northern side of the castle hill and was enclosed by walls running northeast and southwest down the flanks of the hill from the main circuit to the water's edge. Save for the Church of the Panayia no trace of this settlement survives and the modern town now lies entirely to the east. The castle walls encircle the hill forming a rough oval approximately 350m

Gulf of Ambracia

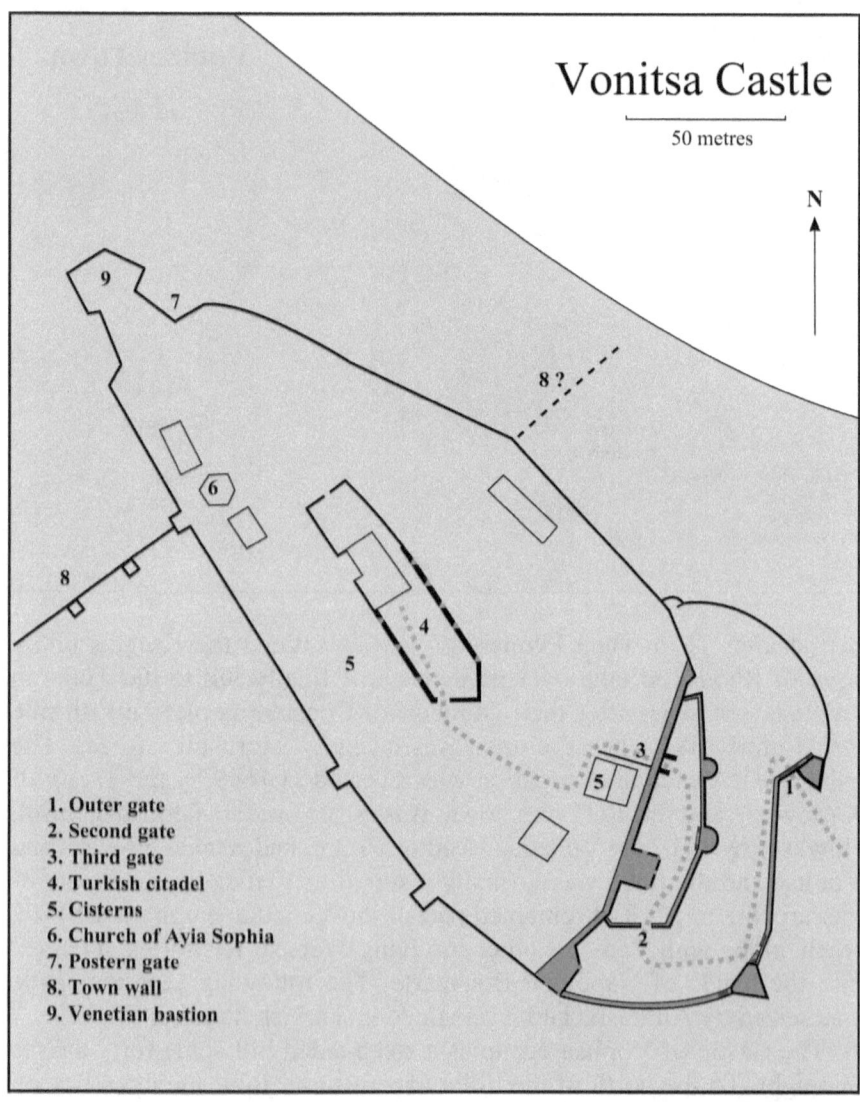

Vonitsa Castle

50 metres

1. Outer gate
2. Second gate
3. Third gate
4. Turkish citadel
5. Cisterns
6. Church of Ayia Sophia
7. Postern gate
8. Town wall
9. Venetian bastion

long and 250m wide aligned northwest to southeast. The circuit that stands today is the product of many centuries of repair, rebuilding and adaptation but the original Byzantine foundation seems to have been built with relatively thin walls reinforced sporadically with square, half round or pointed towers. It appears to have relied on the steep slopes of the hill for much of its strength. To the southeast the ground slopes more gently towards the modern town and the castle's main defences are concentrated here. They consist of a triple line of walls arranged so that entry is gained only by following a serpentine route through three successive gates. The plain outer gate is protected by a sharply projecting beaked tower. Recently restored, this tower has a single chamber in each of its two storeys, and a parapet, with merlons still partially intact, at roof level. An external flight of stone steps on the inner face of the tower gives access via a small landing to the arched doorway of the lower floor. Directly above this entrance a second arched doorway, now walled up, can be seen. The arches above both openings have been embellished with courses of thin red brick. The placement of these doorways and the clear discontinuities visible in the roughly cut masonry of the wall may indicate that another building originally stood against the inner face of the gate. The external stairs continue upwards carried on an arch across the gate passage and give access to the southern section of the outer wall. Its parapet is pierced by narrow loopholes at regular intervals. The intact wallwalk is interrupted by a second two-storeyed triangular tower some sixty metres to the south. At some point a large square gunport has been inserted in the eastern flank of this tower at ground floor level. To the north of the outer gate the wall curves around to the west to meet the inner circuit. The ruins of a hollow tower appear

Figure 3.25 Vonitsa Castle: Outer gate with flanking tower.

Figure 3.26 Vonitsa Castle: Inner face of the outer gate.

Figure 3.27 Vonitsa Castle: Exterior of half-round towers of the second line of defences.

Gulf of Ambracia

Figure 3.28 Vonitsa Castle: Artillery bastion at the southern end of the third line of defence.

to stand at the junction of the two walls. The parapet of this section of the outer wall is now missing and the wall may have been lowered, possibly to provide a better field of fire for artillery mounted on the upper walls. The large outer court, or bailey, within this first line is now bare. The path to the second gate runs south through the bailey beneath the wall and the half-round towers of the second line. A large breach at its southern end marks the position of the gate which was demolished by German forces during the Second World War. The imposing artillery bastion at the southern end of the third line commands the approach to the gate. A second bastion towards the centre of this line overlooks the gate from the north. Beyond the breach the second and third walls form a corridor leading to the third gate. The centre section of the second line of walls is reinforced with two semicircular towers. These rise no higher than the level of the wall itself and simply provide open semicircular platforms at the level of the continuous wallwalk. Around the towers the parapet is provided only with tapering loopholes but elsewhere it is crenellated with a further loophole piercing each merlon. The third gate is now a plain opening in the inner wall but may originally have been a more complex structure. Two irregular projecting walls, or buttresses, of uncertain purpose flank the entrance. Once through the gate it becomes apparent that the greater part of the heavy,

Gulf of Ambracia

battered third wall forms a massive revetment to the steep slope of the hill. The difference in levels between the interior and exterior of the wall is such that the parapet south of the third gate stands a mere two metres or less above the interior ground level. The whole defensive line with its two quadrangular bastions appears to have been constructed in one phase and may be a Turkish reconstruction dating from the 17C. The walls are built of roughly mortared masonry interspersed with broken tile. Their outer faces are still pierced by regular lines of scaffold holes. Both bastions have a square stringcourse moulding at parapet level. The centre bastion is positioned so as to command the second

Figure 3.29 Vonitsa Castle: View of one of the open semi-circular towers of the second line of defence with the outer wall and entrance tower beyond.

Figure 3.30 Vonitsa Castle: Demolished second gate. Behind is the artillery bastion in the centre of the third line of defence.

gate and flank the third. The southern bastion is provided with three artillery embrasures and the centre bastion four, two of them oddly placed above its chamfered corners. The walls themselves have only narrow musketry slits in the plain uncrenellated parapet.

North of the entrance complex the original thin Byzantine walls probably constitute the greater part of the main circuit repaired as necessary over the centuries.[29] The long straight southwest section is reinforced with three irregularly placed solid square towers. Again these walls act partly as revetments to the steep hillside. The surviving sections of plain parapet are provided with small tapering loopholes and

Gulf of Ambracia

probably represent Turkish re-building. An irregular Venetian bastion that forms a level continuation of the earlier walls defends the extreme northern end of the circuit. Its solid gun platform has small open gun embrasures in the parapet, facing north and west, and a single arched gunport covering an adjacent postern gate. This entrance has an external arch of finely carved ashlar and gives access to the area below the hill once occupied by the suburb of Recinto. A footpath still climbs up to the gate from the shore near the church of the Panayia. The gate was also originally overlooked by a round sentry box corbelled out from the wall. Only the base now survives.

Early engravings show the interior of the main enclosure crowded with buildings. Today only a few structures survive scattered about the

Figure 3.31 Vonitsa Castle: Exterior of the Venetian postern gate.

Gulf of Ambracia

Fig 3.32 Vonitsa Castle: Arched gunport covering the approach to the northern postern gate.

site. The largest is the crude citadel on the highest point of the hill. It belongs to the last period of Turkish occupation following the brief period of French tenure, and may have been built by Ali Pasha after 1806 when he re-occupied the town.[30] The citadel consists of a circuit wall approximately eighty metres long by twenty wide, between two and three metres in height, with a two-storey barrack block at its centre. Although it has the appearance of a defensible redoubt it may simply have been built as an additional gun battery commanding the castle as a whole. The entrance is at the southern end where the approach to the gate, now missing, is guarded by a line of musketry slits through the adjacent wall. To the north of the gate as far as the central building the walls on both sides of the circuit thicken to over two metres and are provided with splayed gun embrasures, three to the west and five to the east. The walls of the remainder of the circuit are thin and unprotected. The central barrack block, now ruined and roofless, seems to consist of two separate buildings of differing widths joined end to end. The doorway in the narrower northern façade has an archway identical in style to

Gulf of Ambracia

Figure 3.33 Vonitsa Castle: Southern façade of Turkish barracks.

Figure 3.34 Vonitsa Castle: Wall and embrasures of the Turkish citadel. The roofless barracks is visible to the left.

the Venetian postern gate described above. Over the arch is a moulded surround of brick and stucco. This part of the building may have been the ruined church on the summit mentioned by Leake, subsequently adapted and extended to the south. Below the citadel to the west an opening in the rock, now gated and padlocked, leads into an underground cistern. More cisterns can be found beneath the low, gabled building that stands on a terraced platform immediately to the south of the third gate.

Although there is now no trace of the eastern town wall, that to the west survives almost intact. It runs steeply downhill to the original shoreline of the lagoon from a point below the square tower near to the church of Ayia Sophia. Built of roughly coursed masonry mixed with a large amount of broken brick and tile it is not bonded to the castle wall. It retains much of its wallwalk and crenellated parapet and is reinforced with two square towers. The lower tower still stands to almost its full

Figure 3.35 Vonitsa: Lower tower of the southwest town wall.

Gulf of Ambracia

Figure 3.36 Vonitsa: Gate in southwest town wall.

height one storey above wall level. It commands the gate below that led into the suburb of Recinto. This gate still stands complete with the modern road that encircles the base of the hill running through it.

The castle is constructed entirely of heavily mortared masonry of roughly squared blocks frequently mixed with broken tile and brick and exact dating of its various phases of construction is probably impossible. The beaked towers of the outer wall and the half-round towers of the second line are almost certainly part of the original Byzantine circuit. The parapets with their numerous narrow loopholes probably represent Venetian and Turkish rebuilding. The only provision for artillery among the southeast defences is the two bastions of the third line. These may be Venetian but the irregularly placed gun embrasures and narrow musketry slits are perhaps more indicative of Turkish work. The only part of the fortifications that can definitely be assigned to the Venetians after 1685 is the bastion at the northern tip of the circuit. This is built with the typical Venetian semicircular stringcourse, or cordon, below the parapet. The bastion was added presumably to command the narrow entrance to the harbour in the lagoon.

Today Vonitsa is a small provincial market town with modest tourist facilities. Recent work on the structure of the castle has consolidated much of the crumbling fabric. Opening hours are 8.30 until 15.00 and entrance is free.

Notes

1. For a detailed study of the complex changes to sea levels and coastal geography in the area see Z. Jing and G. Rapp, "The Coastal Evolution of the Ambracian Embayment and Its Relationship to Archaeological Settings", in J. Wiseman and K. Zachos, *Landscape Archaeology of Southern Epirus, Greece I*, pp. 157-198.
2. Eleia, or Elis, was the area around Olympia in the northwest of the Peloponnese.
3. For the context of this myth see A. Brooks, *Myths Games and Conflict*, pp. 16 and 67.
4. Both Leake, *Travels in Northern Greece, Vol. IV*, p. 255, and William Smith, *Dictionary of Greek and Roman Geography, Vol. I*, p. 603, believed that Rogoi should be identified as the site of Charadras, a town mentioned by Polybius (4.63 and 21.26). Leake, following Strabo (7.7.5), thought that Bouchetion was to be found on the coast a little to the east of Parga.
5. N. G. L. Hammond, *Epirus*, pp. 61-63, 475. Strabo (7.7.5) refers to the inland cities of the Cassopaei: Elatria, Pandosia and Baties. Demosthenes (7.32) refers to "the three Elean colonies in Cassopia – Pandosia, Bouchetion and Elatria". Pandosia is the site at Kastri in the Acherontas valley.
6. Jing and Rapp, *The Coastal Evolution of the Ambracian Embayment*, pp. 189-198.

7. For a detailed geological map of the area showing the earlier courses of the rivers see P. N. Doukellis and E. Fouache, *La Centuriation Romaine de la Plaine D'Arta*, p. 377.
8. D. M. Nicol, *The Despotate of Epiros*, p. 58.
9. D. M. Nicol, *The Reluctant Emperor: A Biography of John Cantacuzene*, pp. 38-43.
10. Hammond, *Epirus,* p. 57ff.
11. Cyriac of Ancona visited the church in 1448 and saw the remains of the Evangelist. See E. W. Bodnar, *Cyriac of Ancona Later Travels*, p. 351. Other places claiming relics of St. Luke include Padua, Prague, St. Peter's Rome, Florence and Milan.
12. In 1881 the border was revised again when the Ottoman Empire ceded Thessaly to Greece but Epiros, west of the River Arachthos, and most of the northern shore of the Ambracian Gulf remained in Turkish hands until 1913.
13. George Smyris, Καστρα και Οχυρωσεις Του Αμβρακικου Κολπου.
14. Leake's identification of the original course of the Arachthos (*Travels in Northern Greece, Vol. I*, p. 201) has been confirmed by the work of Doukellis and Fouache.
15. Lieutenant-Colonel Baker, "Memoir on the Northern Frontier of Greece", *Journal of the Royal Geographical Society*, 1837, p. 84.
16. Byzantine forces attempting to recover Epiros for the Empire are recorded landing at Salaora on route to Arta. See Nicol, *The Despotate of Epiros*, p. 42. Cyriaco of Ancona visited the area in 1448 and landed at Koronisia, "near the mouth of the Arachthos river". He makes no mention of a harbour or settlement of Ambrakos (Bodnar, *Cyriac of Ancona Later Travels,* p. 347).
17. Strabo 7.7.6 and 10.2.8.
18. For example, Livy 38.3.
19. Bodnar, *Cyriac of Ancona Later Travels*, pp. 343 and 347.
20. The three sites mentioned by Thucydides (3.105-114) in his description of the Battle of Olpae lie some thirty-three kilometres south of Arta close to the main road. Although the remains here are slight their locations are worth noting because of the importance of the area in the history of Ambracia. All that is left of the town of Argos Amphilochia, abandoned after the founding of Nikopolis, are the foundations of the acropolis circuit and of the long walls that run down the plain. These stand on a ridge approximately one kilometre to the east of the main road. There are also fragmentary remains of a theatre hidden in an olive grove. The site is unenclosed and there are signposts from the main road but there is

actually little to see. Olpae itself occupied an isolated hill on the coast one kilometre to the north of the village of Bouka, which is due east of Argos. In his detailed description of the complex manoeuvres of the battle Thucydides mentions another fortified position to the southwest of Argos, known as Krinai. This fortified hill lies 200m to the west of the main road two kilometres south of Argos and one kilometre before the road rejoins the coast. The outline of the circuit wall can still be seen from the road.

21. Polybius (21.27-28) gives a detailed account of the siege of Ambracia. This involved siege engines, mining and counter-mining and even the use of the use of poisonous smoke.
22. Geoffrey of Malaterra III.39. "He besieged a city called Arta, made determined assaults upon it, and strove with every possible means to capture it."
23. A. Orlandos, "Archeion ton Byzantinon Mnimeion tis Ellados". Cited in A. W. Lawrence, *A Skeletal History of Byzantine Fortification*, p. 223.
24. L. Heuzey, *Le Mont Olympe et L'Arcananie*, p. 326.
25. Nicol, *The Despotate of Epiros*, p.115; Heuzey, *Le Mont Olympe et L'Arcananie,* p. 325.
26. Stanley Lane-Poole, *Sir Richard Church Commander-in–Chief of the Greeks in the War of Independence*, p. 70.
27. William of Apulia, *The Deeds of Robert Guiscard*, book 5.
28. Vonitsa is named as the place of Guiscard's death in the Annales Lupi Protospatherii, 216. However Anna Comnena (Alexiad 6.6) gives a detailed account of his demise on Cephalonia. The town of Fiskardo at the northern tip of the island is supposed to be named after him. William Joseph Churchill, *The Annales Barenses and the Annales Lupi Protospatharii: Critical Edition and Commentary.*
29. The relatively weak walls of the main circuit are probably the reason Leake referred to the castle as "ruinous and ill-constructed" when he visited Vonitsa in 1805. Leake, *Travels in Northern Greece, Vol. I,* p. 166.
30. Ali Pasha had first occupied Vonitsa in 1798 but the treaty of 1800 between Russia and Turkey that created the Septinsular Republic also granted the former Venetian mainland possessions to the Turks. The treaty provided that these dependencies, which included Vonitsa, should continue to enjoy the privileges originally granted by Venice and be subject to their own municipal laws. Ali did not gain full control of the town until 1806 when, using the outbreak of war between Russia and Turkey as a pretext, he re-occupied

Gulf of Ambracia

Vonitsa and Preveza and established his own absolute government. When Leake visited the place in 1805 the only buildings he describes on the summit within the castle are a ruined church and "a house built by Aly Pasha for the Albanian garrison, which he placed here after he had taken Vonitsa from the French". Leake, *Travels in Northern Greece, Vol. I*, p. 169.

4

Epiros

The coastline of western Epiros extends for 75 kilometres north from the Ambracian Gulf to the border with Albania. The range of low mountains along the coast is broken only by the plains of the rivers Acherontas and Kalamas. Twenty-five kilometres north of Preveza the castle of Riniasa guards the narrow pass between the coastal hills and the sea. Built on a conspicuous steep summit, it is thought to have been founded by the despot Thomas (1296-1318) and is therefore also known as Thomokastro. Fifteen kilometres further north lies the plain of the Acherontas, the river Acheron of mythology. Here, near Mesopotamos, can be found the remarkable 3C BC remains of the Oracle of the Dead, or Necromanteio, close to the site of Mycenaean Ephyra. Inland, the village of Glyki stands at the entrance to the Acherontas gorge. Five kilometres due east, but twenty by road, is the well-preserved Castle of Kiafas built by Ali Pasha to control the area after he had defeated the Souliots. The town of Parga is situated on the coast twenty kilometres northwest of the Necromanteio. Its castle has a mediaeval circuit much modified by the Venetians and is crowned by the citadel and serai built by Ali Pasha in 1819 immediately after the British transfer of the town to the Turks. Also visible from Parga is the castle, or gun fort, of Anthousa built by Ali Pasha in 1814 as part of his campaign for control of the area. Inland, overlooking the modern E55, the Ottoman castle of Margariti commands the main route north. North of Igoumenitsa on the Lygia peninsula near the mouth of the river Kalamas stand the fragmentary remains of the Kerkyrean colony of Toroni. The 5C BC city was protected on its eastern side by a fort built on an isolated hill three kilometres inland. In the 19C a Turkish tower, or Kula, known as Pirgos Ragiou was built on one of the corner towers of the original fort. Recently restored, this is a fine example of the many Turkish towers constructed by local Ottoman officials. Above the town of Paramythia, thirty kilometres to the east, the Byzantine castle of Agios Donatos

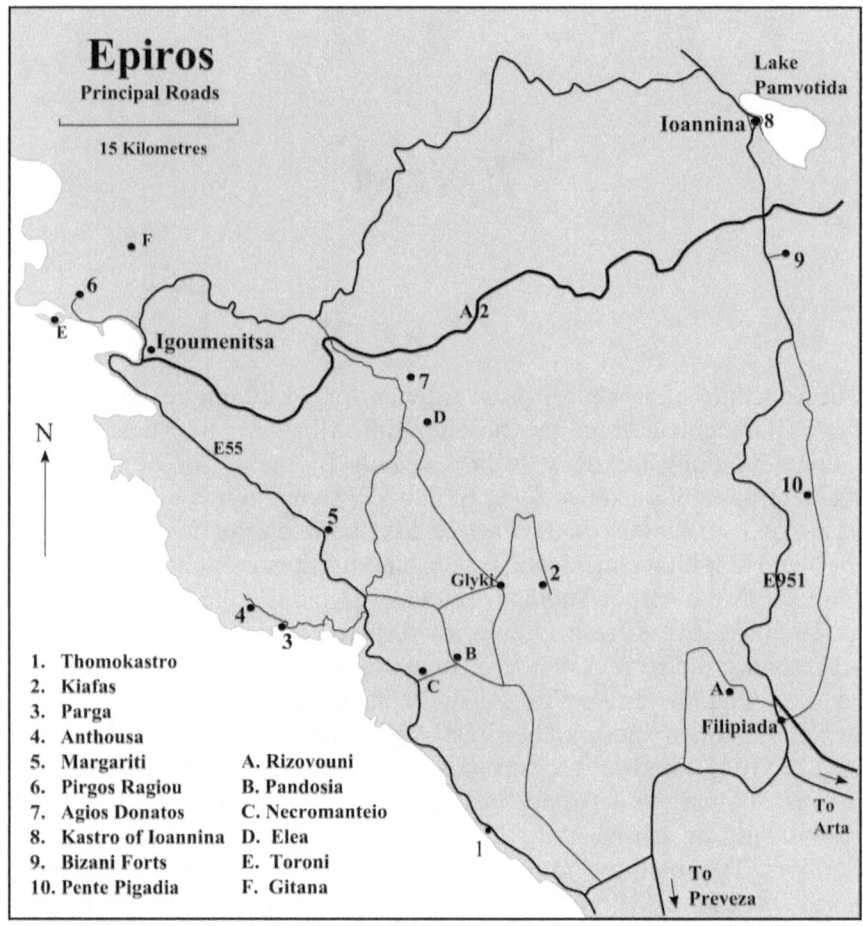

crowns a precipitous hill ringed by cliffs and incorporates an earlier Hellenistic circuit. Ioannina, the largest town of Epiros, dates from the 9C. Its original Byzantine town walls were re-built on a massive scale by Ali Pasha at the beginning of the 19C. Within the enclosed area are the remains of two citadels. The northern enclosure is Byzantine while the southern contains remarkable survivals of Norman work. Ioannina was the Turks' main base in Epiros during the First Balkan War when it was surrounded by a ring of fortified positions. Five kilometres to the south are the surviving structures of the key Turkish fortress of Bizani and the site of the Third Battle of Ioannina in 1913. At Pente Pigadia, a further twenty-five kilometres south, another Turkish fortress guards the original route from Ioannina to Arta. Again this was re-built by Ali Pasha and was the site of another battle of the First Balkan War in 1912.

Epiros

Castle of Riniasa (Thomokastro)

Much of the history of the Castle of Riniasa, or Thomokastro, is obscure. It dates from the beginning of the 14C during the reign of Thomas, the third Despot of Epiros. It saw a brief period of importance after 1338 when the Emperor Andronikos III re-asserted Byzantine control over the territory of the Despotate following the death of John Orsini. Thomokastro became a centre of resistance to this re-unification. The rebels seized Arta and Rogoi and in 1339 brought John Orsini's son, Nikephoros, then still a minor, to Thomokastro from Glarentza in the Peloponnese. Andronikos besieged all three castles. Rogoi and Arta were effectively blockaded and both sieges were brought to a peaceable end by the negotiating skills of the Emperor's Grand Domestic, John Cantacuzene. In contrast Thomokastro could hold out indefinitely against a land-based siege as its position on the coast allowed it to be supplied by sea and Andronikos had no navy. However it too eventually surrendered to the diplomacy of Cantacuzene. It remained in Byzantine

Figure 4.1 Castle of Riniasa: Overall view from the north.

Epiros

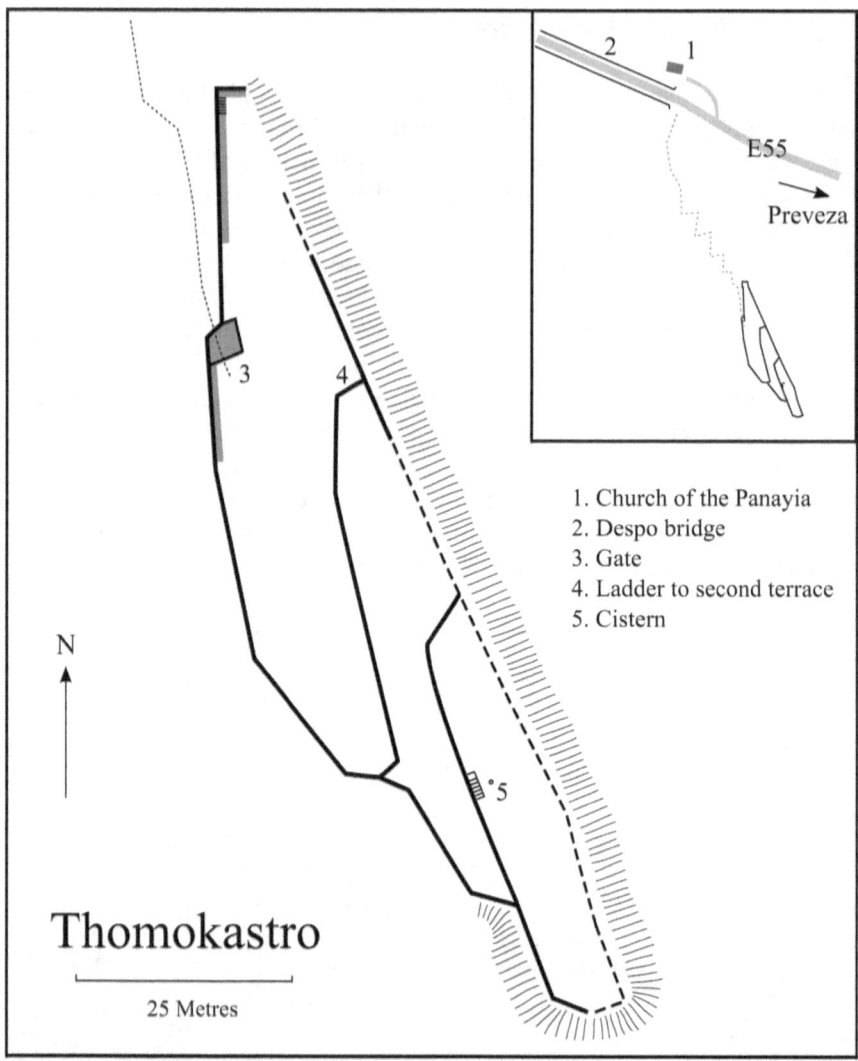

1. Church of the Panayia
2. Despo bridge
3. Gate
4. Ladder to second terrace
5. Cistern

Thomokastro

hands until 1348 when the whole of Epiros fell to the Serbian ruler, Stephen Dušan. After 1366 the Despotate fragmented with the Serbs retaining control in the north based in Ioannina and Albanian rule in the south from Arta. Thomokastro too would have been under Albanian control during this period. By the early 15C Carlo Tocco had purchased the castle and in 1416 he succeeded in reuniting the Despotate. After his death in 1429 the Despotate was again divided and slowly succumbed to the Turks. Arta fell in 1449 and Thomokastro must have also been taken around this date. The castle was last used by Ali Pasha in the early 19C. Leake visited the site in 1809 and records that Ali had made repairs to the walls and built accommodation for his Albanian garrison.[1] The castle may also have been part of the network of forts Ali created a few years earlier during his campaign against the Souliots.

Although it stands close by the main E55 the castle is only visible from the road when travelling south. It stands high on the ridge of an isolated hill half a kilometre inland near the village of Riza. The area enclosed is smaller than it appears at a distance, hardly 100m by 25m, and is composed of three courts that form a series of rising terraces facing west. The eastern side of the hill consists of an unbroken line of cliffs. The rocky slopes to the southwest are almost as steep. There may never have been a continuous line of walls to the east because of these natural defences, but landslip debris is visible along the base of the cliffs and sections of wall have clearly fallen.[2] Originally the castle must have had an outer enclosure that encircled the mediaeval town, probably on the western slopes of the hill below the gate. Leake saw the vestiges of the old town of Riniasa in exactly this position in 1809. Now however the hillside is heavily wooded and completely hides any fragments remaining. Various historical references indicate that Riniasa was a stopping point on mediaeval shipping routes from the north.[3] The exposed nature of the coast and the absence of any natural harbour makes it very unlikely that it actually possessed a port although the bay of Artolithia three kilometres to the south has been suggested as a possible location. Probably the beach itself was used to tranship goods when reasonable weather conditions allowed ships to anchor offshore.

The original approach to the castle must have been from the shore to the west through the lost outer enclosure and then steeply uphill to the surviving gate. Today the route is via a narrow path that starts by the main road at the southern end of the Despo viaduct. The path climbs steeply before passing beneath the northwest wall to the gate. This is set in a jog in the wall and is now in a ruinous state. It appears to have consisted of a vaulted chamber with a second storey, or at least a platform and parapet above, to command the approach. A small part of the vaulting remains. The entrance ramp climbs from the gate into the lower terrace, or bailey, which broadens and forms the largest flat area within the castle. Sections of the ruined west parapet survive to the south of the gate. On the eastern side of the bailey a massive, battered retaining wall supports the higher terrace of the second court. To the north of the gate the lower bailey narrows, ending at a small open tower that rises only a few feet above the level of the west wall. Both wall and tower retain their crenellated parapets and wallwalks although they are now in a

Epiros

Figure 4.2 Castle of Riniasa: The approach to the main gate.

Figure 4.3 Castle of Riniasa: The remains of the northern tower.

Epiros

Figure 4.4 Castle of Riniasa: Lower bailey
and the supporting wall of the second terrace.

poor state of repair. A short flight of steps leads from the wall to the narrow wallwalk of the tower. The eastern corner of the tower and a long stretch of the east perimeter wall have collapsed. Access to the second terrace is currently via a precarious, improvised wooden ladder at its northern tip. No trace of the original approach can be seen. This overgrown second bailey is smaller but of similar shape to the first. The western parapet has completely disappeared. To the east another retaining wall revets the third terrace. Access to this final level is via a ruined stairway halfway along the retaining wall. Near the top of the stair an open shaft marks the position of an underground cistern. The remainder of the summit is an overgrown ridge dotted with fragments of masonry. The castle's walls are built entirely of heavily mortared rough blocks and tile fragments. The parapets that survive are thin crenellated lines that appear almost unchanged from the original mediaeval work. There is no visible evidence that the castle was ever adapted for artillery. Surprisingly there is also no evidence of Ali Pasha's early 19C additions.

As the walls function chiefly as revetments to the terraced interior they are more impressive from below than within. The best overall views are from the old road that runs close the shoreline below the hill. To reach the castle follow the E55 north from Preveza. Half a kilometre after the Riza crossroads the small chapel of the Panayia stands on the east side of the road immediately before it crosses a ravine on a high viaduct known as the Despo bridge. It is possible to park by the chapel. The path to the main gate is concealed beneath trees on the opposite side of the road a few metres from the end of the roadbridge. The entire site is steep and overgrown and exploration requires care.

Kiafas Castle

The Castle of Kiafas, also misleadingly sometimes referred to as the Castle of Souli, was built by Ali Pasha between 1803 and 1805 after his final victory against the Souliots. The tribesmen known as the Souliots were Greek speaking Orthodox Christians of Albanian origin who had probably first occupied the area around the Acherontas gorge in the 17C.[4] They had originally been granted the right to bear arms by the Ottoman government in an attempt to suppress local bands of brigands. The number of Souliot families grew in number and power throughout the 18C. They eventually controlled and protected over sixty villages across a large territory from their four central settlements of Souli, Kiafas, Avariko and Samoniva. Located high above the gorge of the Acherontas these settlements were shielded on all sides by mountains and narrow passes. Ali Pasha became ruler of Ioannina in 1788 and from this base he continued his campaigns to extend his rule throughout northern Greece. The independent Souliots represented a major challenge to his plans for absolute authority throughout the territory and he was to spend the next fifteen years in sporadic attempts to expel them from their mountain strongholds by a combination of intrigue, bribery and direct attacks. Finally in May 1803 the Ottoman government, to whom he still owed allegiance, ordered him to break the power of the Souliots and bring his campaign to a close. The villages were overcome one by one and in December 1803 an agreement was signed whereby the Souliots abandoned their remaining positions and were allowed to retire to safety. Although Ali immediately broke his word and attempted to ambush the retreating Souliots, many succeeded in reaching the Ionian Islands from Parga.[5] To consolidate his hold on the Souliot territory Ali ordered the immediate construction of a fortress on the hill above the village of Kiafas. When Leake visited the site in July 1805 with the fort's architect, Petros of Koritsa, the fortifications were largely complete and the construction of a serai, or palace, within the walls had begun.[6] Henry Holland was entertained in the completed

Epiros

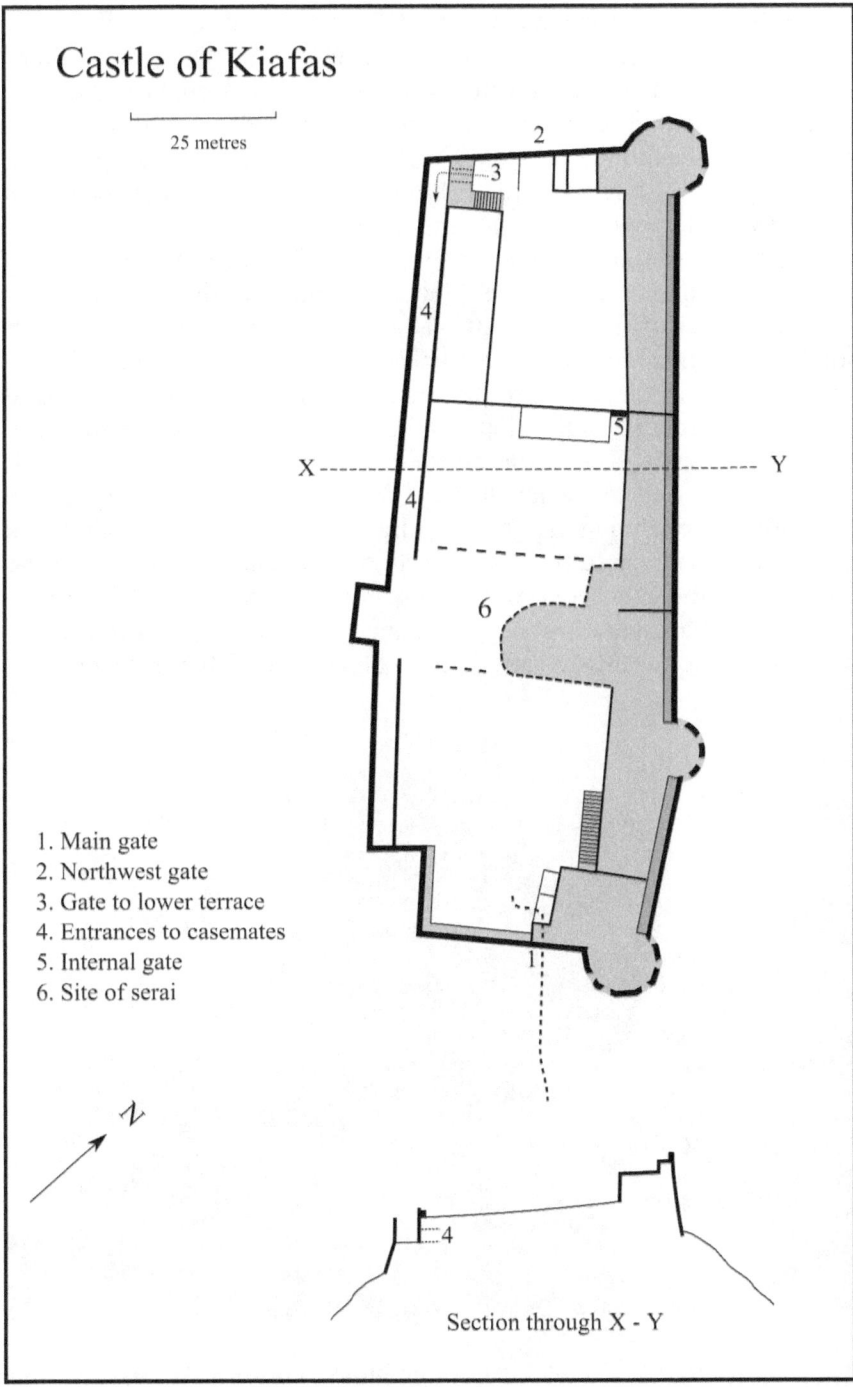

Epiros

palace by the fort's commandant in 1813.[7] After Ali's downfall and assassination in 1822 the fort remained in use as an Ottoman military post. Edward Lear visited the area in 1849 staying overnight in the serai which he describes as already dilapidated.[8] The fort appears to have been finally abandoned after the Greek conquest of Epiros in 1913 and at some point its internal buildings have been totally demolished. The area remains de-populated to the present day.

The castle is built astride a narrow ridge called the hill of Trypa connected to the main range of the Souliot mountains to the east by a high saddle, the site of the village of Kiafas. Numerous ruined houses can still be seen scattered across the hillside. The road along the saddle connected Kiafas with Avariko to the south and Samoniva and Souli to the north. To the southwest the slopes of Trypa fall some 600m to the gorge of the Acherontas. The castle occupies the centre of the ridge, which Leake reports had to be levelled before work could commence. The walls form a rough quadrangle 120m by 50m with a gate in each of the short faces. The circuit is reinforced by multangular towers at the northwest and southeast corners, a half-round tower in the long northeast face and a square bastion projecting from the centre of the southwest face. The northwest gate is now blocked by fallen masonry and

Figure 4.5 Kiafas Castle: The blocked northwest gate.

Epiros

Figure 4.6 Kiafas Castle: Exterior of southeast gate.

Figure 4.7 Kiafas Castle: Interior of southeast gate.

entry is via its southeast counterpart. Here a plain outer arch leads via a barrel vaulted corridor through the thickness of the walls to an inner gatehouse now reduced virtually to its foundations. A right-angled turn through this building seems to have led into the interior. Within, the fort is divided by a cross wall into two unequal enclosures. The larger court to the south contained the buildings of Ali Pasha's serai, now reduced to large mounds of rubble. This two-storeyed building seems to have been built across the full width of the fort, further dividing the southern court in two.[9] Beyond the ruins of the serai a plain arched gate at the eastern end of the crosswall leads into the northern enclosure. Again the internal buildings of this court have been reduced to ruins. They presumably provided accommodation for the garrison and may have contained the house of the commandant mentioned by Leake. The best-preserved elements of the fort are the ramparts themselves. The walls facing

Figure 4.8 Kiafas Castle: Gate in interior crosswall.

Epiros

Figure 4.9 Kiafas Castle: The rampart overlooking Kiafas village.

towards the village of Kiafas are up to ten metres thick. The slightly battered external faces are built of roughly dressed and squared blocks laid in regular courses. A continuous, square stringcourse marks the level of the parapet externally. The interior faces are more crudely constructed. The internal fill is presumably of rubble and earth. The great thickness of the walls provides one continuous platform from one corner tower to the other. To the southeast a broad ramp gives access to the platform from the southern courtyard. Only the parapets of the three towers are provided with embrasures for cannon. The intervening curtain walls are equipped simply with musketry loopholes in a thin parapet above a separate higher-level wallwalk. If gun embrasures were intended elsewhere they were never completed. The projecting corner towers provide flanking cover along the faces of the walls. The short southeast and northwest walls and the approaches to the gates are also protected with loopholes in the parapet, rectangular on the interior and tapering to a narrow vertical slit on the exterior. The long southwest face of the fort overlooking the gorge has a double wall on two levels. The lower half of the outer wall forms a revetment to the hillside while

Epiros

Figure 4.10 Kiafas Castle: Section of the corridor between the inner and outer southwest walls north of the square bastion. The arched casemate entrances are visible.

the upper part screens a series of arched entrances in the base of the inner wall. These open into chambers, or casemates, built into the hill beneath the courtyard above. The two walls form a long corridor that may have been roofed over when first built. Leake described the chambers as bomb-proof magazines, casemates and cisterns. The inner wall also forms a revetment to the hill and on its inner side seems to have had only a low level parapet. While the area of the walls around the square bastion is now merely a confused ruin, the northwestern section of the corridor is well preserved. The original entrance route to the corridor, a sloping ramp leading down from the western corner of the north court through an arched gate beneath the parapet, is still accessible.

Ali Pasha built numerous fortresses and palaces, partly to impress and intimidate the local populations, and partly to facilitate his habit of travelling regularly around his territories.[10] The Castle of Kiafas was a

Epiros

Figure 4.11 Kiafas Castle: Northwestern corner tower.

good example of this dual role with a superficially formidable external appearance and impressive accommodation within. However when considered purely as an artillery fort the weakness of its position is apparent. It was placed to overlook the village of Kiafas and the track along the saddle below. No other route of any strategic importance passed beneath its guns. It was designed merely to confront the guerrilla tactics of the Souliots and prevent any possibility of their return. The limitations of its position if faced by a better equipped force were first remarked upon by Leake while it was still under construction. He noted the

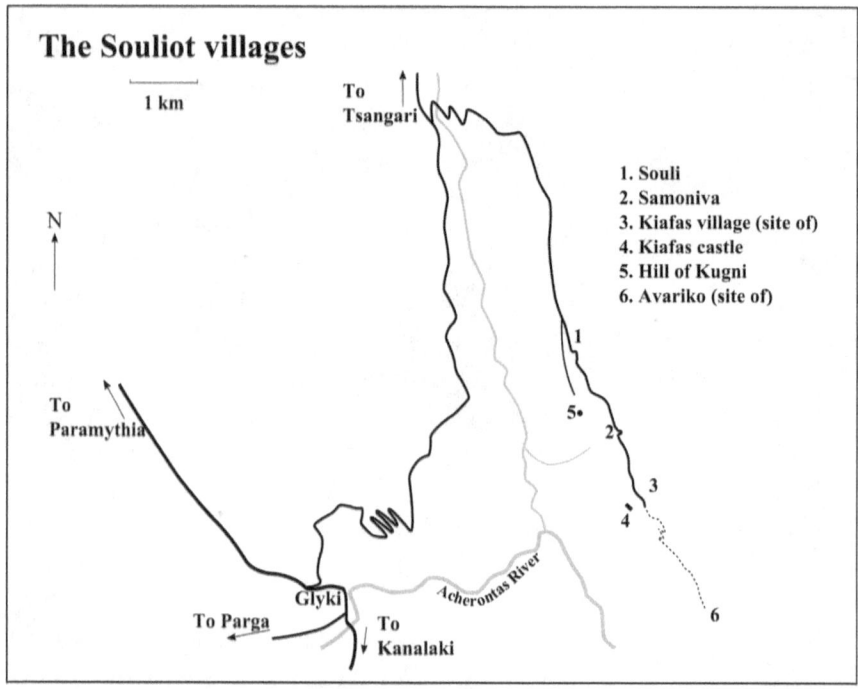

general weakness of the fort's armaments and that its position was well within range of any field artillery of the period if placed on the higher ground to the northeast. Nevertheless the castle remained in use until the end of the Turkish period although it appears to have taken no part in the struggles of the Greek Revolution.

On the outskirts of Glyki a turning from the main road to Paramythia, prominently indicated by a commemorative arch, marks the start of the circuitous route to the Souliot villages. To avoid the impassable Acherontas gorge the tarmac road runs north on the western side of a tributary valley. After ten kilometres a right fork leads across a bridge over the seasonal stream and then south on the valley's eastern side for five kilometres to Souli. On the village outskirts a road forks left and descends the hill towards Samoniva. Above the road to the west rises the hill of Kugni, the last position held by the Souliots before their expulsion. At the entrance to Samoniva a newly surfaced road continues south climbing the hill towards the ruined settlement of Kiafas where the tarmac surface ends. The deserted castle dominates the ridge above the scattered ruins of houses. A rough track leads steeply uphill to the open south gate. Serious walkers can also reach the castle on foot from Glyki by a dramatic footpath along the southern side of the gorge.

Parga Castle

Parga is now a successful holiday resort sixty kilometres to the north of Preveza. Its castle stands on a high, rocky promontory surrounded on three sides by the sea and it must have once dominated the small town that grew up both within and below its walls. Rapid tourist development and the overgrown state of the site today have diminished the castle's visual impact, but the Venetian defences and the well preserved citadel built during Ali Pasha's brief tenure remain impressively intact.

Parga's early history is obscure and probably followed that of the Despotate of Epiros as a whole. It first appears in the historical record in 1320 when Nicholas Orsini is known to have offered the territory to Venice in exchange for military support; an offer which the Republic declined.[11] In 1339 John Cantacuzene lists it among the places remaining loyal to the Byzantine empire. In 1386 the Venetians gained control of Corfu and as a result Parga's position on the mainland acquired greater importance. It became a Venetian protectorate in 1401 and its administration was thereafter linked with that of Corfu. Although the town was periodically attacked by the Turks, and indeed was sacked in 1537 and again in 1571, it remained in Venetian hands for four hundred years until 1797. With the fall of Venice to Napoleon Parga passed to the French along with the Ionian Islands. However their occupation was extremely brief and by 1799 the combined forces of Russia and Turkey had expelled all of the French garrisons. In 1800 the two powers signed an agreement in Constantinople, ratified by Great Britain, which formed an autonomous state of the Ionian Islands known as the Septinsular Republic. This treaty, or convention, also ceded to Turkey all of Venice's mainland possessions to the east of the islands, including Parga.[12] Although the town was nominally under Ottoman control from 1800 to 1807, its autonomy during this period was guaranteed by Russia. The Treaty of Tilsit, signed in 1807, ceded the Ionian Islands back to the French. They included Parga in their re-occupation and built a small fort on the island in the harbour in 1808. Again the French occupation was short-lived. The British progressively expelled their forces from the islands taking Zante in 1809, Lefkas in 1810 and Corfu in 1814. Finally in 1815 the Treaty of Paris re-created the single state of the Ionian islands under British protection.[13] In 1814 the British also occupied Parga following an appeal for British assistance from its inhabitants who realized that the French were no longer willing or capable of protecting them from Ali Pasha. However the Treaty of Paris recognised the agreement between Russia and the Ottoman Empire of 1800 and hence

Epiros

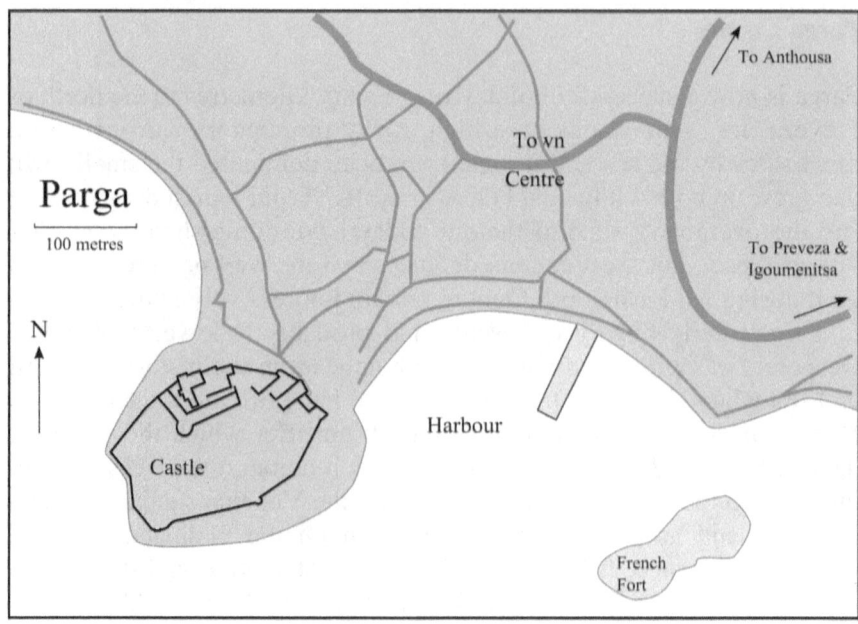

Turkish claims to the old Venetian possessions on the mainland. The Turks therefore called upon Britain to hand over Parga and eventually Sir Thomas Maitland, the High Commissioner of the Ionian Islands, agreed to do so in 1817.[14] Ottoman power in the area was in the hands of Ali Pasha and the majority of Parga's inhabitants were determined to emigrate rather than be subjects of his harsh regime. Negotiations over compensation for the property that would be abandoned lasted until 1819. In April of that year almost the entire population sailed to Corfu leaving the town to Ali Pasha's forces. Ali held the town for three years until his death in 1822 but it remained in Turkish hands until 1913 when Epiros became part of Greece.

It may be a misnomer to refer to Parga's fortifications as a castle. Commentators at the beginning of the 19C refer to it as a walled town. De Bossett described it as a small town surrounded by walls, built on a conical hill and "crowned by a sort of citadel".[15] In 1806 Leake also described the town standing on the steep side of a conical hill, while outside the walls he mentions only a single street of houses on the neck of the promontory and another along the beach of the east bay.[16] The outline of the walls forms a rough oval. To the north they run along the highest part of the hill above precipitous cliffs. To the south the circuit encloses the slopes occupied by the derelict houses of the early town and the few areas of level ground. The Venetian defensive works are

Epiros

concentrated on the eastern side where they command the neck of the peninsula and the single entrance. As a maritime state the security of the harbour must always have been of prime importance to the Venetians. Although the anchorages in both bays on either side of the castle headland are exposed to the southwest the Venetians must have found the eastern bay usable as a harbour. Their fortifications include batteries to cover the entrance to the bay between the headland and the small island to the east. At the highest point of the promontory stand the citadel and serai built by Ali Pasha. The serai overlooks the west bay and must stand upon, or incorporate, the earlier citadel mentioned by De Bossett.

Narrow lanes climb through the houses of modern Parga to the outer gate of the castle. This is a late addition to the defences. An inscription above the gate records that it was constructed in 1707 by Count Marco Teotochi, Governor and Captain of Parga. The arched entrance has been rebuilt and now houses a square modern gate. Beyond the gate a narrow corridor formed by a low loop-holed wall built beneath the main defences leads to the original gate set in an angle of the main wall. Above this gate is the lion of Saint Mark and another well-worn inscription.

Figure 4.12 Parga Castle: Entrance corridor looking north towards the modern outer gate.

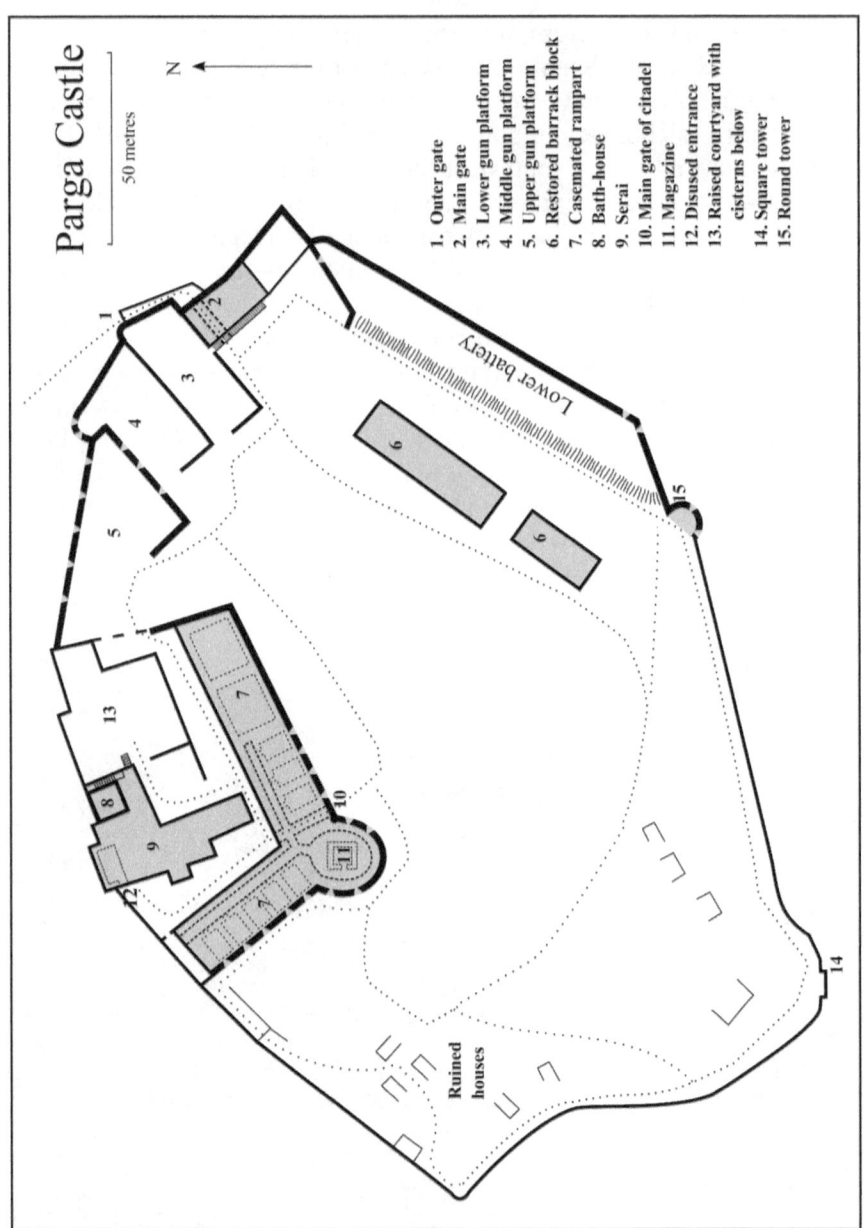

Parga Castle

1. Outer gate
2. Main gate
3. Lower gun platform
4. Middle gun platform
5. Upper gun platform
6. Restored barrack block
7. Casemated rampart
8. Bath-house
9. Serai
10. Main gate of citadel
11. Magazine
12. Disused entrance
13. Raised courtyard with cisterns below
14. Square tower
15. Round tower

Although the date on this inscription is no longer visible it refers to Paulo Caotorta who was Proveditore and Captain of Corfu around 1626. The well-preserved outer arch of the gate leads into a barrel-vaulted tunnel that runs for twelve metres through the solid gun platform built

Epiros

Figure 4.13 Parga Castle: The Venetian northeast defences.

against the outer wall at this point. It emerges into the interior beneath a long stairway that gives access to the platform above. From within the castle it is apparent that the tall external walls in this section of the circuit are for the most part revetments built partly against the natural slope of the hill and partly against the terraced gun platforms that rise in steps to the west of the main gate. These were built by the Venetians to provide three tiers of fire towards the harbour and also to command the narrow neck of high land that connects the promontory to the mainland. This arrangement is clearest on the upper terrace where the gun embrasures are well preserved. Three face southeast towards the harbour and five are directed to the landward approach. Within the limitations of the steep site the lower and middle terraces also provide a degree of flanking cover along the face of the walls from their curved projecting northern corners. Thirty metres east of the main gate the circuit turns sharply southwest. The structures that stood at this corner are almost completely demolished. A long Venetian battery, now overgrown, runs southwest from this point for one hundred metres. Built on a step cut in the slope

Epiros

Figure 4.14 Parga Castle: The exterior of the main gate.

of the hill with its parapet at internal ground level, it commands the harbour entrance below. At its southern end the parapet makes a shallow turn to rejoin what may be the line of an earlier upper wall at a round tower. The tower is equipped with two gun embrasures in the

Figure 4.15 Parga Castle: Southern round tower.

parapet but the underlying structure probably pre-dates the Venetian work. The western continuation of the circuit is also earlier. Here the walls are relatively thin and for the most part are simply revetments to the slope of the hill with little projection above ground level on their interior sides. The rocks and cliffs rising abruptly from sea level presumably were thought to provide sufficient natural defence on this side of the circuit. A square tower, mediaeval in appearance, marks the southernmost point of the walls. To the north the slopes rising up to the citadel are covered with the confused ruins of houses. Stairways and

Epiros

Figure 4.16 Parga Castle: Southern square tower.

Figure 4.17 Parga Castle: Entrance to Ali Pasha's citadel.

Epiros

Figure 4.18 Parga Castle: Plaque above the citadel entrance.

alleys can still be made out on the overgrown hillside. From the square tower the walls run northwards to the western salient of the circuit, which now forms a crude belvedere overlooking the west bay. From here the wall climbs northeast to meet the mass of Ali Pasha's citadel.

Ali Pasha finally gained possession of Parga in 1819. He assigned the abandoned properties of the exiled inhabitants to his followers and within a year had built substantial new structures within the castle circuit. On the highest point of the hill overlooking the west bay he erected a serai, or palace, replacing or incorporating earlier buildings. To protect and enclose the serai he built an imposing artillery work in the form of a V-shaped casemated rampart with a large horseshoe bastion projecting boldly from its apex. Recent tree growth now makes the scale of these structures difficult to appreciate from within the castle but

Figure 4.19 Parga Castle: Tunnel vaulted corridor within the rampart. The casemate entrances can be seen on the right.

the buildings are still readily accessible. The entrance to the citadel complex is set in the flat wall immediately east of the horseshoe bastion. It mimics the Venetian main gate in appearance with the plain arched opening in the face of the wall leading via a tunnel vaulted corridor through the thickness of the work to the buildings of the serai

Epiros

Figure 4.20 Parga Castle: Overall view of Ali Pasha's citadel from the north. The west end of the rampart is to the right; the bathhouse on the roof of the serai is to the extreme left.

within. On either side of the outer arch are two inscribed plaques adorned with the symbols of Ali Pasha's regime. There can be no doubt over the construction date as the left hand plaque records Ali Pasha's name in crude lettering, in Greek, with the date May 1820. At the inner end of the entrance passage two further corridors branch left and right giving access to the vaulted casemates that form the interior of the rampart and support the terreplein above. An opening near the beginning of the western corridor also gives access to the interior of the horseshoe bastion. This consists of a domed chamber apparently reinforced by a massive central pillar. However the pillar is itself hollow with a further square chamber within. This curious double arrangement may have been designed as a powder magazine. The bastion's gun platform above is provided with four gun embrasures in the parapet placed to cover the flanks of the two arms of the main rampart. A round stone sentry

Epiros

Figure 4.21 Parga Castle: Ali Pasha's bathhouse.

box overlooks the approach to the gate below. The pentagonal concrete structure standing in the centre of the platform appears to be a legacy from the Italian occupation during the Second World War.[17] The western corridor is illuminated by square openings through the inner face of the rampart and leads past the entrances to five casemates to another arched gateway. This opens into a narrow court formed between the northwest face of the rampart and the circuit wall. A short crosswall blocks off the southwest end of the court and completes the enclosure of the serai on this side of the citadel. The east arm of the rampart is in a more ruinous condition. Three casemates lead off the interior corridor but the vaulting of the larger chambers at the east end has partially collapsed. Formerly this end of the rampart was also connected by a crosswall to the north circuit wall. A large modern breach now provides a second entrance into the irregular courtyard between the rampart and the serai. The two arms of the rampart and the central horseshoe bastion form one continuous gun platform and are well provided with gun

Epiros

embrasures. The platform is now overgrown and derelict with gun barrels abandoned and half hidden in the vegetation. A second square sentry box with a domed roof is mounted on the extreme western corner overlooking the bay.

The serai occupies most of the internal area enclosed by the rampart leaving only a narrow courtyard between the two buildings. The western half of the accommodation Ali built for himself consists of an L-shaped range of vaulted chambers. The eastern part is a raised walled court standing over substantial cisterns. This may have been surrounded by further structures now demolished. A flight of steps leads up from this courtyard to a freestanding structure on the roof of the main range. Although a ruin, the form of a domed Turkish bathhouse is still clear. It is known inevitably as Ali Pasha's bath. An arched passageway leads beyond the bathhouse onto the flat roof. Here virtually all traces of the parapet have disappeared apart from fragments around the square tower projecting from the centre of the western side. At the extreme northwestern corner of the serai a hollow, two storey vaulted structure is built out over the slope of the hill. Two massive plain arched openings pierce

Figure 4.22 Parga Castle: The west face of Ali Pasha's serai with the projecting square tower. The arched opening leads into the two-storey structure isolated from the rest of the complex.

Epiros

Figure 4.23 Parga Castle: The walled lane leading uphill inside the outer curtain through an archway towards the citadel.

the north face of the upper storey with two smaller splayed openings below (visible in Fig 4.20). A large arched gateway in the west face close to the outer circuit wall leads into the tall vaulted interior space. This is isolated from the main serai complex by an internal wall that appears to be a later insertion into the fabric of the building. Two square openings high in this wall seem to function only as windows admitting light into the main level above. It is possible that the western side of the serai is a survival from the earlier citadel mentioned by de Bossett. The gateway here, although subsequently blocked up internally, may then be the original entrance from the town on the hill below. Evidence for such a route can be seen in the remains of a walled lane running inside the circuit wall below the citadel now blocked off by the crosswall at the western end of the rampart

The origins and extent of the first walls on the castle hill remain obscure. The visible Venetian defences are said to date from 1571. In that year the inhabitants evacuated the town and fled to Corfu in response to the threat from the Turkish fleet operating in the Adriatic. The Turks held the town briefly but, after the Battle of Lepanto, the Venetians reoccupied their territory and over the next four years the defences were rebuilt.[18] The process of repair and rebuilding continued throughout the Venetian period as the later inscriptions of 1626 and 1727 attest and also must have begun before 1571. However the identification of earlier work is virtually impossible as almost all elements of the structures still standing are built of the same heavily mortared rubble masonry, with dressed stone used only for archways and corners.

The castle is normally open during daylight hours. The interior is generally overgrown and much obscured by pine trees. However a network of rough paths gives access to all of the features mentioned above. The only restored structures within the walls are two barrack blocks. The larger of these two-storeyed buildings has been converted into a café and an exhibition space. The best overall view of the defences is from the west bay. The castle gate is most easily approached on foot. Parga is a busy tourist resort during the summer months and parking is normally only possible on the outskirts of the town.

Castle of Anthousa

At the beginning of the 19C the territory of Parga consisted of the town itself and a handful of villages in the immediate area. Its autonomy had always depended on the power of others but in the last years of the Venetian protectorate Ali Pasha had slowly encroached on this small territory, detaching the more isolated villages one by one by a process of intimidation or direct attack. After the fall of Venice in 1797 Parga relied on Russian and then French protection. In 1814 Ali Pasha's forces threatened the village of Aghia on the border of Pargiot territory and although the French still maintained a garrison in Parga they were unable to prevent Ali seizing the village.[19] This failure prompted the inhabitants of Parga to petition the British for help. By the end of March 1814

Epiros

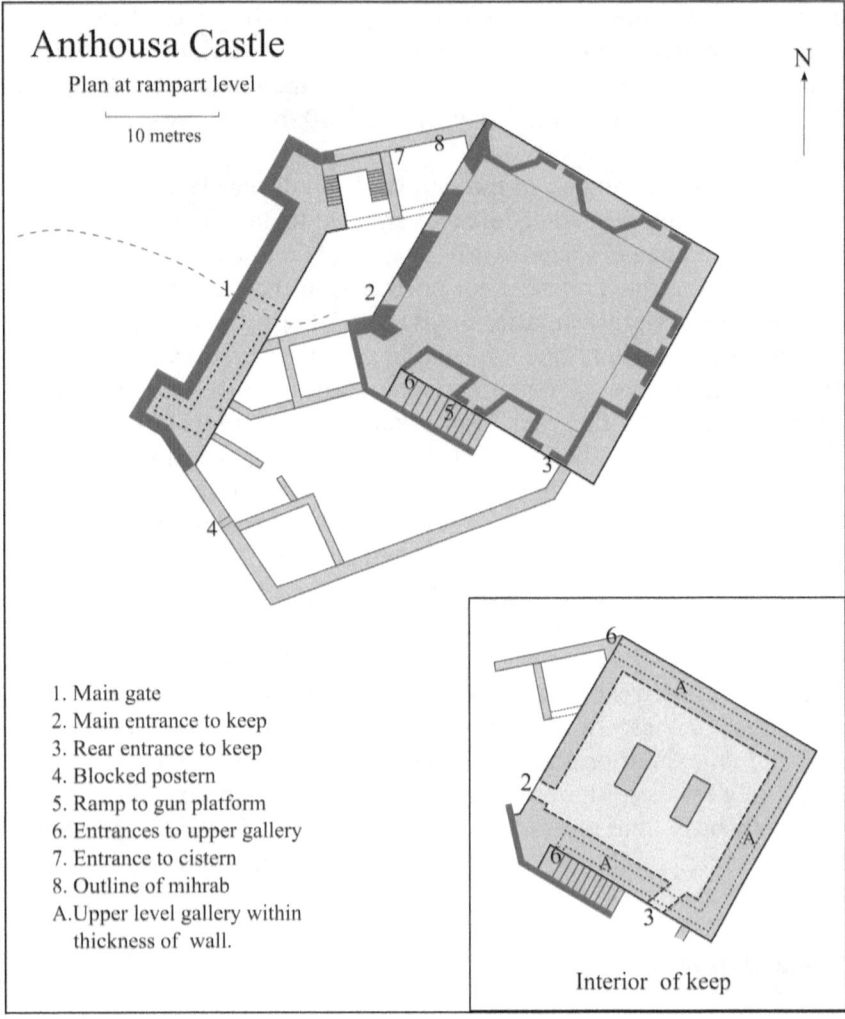

Anthousa Castle

Plan at rampart level

10 metres

1. Main gate
2. Main entrance to keep
3. Rear entrance to keep
4. Blocked postern
5. Ramp to gun platform
6. Entrances to upper gallery
7. Entrance to cistern
8. Outline of mihrab
A. Upper level gallery within thickness of wall.

Interior of keep

the French troops had been ejected and transferred to Corfu and a small British force occupied the castle. However these events did not prevent Ali building a new fort that same year on a prominent hill a little to the south of Aghia. Its walls are clearly visible from Parga some three and a half kilometres to the southeast. Whatever its strategic importance it was evidently located to intimidate the local population although the town itself would have been out of range of the relatively small guns actually mounted in the fort. Examples of these still lie abandoned on the ramparts. Known at the time as the Fort of Aghia it is now generally called the Castle of Anthousa after the larger village a little to the south.

Epiros

The fort stands on a conspicuous hill with steep slopes on all sides other than the approach from the west. The walls are built out over these slopes and are particularly imposing from the east and south, rising over fifteen metres from ground level. However over half of this height consists simply of a solid platform supporting the main block of the fort. This has the appearance of a square keep and is essentially a single-storeyed squat tower approximately twenty metres square with a vaulted interior and gun batteries on its roof. To the west, where the final approach to the main gate is across level ground, the true height of the walls becomes apparent. Here a six-metre high curtain wall encloses two irregular courts to the west and south of the keep. The gate is set in the northwest face of the curtain between shallow square towers. A monumental façade surrounds the opening although it is now partly

Figure 4.24 Castle of Anthousa: View from the east with the main block in the right foreground and the south court to the left.

Figure 4.25 Castle of Anthousa: Northwest front and main gate.

destroyed and badly weathered. The two towers, which seem to have been designed as vestigial flanking bastions, were originally each equipped with a single arched gunport at ground level, now walled up. As is often the case with the Ali Pasha's forts, the walls' impression of strength is superficial. The entire northwest face is hollow with a vaulted interior supporting the walkway and parapet. The outer skin is hardly one metre thick. The platform above would have been too narrow to mount cannon and the partly ruined plain parapet is equipped only with tapering loopholes for small arms. The vaulting above the entrance has now partly collapsed. The western entrance to the keep is visible ahead on the other side of the narrow north court. To the right a corridor leads through the interior of the wall to the southern flanking tower. An archway opposite the tower opens into the larger southern courtyard. The two courtyards are separated by a two-storeyed building, now roofless, that connects the rear of the northwest wall with the western corner of the keep. The north court had another range of two storeys on its northern side divided by a crosswall. This range appears to have had some domestic function. On the upper floor of the right hand chamber the clear outline of a mihrab can be seen in the wall although it does

Epiros

Figure 4.26 Castle of Anthousa: Monumental façade of the main gate. Within can be seen the west entrance to the keep.

not face directly east. A stairway leads from the left hand chamber up to parapet level. Below this stairway an arched opening at the rear of the right hand chamber give access to steps down into a large plastered underground cistern still in good condition. Both ranges of buildings seem

Figure 4.27 Castle of Anthousa: Outline of mihrab in the upper floor of the buildings of the north courtyard. Both the line of the roof joists and the parapet above are clearly visible.

to have been of two storeys with wooden floors and possibly pitched roofs. The southern court had further buildings along its southwest side now reduced to ruins. Here a partially buried postern gate is still visible although its inner arch has been walled up at some point. The arched opening can be seen clearly from outside the fort. At the eastern end of the court an archway in the southwestern face of the keep provides a second entrance to the interior. The trace of a pitched roofline in the face of the wall just below parapet level indicates that this entrance was masked by a forebuilding. A substantial ramp built against this face of the keep rises to a gap in the line of the parapet and provides access to the gun platforms on the roof.

An unusual feature of the keep is the barrel vaulted corridor, or gallery, that runs around three sides of the block within the thickness of the wall immediately below the level of the parapet. There is no access to the gallery from within the keep. A square opening in the outer face of the wall at the top of the external ramp forms one entrance; a second is to be found at the northern corner of the keep where the corridor seems to have opened onto the roof of the adjoining range of buildings. Narrow angled loopholes pointing sharply downwards pierce both walls

Figure 4.28 Castle of Anthousa: Eastern entrance to keep. The outline of a pitched roof is visible beneath the parapet.

of the gallery so that small arms fire could be directed both externally and into the interior of the keep. This consists of one large open chamber with two central pillars. The roof is divided into nine bays with groin vaults separated by semi-circular arches. The gallery in the wall runs above the level of the vault springing and just below the base of

Epiros

Figure 4.29 Castle of Anthousa: The thin walls of the parapet and embrasures. The entrance to the internal gallery can be seen below.

the parapet. The builders clearly believed that the gallery's tunnel vault would be too weak to support the weight of a normal solid parapet and they therefore constructed a skeleton of thin walls on the three weakened sides. The walls form a series of box shaped structures that create the outline of a conventional artillery parapet with two embrasures in each face. On the northwest side where the wall is solid the parapet is of conventional construction with three tapering embrasures. On the southeast side steel studs set in concrete mark the position of the mountings for armaments installed during the Italian occupation of 1941.

The fort's architect is said to have been a Don Santo di Monteleone who apparently served in Ali Pasha's army.[20] The work was clearly designed to be a symbol of Ali's power and this symbolism seems to have been more important than real strength. As mentioned above the walls are relatively thin and the skeletal parapet of the keep could never have withstood serious bombardment. The fort, known locally as Ali Pasha's castle, is reached by taking the road from Parga north through Anthousa village. Bear right in the village and after a further kilometre turn left signposted to Trikorfo and the Kastro. The path from the car park leads directly to the entrance in the northwest face of the castle. Excursions from Parga visit the site in summer.

Epiros

Castle of Margariti

Eight kilometres north of Parga the castle, or fort, of Margariti stands neglected and overgrown on a small hill overlooking what must always have been the main route to Igoumenitsa. The castle is a purely Turkish construction and dates from 1549.[21] It seems to have been constructed to counter Venetian influence in the area and stands just outside the boundary of the territory of Parga at its maximum extent.[22] The Venetians first contemplated attacking the fort in 1571 in the build-up to the Battle of Lepanto later that year. After the Ottoman naval defeat Venice attempted to maintain the momentum of the victory and was able to take Margariti in November 1571.[23] However the failure of the Holy League to engage the re-built Ottoman fleet during 1572 led the Venetians to seek an independent peace with the Turks in the spring of 1573. The weakness of the Venetian bargaining position meant that they were forced to abandon their claims to Cyprus, which had fallen to the Turks in their campaign of 1570-71, and relinquish their conquests on the coast of Epiros including Margariti. The Venetians' only gain from the

Figure 4.30 Castle of Margariti: Northwest corner of the circuit. The horizontal lines of scaffold holes are still visible.

treaty was the re-establishment of free trade in the eastern Mediterranean. Margariti remained an Ottoman stronghold and by the 18C it had become the capital of a semi-autonomous region with its own bey or lord. By the beginning of the 19C its independence had made it a target for Ali Pasha's aggression and it fell to his forces in 1811 becoming a base for his campaign against Parga. There had been a strong Albanian presence in the area from the 14C onwards and from the 17C Albanian Muslims probably formed the majority of the population. The district of Margariti along with those of Paramythia and Filiates was then known as Chameria, or Tsamouria, and covered approximately the same area as modern Thesprotia. It became part of Greece in 1913 when the international treaties agreed after the Balkan Wars of 1912-13 assigned

Figure 4.31 Castle of Margariti: Southern corner of the main circuit viewed from the platform of the round bastion. The archway gave access to the bastion from the interior of the fort.

Epiros

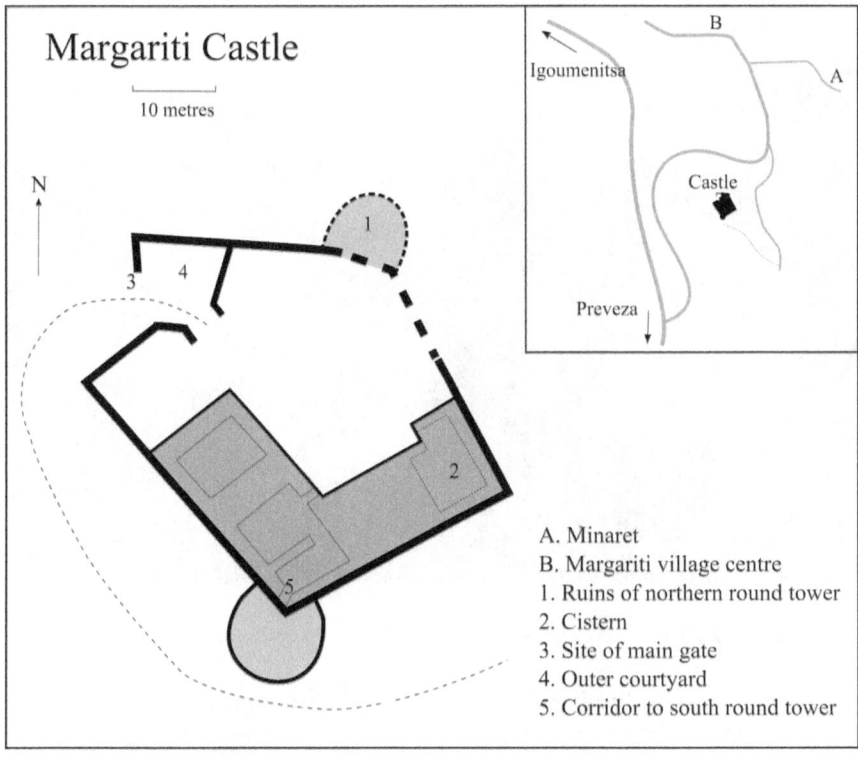

A. Minaret
B. Margariti village centre
1. Ruins of northern round tower
2. Cistern
3. Site of main gate
4. Outer courtyard
5. Corridor to south round tower

the southern part of Epiros to Greece and also recognised the new state of Albania.[24] Many of the Muslim population emigrated or were forced from the area at this time. More left during the exchange of populations agreed between Greece and Turkey at Lausanne in January 1923. The remainder of the Muslim population fled to Albania at the end of the Second World War.[25]

The continuing depopulation of rural Thesprotia has caused much of the once heavily grazed hillsides to revert to nature. As a result the imposing walls of the castle, which still stand to a height of ten metres on the south and west sides, are now largely obscured by trees and scrub. The castle is roughly quadrangular with a large solid circular bastion projecting from the southern angle at a lower level. The bastion's gun platform is some three metres below the main parapet and the whole structure appears almost detached from the remainder of the fort. It is possible that it was a late addition to the defences and may date from the period of Ali Pasha's control. No trace of its parapet remains. An arched opening in the face of the main wall leads from the rear of the platform through the thickness of the wall into a vaulted chamber that

Epiros

Figure 4.32 Castle of Margariti: Southeast face.

provides access to the interior of the fort. There appears to have been a second circular bastion at the northern angle of the fortress. Although the structure has collapsed its lower courses can still be distinguished. The main rampart on this side of the fort is also largely destroyed. The entrance complex is now much ruined but seems to have consisted of an outer gate, now missing, that led into a small courtyard. An inner gate then gave access to the main enclosure. The overgrown interior has an L-shaped range of single-storey vaulted chambers built against the inner faces of the west and south walls. These must have provided accommodation for the garrison. Although partially ruined much of the vaulting survives and a cistern can still be seen at the eastern corner of the range. The flat roof of these chambers must have functioned as a gun platform but it is no longer possible to distinguish any artillery features in the completely ruined parapet.

The castle stands to the south of the village of Margariti on the eastern side of the main Igoumenitsa road. From this direction the by-road into the village sweeps around the north of the castle hill. A tarmac lane leads up the eastern side of the hill. There is room to park where an obvious rough path winds uphill to the castle. In addition to the castle, relics from the long period of Albanian Muslim occupation still survive in the area. At the end of the 19C Margariti was a substantial town with several mosques and a madrasah.²⁶ A single minaret in the centre of the village survives from this period. The numerous ruined houses on the hillsides above the modern village remain as the main evidence of its earlier population.

Igoumenitsa and Pirgos Ragiou

The town of Igoumenitsa, now Greece's third largest port, is approximately twenty five kilometres north of Margariti and stands on a broad bay at the southern edge of the coastal plain of the river Kalamas, or Thyamis. Its history is often conflated with that of Gitana, the 4C BC walled city ten kilometres to the north.²⁷ The town developed as the major port linking Greece with Italy after the end of the Second World War. Before this date it was hardly more than a small village. In the mediaeval period it was known as Gomenitsa, or Gumenizza, but was of little importance. The main Venetian port for trade between Epiros and Corfu was at Sagiada, known to the Venetians as Bastia, some fifteen kilometres further north.²⁸ Igoumenitsa appears fleetingly in the historical record. In 1571 the combined fleet of the Holy League anchored briefly in the bay to take on water and stores. Although there were some minor skirmishes with Ottoman troops from Margariti, Igoumenitsa at that time appears to have been undefended.²⁹ However by 1685 fortifications of some form existed as Morosini, en route to Santa Maura from Corfu, was reported as having "taken and demolished the castle of Gumenizza".³⁰ The Treaty of Passarowitz confirmed Venetian possession of their conquests on the coast. A later fort still stands on the same site; a hill three hundred metres east of the quays of the modern harbour. Much of the circuit of crudely built rubble masonry survives hidden within a wood of pine trees. The curtain wall is roughly quadrangular and is reinforced with square towers. It dates to 1798 and was probably built or re-built by Ali Pasha after he had expelled the French from the old Venetian coastal strongholds.

Pirgos Ragiou, the Tower of Ragio, is a Turkish work of the early 19C built by the Aga of Igoumenitsa to house the local guard. It stands on part of a much older fort that encircles the flat top of a conical hill rising abruptly from the plain on the northern side of the bay of Igoumenitsa. The site overlooks the old southern course of the Kalamas and at one time it may have been an island surrounded by marsh. The first fortifications on the hill date from the fifth or fourth century BC and were designed to protect the eastern approaches to the Kerkyrean

Figure 4.33 Pirgos Ragiou: The Turkish tower from the west. Four courses of the 5C BC walls are visible.

colony of Toroni.[31] The walls form a five-sided enclosure reinforced with four square towers. Their external faces stand to four or more courses. The greater part of the circuit is of regular isodomic masonry but on the southwest, where the walls incorporate several large masses of natural rock, there are sections that are purely polygonal. The fort had two entrances; the main gate to the south and a narrow postern in the north wall guarded by the adjacent tower. This was later incorporated ingeniously into the entrance arrangements of the Turkish tower house. In the centre of the enclosure a large water cistern can be seen, hollowed out of the rock. The remainder of the interior is a confused jumble of foundations that represent buildings of the Ottoman period.

The Turkish tower itself consists of a main square block of two storeys with a narrower wing projecting to the south. The external walls of

Epiros

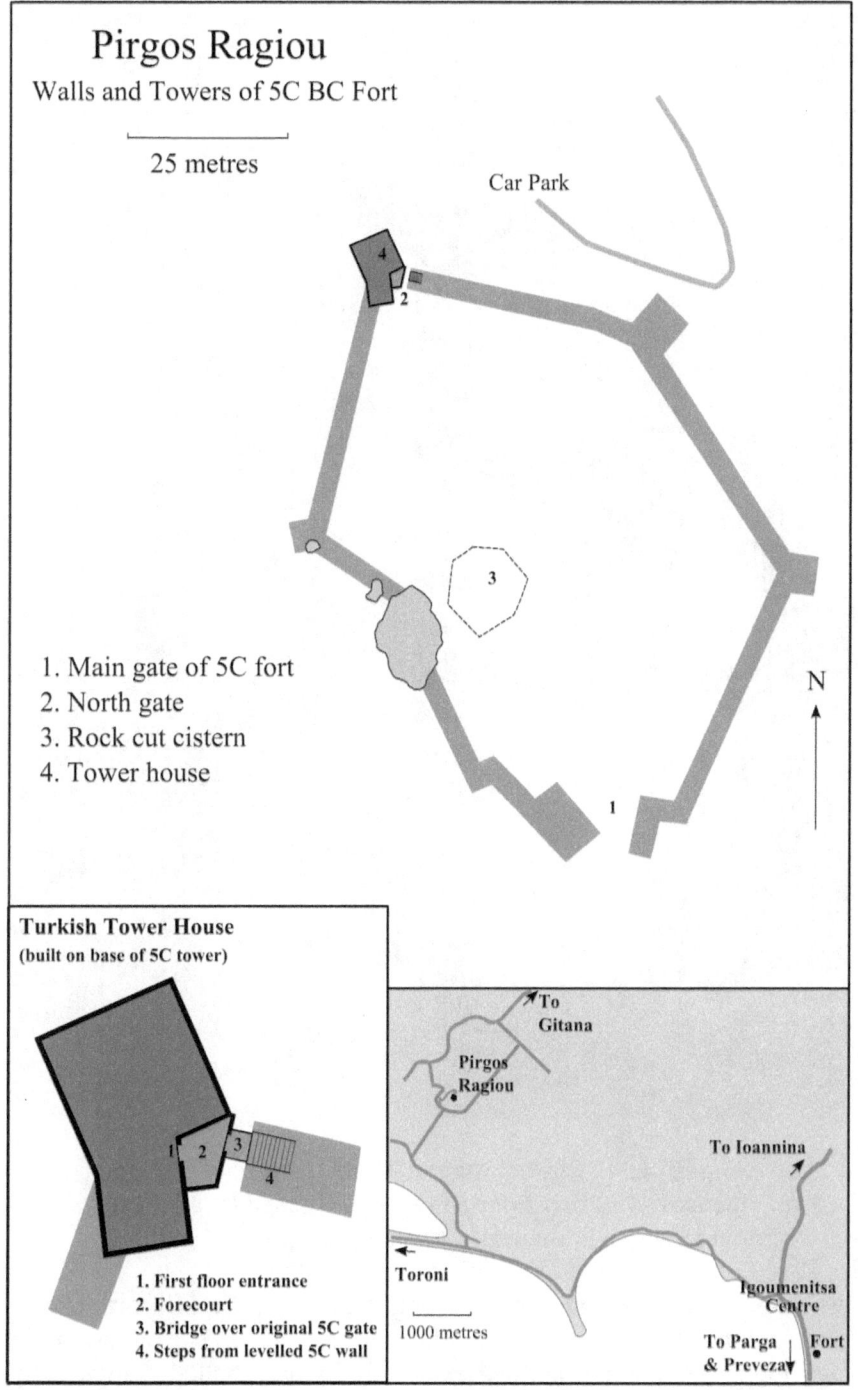

Epiros

Figure 4.34 Pirgos Ragiou: View of the tower from the east. The first floor entrance is reached by a bridge over the gap in the wall formed by the postern gate.

the main block stand on the surviving courses of the 5C north tower. The roof forms one continuous flat platform and is surrounded by a high loopholed parapet defined externally by a corbelled stringcourse.

Epiros

Figure 4.35 Pirgos Ragiou: The tower from the interior of the fort.

The tower entrance is at first floor level and is protected by a small walled forecourt built on a raised plinth in the angle of the two wings of the tower. A bridge over the gap in the fifth century wall formed by the postern gate connects the outer door of the forecourt to a flight of eight stone steps built on the levelled surface of the east wall. Originally the bridge was probably removable. Loopholes in the forecourt wall defend the approach. The upper floor of the tower is provided with small shuttered windows. The interior has been restored with aid from an EU interregional fund. The internal rooms are used to display information about the general history of the area. One room has been restored to show a typical Ottoman living space of the early 19C. The tower is locked but the custodian will open it on request.

The Tower of Ragio is a more developed example of the simple square towers to be found throughout Greece. The Turkish versions are known as Kula, or Koulia. Another restored example can be seen at Paramythia. Ragio is most easily reached by following the coastal road west from Igoumenitsa towards the Lygia peninsula. A road forks north near the head of the Lygia lagoon towards the hill of Ragio. At the base of the hill a modern steel gate, open during standard opening hours (8.30 to 15.00), gives access to the approach road that climbs to a car park close to the tower.

Paramythia, the Castle of Agios Donatos

Paramythia is a small hillside town near the head of the valley of the river Kokytos. The river flows south towards Glyki and joins the Acherontas near the Necromanteio. The high ridge of the Paramythias range forms the eastern side of the valley and reaches its maximum height at Mount Korilas above Paramythia. The Castle of Agios Donatos stands on a cliff edged spur in the foothills above the town.[32] The fortress had three distinct phases of construction, Hellenistic, Byzantine and Turkish with the final period of Ottoman occupation lasting until the beginning of the 19C. The first walls on the hill may date from the period of the rise of the Molossian state in the 4C BC.[33] The site was abandoned after the Roman sack of Epiros in 167 BC. At some point in the 1C BC the Romans founded a new town, Photike, in the valley a little to the northwest of modern Paramythia. The site has never been excavated but its extent may be indicated by the ruins of a number of Byzantine churches that incorporate elements of early Christian basilicas. Photike is thought to have been occupied until the 6C AD when Justinian, according to Procopius, relocated the town to the original hilltop site of Agios Donatos.[34] This period of re-occupation may have been brief and the area may have been lost to Byzantine control until the 9C. In fact the range of possible dates for the rebuilding of the walls may extend to the early part of the 13C after the establishment of the Despotate of Epiros. A settlement below the castle on the site of modern Paramythia probably first developed in the early years of the Despotate. Surviving monuments within the town include the 14C church of the Panayia and the remains of a Byzantine bathhouse. From the 13C onwards the history of Agios Donatos follows closely that of Ioannina. In 1380 the castle was acquired by Thomas Preljubovič. In 1411 it passed to Carlo Tocco but in 1430 it fell, with Ioannina, to the Turks.

The Turkish name for the castle was Aidonat Kalesi, the Castle of Aidonat, a corruption of Donatos. Although central control from Constantinople was strong enough to suppress a revolt that broke out in Paramythia in 1611, by the end of the 17C the area had developed, like Margariti, into a semi-autonomous province with its own bey.[35] At the end of the 18C Ali Pasha began to threaten its independence and he sacked the town sometime after the defeat of the Souliots in 1803. Leake, writing in 1809 after Ali had expelled the ruling families, described the lower town as half populated and the upper town within the castle walls as ruined and deserted. Thereafter the castle was used to house Ali's Albanian garrison. Ali's governor however established

Epiros

himself in the fortified house of one of the leading families. This may be the three-storeyed tower house, or Koulia, recently restored, that can be seen on the edge of the town on the lower slopes of the castle hill. Agios Donatos was finally abandoned after Ali's death in 1822. Paramythia became part of Greece in 1913 and the district's Albanian Muslim population migrated or fled the area over the next three decades along with those of the Margariti and Filiates districts.

The castle spur is connected to the main body of the hill by a narrow saddle to the east. To the south and west its steep sides provide considerable natural protection while the overhanging cliffs to the north allowed the builders to dispense almost entirely with walls on this side of the circuit. The area enclosed forms a rough oval, approximately 300m by 120m, with a second inner enclosure, or acropolis, at the highest point of the site placed to dominate the more accessible eastern approach. The lower southwest gate can be reached by a steep footpath from the town but the easiest approach is by an indirect road to the east upper gate. Here a short path leads along the wooded saddle past a section of Hellenistic wall to a ramp supported by ancient foundations. The track then runs beneath the acropolis to the site of the east gate, now

Figure 4.36 Castle of Agios Donatos: The east gate.

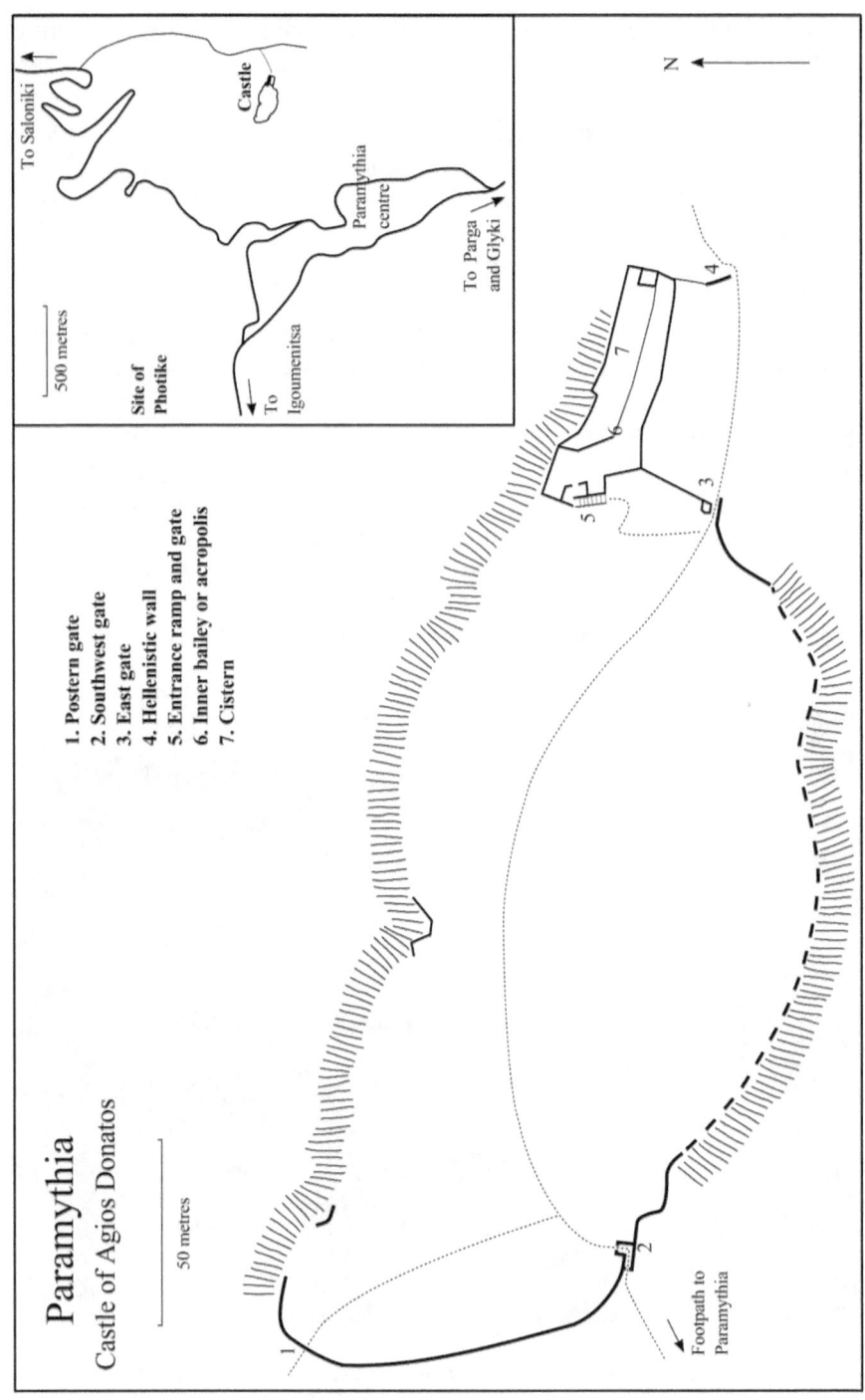

Epiros

Figure 4.37 Castle of Agios Donatos: North wall of acropolis. The arches allowed fire to be directed through ground-level slits down the face of the cliff below.

largely destroyed. The surviving walls are of heavily mortared rubble masonry. Within the gate a rough path snakes uphill to the acropolis. The entrance complex here consisted of a ramp and a double gate involving several changes of direction, although again the walls have been reduced to a fraction of their original height. The terraced interior is on two levels. The distinctive Byzantine construction of alternating bands of rubble masonry and brick can still be seen in the surviving walls. There are concealed cisterns below the upper terrace. The most distinctive surviving features are the three man-sized shallow arched chambers in the north wall close to the gate. These are provided with slits at their bases allowing fire to be directed almost vertically down the face of the cliff below. From the upper gate a lane, paved with cobbles and with rock-cut steps in sections, runs the length of the site down to the southwest gate. The foundations, ruined walls and supporting terracing of the Turkish houses of the upper town are visible on either side. The western side of the site is the best preserved. The southwest gate itself, the adjoining sections of the circuit wall and the surviving walls of the domestic buildings to the north of the gate have all been recently cleared and consolidated. The three phases of construction can be seen on either side of the gate where the massive blocks of the first Hellenistic wall support a mixture of Byzantine and later Turkish work. One hundred metres to the north an original Hellenistic postern gate survives intact. When Leake inspected it in 1809 it was walled up and its excellent state of preservation may indicate that it was blocked at an early stage of the site's re-occupation. The gate itself is formed of massive squared blocks with a monolithic lintel, but the walls on either side are purely polygonal. It has now been cleared and restored. Immediately to the north of the postern gate the wall ends at the edge of the overhanging northern cliffs. With the exception of two short stretches of wall above accessible gullies, the cliffs were thought to provide sufficient natural defence from here to the acropolis. The fortifications were

Figure 4.38 Castle of Agios Donatos: The Hellenistic postern gate.

Epiros

Figure 4.39 Castle of Agios Donatos: Exterior of the southwest gate.

never updated for artillery. The successive re-building works always followed the line of the Hellenistic circuit and the castle retained its mediaeval appearance until it was abandoned in the 19C.

To reach the upper gate by car take the road north from Paramythia towards Saloniki and Agios Kiriaki. This climbs the mountainside in serpentine curves. After approximately three kilometres the ascent reaches the height of the wooded castle spur, visible one kilometre to the south. Take the unsigned gravel road that can be seen running across the scree-lined hillside towards the castle. Four hundred metres after the road first enters the wood a surprising children's playground on the left marks the point where a footpath leads off to the right towards the upper gate of the castle.

Ioannina

Modern Ioannina is a large town standing on the western shore of Lake Pamvotitha some forty kilometres to the northwest of Paramythia. The lake occupies a closed basin in the western flanks of the Pindos Mountains. It is fed by springs and has no surface outlet. The old walled town, or Kastro, is built on a promontory projecting into the lake. Although now surrounded by considerable urban sprawl, when seen from the north or east the intact mosques and minarets of the Kastro still give Ioannina the feel of an Ottoman city. This legacy is due at least in part to the political ambitions of Ali Pasha who replaced the earlier defences with massive new walls and transformed the town into his own vision of a fortified capital at the beginning of the 19C.

Ioannina was originally a Byzantine foundation of unknown date. It does not appear in the written record until the late 9C AD when there is a reference to a bishopric.[36] Town walls of some description must have existed by 1082. In the previous year Robert Guiscard had attacked the Byzantine Empire from his Norman power base in southern Italy and he and his son, Bohemond, succeeded in taking possession of the coast of northern Epiros (now Albania). Although Guiscard was forced to return to Italy in 1082 to suppress a revolt, Bohemond advanced inland and captured Ioannina that year. Anna Comnena claims that he surveyed the walls, restored the dilapidated citadel and built a second citadel in a stronger position.[37] However the Norman occupation was short-lived and by the end of 1084 the Byzantines had recovered virtually all of their lost territory. In 1204 the sack of Constantinople by the forces of the Fourth Crusade led indirectly to a dramatic expansion in both the size and importance of Ioannina. The new state of Epiros, later the Despotate, founded by Michael Comnenus in the decade after 1204, became a place of asylum for large numbers of refugees from Constantinople. Many came to Ioannina where Michael granted them both citizenship and space within the town to settle. To protect the expanded settlement he built a new circuit of walls and Ioannina became the second city of the state of Epiros after Arta, the capital.[38]

When Nicholas Orsini seized Arta in 1318 the citizens of Ioannina took the opportunity cut themselves free from the Despotate and reunite their city with the rump of the Byzantine Empire, restored when Constantinople was recovered in 1261. The extensive list of privileges granted by the Emperor Andronikos II in return for the city's allegiance gave it almost the status of a separate city-state.[39] In 1323 John Orsini killed his brother Nicholas and gained control of Epiros. He persuaded

Epiros

the citizens of Ioannina to accept him as governor of the city on behalf of the Emperor and the city's privileges continued. John Orsini was murdered by his wife Anna in 1337. Ioannina was again given a Byzantine governor, and by 1340 the entire territory of the Despotate was restored to the Empire.

On the death of Andronikos III in 1341 civil war broke out in Byzantium. The ensuing conflict left the Empire unable to resist a Serbian invasion and by 1348 virtually all of Epiros and Thessaly were in the hands of the Serb ruler Stephen Dušan who assigned Epiros to his half-brother, Symeon Uroš. The Serbs in turn then had to face Albanian incursions into the territory of Epiros. By 1367 the situation had been resolved by partitioning the Despotate. Albanian control in the south was divided between Peter Losha who held Arta and Rogoi and Gjin Boua Spata who held Angelokastro. Ioannina was assigned to Symeon's son-in-law, Thomas Preljubovič. Once again Ioannina was a separate state with its own ruler, albeit a Serbian. It was repeatedly attacked, unsuccessfully, by Albanian forces from 1367 to 1379. In 1384 Thomas Preljubovič was assassinated and his widow quickly married the Florentine Esau Buondelmonti. The following year Esau was granted the title of Despot by the Emperor John V. From 1399 onwards the balance of power in the region began to change. Carlo Tocco began a campaign to extend his domain beyond Lefkas and Vonitsa and attacked the Albanian territories in southern Epiros. By 1408 he was in control of all of Akarnania. In 1411 Esau Buondelmonti died. The citizens of Ioannina swiftly invited Carlo, who was Buondelmonti's nephew, to be their new Despot. His adoption of the title was confirmed by the Emperor Manuel II in 1415. The following year Carlo and his brother, Leonardo, seized Arta and Rogoi and the reunification of the Despotate was complete. It was to last a mere fifteen years. In 1429 Carlo died and his nephew, Carlo II, inherited Ioannina and Arta. The following year the Turks under the Sultan Murad II seized and plundered Thessalonica and proceeded to march on Ioannina. To avoid the destruction of their city the leading citizens surrendered to the besieging Turks in October 1430.[40] Carlo II remained as ruler in Arta but only as a vassal of the Sultan. By surrendering their city and pledging loyalty to the Sultan the citizens of Ioannina were able to retain many of their privileges and a great deal of

Overleaf: Figure 4.40. Ioannina: View of the southeast acropolis. The Fetihe mosque is top left. Below it is the arched main gate to Ali Pasha's citadel. Centre left is the Royal Pavilion, now the Byzantine Museum. Centre right is the round tower attributed to Bohemond.

Epiros

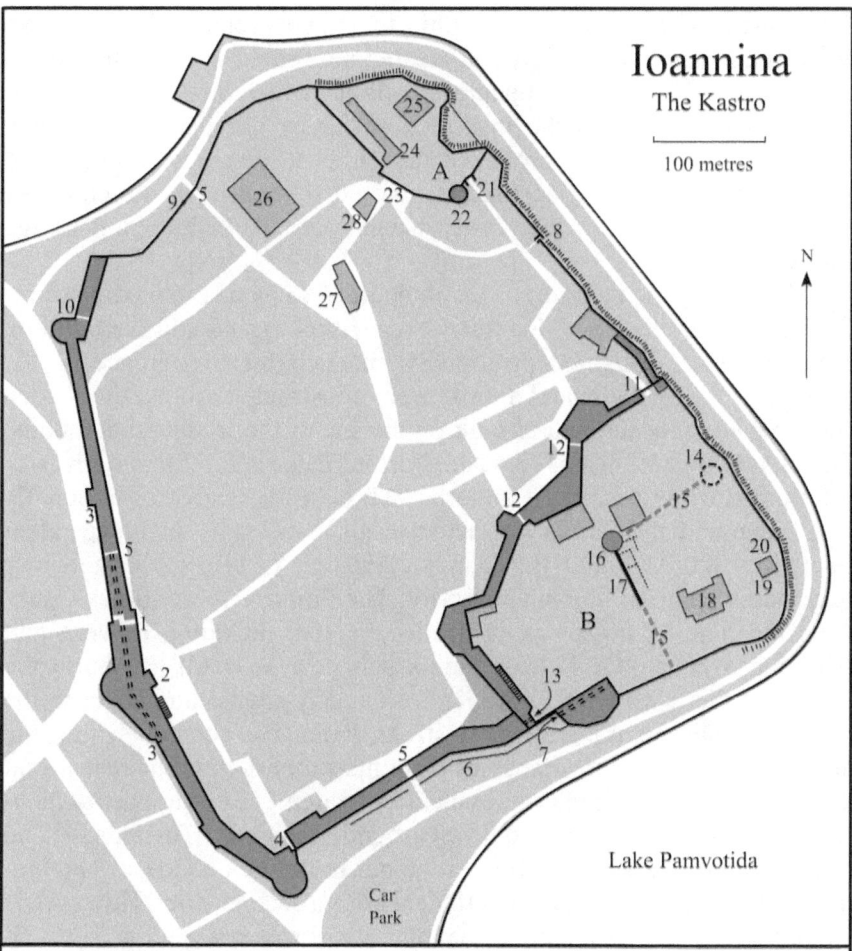

Ioannina
The Kastro

100 metres

Lake Pamvotida

Car Park

A. Northeast acropolis or citadel
B. Ali Pasha's citadel partially on site of the southeast acropolis
1. Main gate
2. Thomas tower
3. Postern gates
4. Skala gate
5. Modern entrances
6, Outer wall
7. South gate to citadel
8. Gate and stairs to lakeside
9. North gate
10. Molos gate
11. Main gate to citadel
12. Subsidiary gates to citadel
13. Gate from citadel to outer rampart
14. Foundations of early circular tower
15. Possible extent of southeast acropolis
16. Tower of Bohemund
17. West wall of southeast acropolis
18. Byzantine Museum
19. Fetihe mosque
20. Tomb of Ali Pasha
21. Original gate to northwest citadel
22. Byzantine tower
23. Modern entrance to northwest citadel
24. Madrasah
25. Aslan Pasha mosque
26. Riding school
27. Turkish baths (17C)
28. Turkish library

their independence. The town within the Kastro remained a Christian enclave and Turkish immigration created new suburbs built outside the mediaeval walls. This arrangement continued for almost two hundred years until 1611 when the insurrection led by Dionysios, the Greek Metropolitan of Larissa, provoked the Turks to take possession of the Kastro, expel its Christian inhabitants and demolish all the churches within.[41] From then on the Kastro became the Turkish administrative and religious centre.

Ali Pasha gained control of Ioannina in 1786 by a combination of intimidation and trickery.[42] Ioannina became his capital and the building programme he instigated profoundly changed the appearance of the town. Thick new walls and a moat were constructed around the Kastro and a new citadel and palace built on the site of the southeast acropolis. The citadel was known as Its-Kalé. Further palaces for Ali and his sons were constructed within the suburbs. Ali held his territories notionally as an agent of the Sultan but acted in all respects as an independent ruler. In 1820 Mahmud II began a campaign to bring Ali's territory back under central Ottoman authority. The Sultan's forces quickly subdued the other main towns controlled by Ali, including Preveza and Arta, and by October 1820 Ioannina was besieged. Ali had burnt the houses of the town outside the Kastro to deny shelter and cover to the besiegers. The combination of a strong defensive position within the new walls and counter offensives from his supporters in the rear meant that the siege made little progress and by March 1821 over twenty thousand Turkish troops were tied down around Ioannina.[43] Towards the end of March the Greek Revolution broke out in the Peloponnese. The limited Turkish resources now had to deal with a second front. However in October 1821 the stalemate at Ioannina was broken when the Turks finally took the bastion of Litharitsia, a strongpoint to the south of the Kastro that controlled the approaches to Ali's fortress.[44] The Turks could now bombard the interior of the main fortress. In January 1822 they finally entered the Kastro and in February Ali Pasha was killed while attempting to negotiate his freedom.

Ioannina remained in Turkish hands throughout the period of the Greek Revolution. The establishment of the northern border of the new state on the Arta–Volos line in 1832 left the town firmly part of the shrinking Ottoman Empire. In 1870 most of the buildings of Ali Pasha's citadel burnt down and the administration centre of the town moved permanently beyond the walls. The citadel became simply a military stronghold and a military hospital was built on the site of Ali's palace.[45] Towards the end of the 19C the Ottoman Empire sought German help to modernise its army and defences, and Ioannina was re-established as the principal fortress of Epiros. The programme of fortification was directed by the German General van der Goltz. He followed the principles of the day in constructing a ring of detached forts, self-contained bunkers and trenches to form a defensible line some five to ten kilometres beyond the limits of the town. The original citadel of Its-Kalé with its military hospital became the fortress headquarters connected to the outlying forts by telephone lines.[46] In October 1912 Bulgaria, Serbia, Montenegro and Greece, acting as a Balkan alliance, declared war on the Ottoman Empire. Greek forces began to blockade Ioannina the following month and after three months of fierce fighting the Turks surrendered the town on the 6th March 1913.[47] In Greek hands Its-Kalé continued to be used by the military well into the twentieth century. The military hospital was demolished in 1958 in order to build the Royal Pavilion, now the Byzantine Museum. The remainder of the Kastro is now a quiet residential suburb.

The Town Walls

The promontory enclosed by the Kastro walls forms an area approximately 600m by 700m. The growth of the modern town and the reclamation of land from the lake and its marshy foreshore have disguised the full extent of the Kastro's natural defences. The waters of the lake once reached the rocky cliffs that form the eastern side of the promontory. Areas of marsh lay to the north and south. A wet moat ran the full length of the western face of the Kastro and connected to the lake at each end. Today a broad tree-lined esplanade built on reclaimed land runs along the lakeshore beneath the cliffs. The marshes have been drained and built over and the moat has been filled in. The walls now visible are almost entirely the work of Ali Pasha's engineers. They follow the line of the earlier Byzantine enceinte which may have resembled the circuit at Arta with tall, thin walls reinforced by a mixture of square, round and beaked towers. On the vulnerable western and southern sides Ali's new walls are up to twenty metres thick. Although apparently of massive construction they are in fact hollow. They were formed by building a new outer wall parallel to the Byzantine original. The space between was vaulted over to form internal galleries and corridors supporting a continuous wide walkway at parapet level.[48]

The main gate to the Kastro is in the centre of the western wall. The street that runs outside this face of the fortress marks the position of the moat isolating the Kastro from the rest of the town. A bridge provided

Epiros

Figure 4.41 Ioannina: Outer face of the main gate of the Kastro. Above the arch are engravings of Ali's lion symbol.

access to the gate passage which takes a dogleg course through the thickness of the wall. Above the entrance are carved reliefs of Ali's symbol of the lion. The clock tower that flanks the gate to the south is a later addition. Fifty metres to the north a second gate, probably modern, pierces the wall. Internal galleries run the length of the wall between the gates and are visible from their entrance passages. A further fifty metres

Epiros

Figure 4.42 Ioannina: The blocked Molos gate.

to the north the wall is reinforced by a square tower with a postern gate in its southern flank. Towards the northern end of the west walls the Molos gate pierces the wall hard against the north flank of a projecting round bastion. The gate is no longer in use and is closed by its original door of wood reinforced by studded iron plates. The finely carved arched entrance is surmounted by an ornate ogee arch. As the name implies the Molos gate gave access to a mole, or jetty, on the lakeshore nearby. Fifty metres further north the broad west wall ends on the line of the early nineteenth century lakeshore. From here a narrower wall runs along the old shoreline before climbing to meet the northeast acropolis circuit. At its midpoint another disused gate close by a modern breach in the wall provided direct access to the shore.

Epiros

Returning to the south of the main gate the wall thickens further and incorporates a massive curved bastion that enfilades the gate itself and the full length of the wall beyond. The rear of the bastion encloses a Byzantine square tower. Known as the Thomas tower, after Thomas Preljubovič, it dates from the second half of the 14C. Athough the bulk of the tower is embedded in the bastion its rear face and entrance arch are still visible. The name Thomas has been recognised in the brick inscriptions on either side of the arch.[49] The bastion and the wide walkway of the adjacent sections of wall seem to have formed a major artillery position in the centre of the landward defences. The embrasures in the parapet are largely intact and access to the gun platform was provided by a substantial ramp built against the inner face adjacent to the Thomas tower. An arched gate in the wall abutting the bastion's south flank gives access to the galleries within and may have functioned as a sally port. From this point the west wall runs south for a further 170m

Figure 4.43 Ioannina: The upper part of the rear face of the Thomas tower with brick entrance arch and cloisonné masonry.

Epiros

Figure 4.44 Ioannina: The southern flank of the central bastion with the arched sally port visible in the angle of the wall.

broken only by a shallow square tower. A substantial circular bastion designed to protect the southern lakeshore stands at the southwestern corner of the circuit. It projects some thirty metres beyond the south face of the Kastro and is provided with gun embrasures and musketry slits in the parapet. The bastion also protects the approach to the Skala gate which must have led to a landing place or wharf. Again the shoreline would once have been much closer to the walls. There is evidence of damage and repairs to the masonry of the bastion which is not bonded to the adjacent arcaded stretch of wall. This arches over the gate and links the bastion to the south wall. The gate itself is the only entrance to the Kastro not provided with an arched façade and inscribed with Ali Pasha's symbols. As such it may pre-date Ali's work. The Kastro's thick south wall continues east for 250m where it joins the circuit

Epiros

Figure 4.45 Ioannina: The southwestern round bastion.

Figure 4.46 Ioannina: The Skala gate.

Epiros

Figure 4.47 Ioannina: The south gate to Ali Pasha's citadel. In the right foreground are the lower courses of an outer wall that ran from this point west to the Skala gate. The height of the wall to the left reflects the higher ground level within the citadel.

of Ali's citadel at its southwestern corner. Originally a low outer wall ran in front of this section of the defences from the Skala gate to the southern multangular bastion of the citadel. The fragments that remain indicate that this wall was equipped with low-level gunports. A monumental gate is set in the west flank of the multangular bastion. Above the gate's arch are empty niches that would have once held the usual symbols of Ali's power. This entrance leads not into the Kastro but directly into the southeastern citadel via a long barrel vaulted tunnel through the thickness of the bastion. To the east of the multangular bastion the circuit reverts to a single solid wall on the line of its Byzantine

Epiros

Figure 4.48 Ioannina: The casemates of the south wall of the Kastro circuit where it meets the high wall of the southeast citadel.

Figure 4.49 Ioannina: Interior view of the gate from the southeast citadel onto the wallwalk of the south curtain of the Kastro.

predecessor. Sections of the earlier structure must be embedded in Ali Pasha's rebuilding of the circuit. The wall turns north along the edge of the cliffs above the lake eventually meeting the circuit of the old northeast acropolis. From the Skala gate, or the modern opening a little to the east, it is possible to inspect the internal face of the south wall of the Kastro circuit from the streets within. The hollow wall contains a series of casemates with arched doors and windows. A gate opens from the interior of the citadel directly onto the wallwalk above the casemates. There is an eight-metre difference in ground level here. When Ali Pasha constructed the citadel the internal area of the acropolis was greatly increased by levelling and raising the uneven ground surface.[50] As a result half of the external height of the southwest wall of the citadel is a revetment to the raised ground level within.

The citadel of Ali Pasha (Its Kalé)

The citadel is separated from the remainder of the Kastro by thick walls to the north and west reinforced with three irregular polygonal bastions. These defences enclosed Ali's seraglio. They were built around 1815 and were the last works he completed. Like the main Kastro circuit the walls and bastions are hollow with vaulted chambers and corridors supporting a continuous wide gun platform. This method of construction is

Figure 4.50 Ioannina: Arcaded central section of the citadel wall.

visible in the central section of the walls where the gun platform is supported by an open two-storey arcade. Elsewhere an outer wall screens the internal vaults that formed storerooms, magazines and accommodation for the garrison. The main gate is at the northeast corner of the citadel with two further gates between the north and the central bastions. Each had the same style of arched façade with carved reliefs above. The gates and the exterior of the walls and bastions can be inspected from the streets of the Kastro that encircle the citadel. The north bastion flanks the main gate. In addition to the usual gun embrasures in the parapet, now largely destroyed, this bastion is equipped with irregular arched openings in its faces and flanks which must also have been designed for artillery. Early photographs show that the main gate stood within a large two-storeyed gatehouse, with a pitched roof, which extended eastward as far as the cliff edge. Most of this structure has been long demolished. Only foundations and the lower half of the outer wall with the gate's façade now survive.

Until the fires of 1870 the buildings of Ali Pasha's seraglio occupied much of the interior of the citadel. As well as altering the ground level

Figure 4.51 Ioannina: The large gunports in the northeast bastion commanding the approach to the main gate of Ali Pasha's citadel.

Figure 4.52 Ioannina: The elaborate façade of the main gate to the citadel. The empty niches held Ali Pasha's symbols.

Ali demolished most of the earlier structures of the southeast acropolis to build his new palace. Leake describes the seraglio in 1809 as follows. "The entire southern shore of the peninsula is thus occupied by the harem of the great palace of Aly Pasha ... A long narrow court separates the harem from the public apartments: these form the grand front of the palace which faces the north, and occupies, like the harem, the whole breadth of the promontory."[51] Ali had also built the fortifications and palaces at Litharitsia by this date, but had not yet built the citadel walls. By 1813 the palace on the promontory seems to have become known as the "old seraglio".[52] Leake does not mention that Ali incorporated into his palace a round tower now thought to be that built by

Bohemond in 1082. After the destruction of the palace buildings the tower was again visible and now stands isolated in the centre of the enclosure. Recent investigations have also revealed the base of the western wall of the first acropolis and the foundations of another circular tower close to the cliff edge. These features appear to define the extent of the earlier circuit. Much of the foundations of the elaborate complex of buildings that constituted Ali's seraglio have also been revealed.[53]

Of the remaining intact buildings within the citadel walls only the Fetihe mosque pre-dates Ali Pasha's works. It dates from 1597 and stands on the site of the church of the Archangel Michael built in the early 14C and designated as the metropolis of Ioannina in 1319.[54] The church may have contained the tomb of Thomas Preljubovič found by Ali Pasha's builders in 1795 close by the mosque.[55] The mosque was renovated by Ali Pasha who also built his own tomb nearby. The tomb was intact until 1940 but the ornate railings that now surround it are a modern restoration. Alongside the mosque is the former Royal Pavilion, built in 1958 on the site of the late 19C Turkish military hospital and now the Byzantine Museum. To the north of Bohemond's tower are

Figure 4.53 Ioannina: Bohemond's tower. This appears to have formed the northwest corner of the original southeast acropolis.

Epiros

Figure 4.54 Ioannina: The Fetihe mosque from the west. To the right is the Byzantine Museum. To the left the restored tomb of Ali Pasha. In the foreground can be seen the lower courses of "Bohemond's wall", the western wall of the first acropolis.

two large pitched roofed buildings with slate tiles, one free-standing, the other built against the citadel wall. Their original purpose is uncertain and they are now used by the Byzantine Museum. Near to the main gate another slate roofed single storey building with distinctive chimneys has been converted to serve as a café but was originally a kitchen.

The northeast citadel

The northeast citadel was the first acropolis of Byzantine Ioannina. Here stood the monastery of John the Baptist after whom traditionally the town was named.[56] The walls still retain some Byzantine elements notably the circular southern tower and the adjacent gate, now disused. After the revolt of 1611 and the expulsion of the Christian inhabitants

Figure 4.55 Ioannina: The disused gate of the northeast acropolis. The extensive use of thin bricks in the construction of the walls can be clearly seen.

from the Kastro, Aslan Pasha demolished the buildings within the citadel and built a mosque on the site of the monastery. Named after its builder it is surrounded by a Muslim cemetery. Among the tombs is an octagonal mausoleum, sometimes ascribed to Ali Pasha but probably the burial place of Aslan Pasha himself.[57] The largest building within the citadel is the long narrow madrasah consisting of series of rooms behind a continuous brick arched portico. This also dates from the 17C. The mosque now houses the Municipal Museum while the madrasah hosts the collections of the Museum of Fotis Rapakousis. Just outside the modern entrance to the acropolis stands the well-preserved library of the madrasah with a triple-domed roof and an open entrance portico. A little to the southwest of the library are the unrestored remains of an

Figure 4.56 Ioannina: The arched portico of the madrasah.

Ottoman public bath-house, while to the west is the substantial mass of Ali Pasha's cavalry school, a large, rectangular, two-storeyed building in a relatively good state of repair.

The sheer size of the walls of Ioannina remains an impressive statement of Ali Pasha's political power but seen as a work of fortification they appear idiosyncratic and ill designed. For nearly three hundred years prior to their construction the science of fortification had been refining the defensive response to gunpowder artillery. Thick low-set solid ramparts of earth with angle bastions providing flanking fire for every face of the work had become almost the universal standard for fortresses and city defences. Ali Pasha employed French engineers but, according to Davenport, their plans were often ignored.[58] As a result, despite the complexity and expense of their elaborate vaulted construction, the Kastro was surrounded by walls incapable of absorbing cannon shot, and with bastions that only provided partial flanking fire. In fact, as the Turkish attack of 1821 showed, the Kastro relied on the separate artillery position at Litharitsia to defend the southern approaches. Ultimately the Turks had to build a ring of outer works around the town to bring the defences up to date at the end of the 19C.

The Kastro is still part of the modern town and its monuments and walls are readily accessible, at least externally. Its Kalé is open during daylight hours. The museums within the Kastro are open during standard opening hours (8.00 – 15.00). The town is crowded with traffic but parking is possible by the lakeside.

Fort Bizani

At the end of the 19C the Turks re-fortified Ioannina by building a chain of detached forts and bunkers to the west and south of the town placed to take advantage of the high ground at the edge of the plain. Lake Pamvotida provided a natural barrier to the east. Bizani is the Greek name for Fort Bijan, the largest of these new works. Along with the fortifications on the hill of Kastritsa some five kilometres to the northeast, it controlled the main route from the south. The whole defensive system was known to the Turks as the Yanya Fortified Area. Despite enduring heavy bombardment in the First Balkan war the fortifications of Bizani are a remarkable survival from this period.

The Turks had been forced by the European powers to cede Thessaly and the Arta district of Epiros to Greece in 1881. The new border followed the course of the Arachthos valley north from Arta to within twenty-five kilometres of Ioannina. The first Greek attempt to take the remainder of Epiros occurred in 1897 when a revolt on Crete, at that date still in Turkish hands, led to a general mobilisation on the Greek mainland. The conflict, which became known as the Thirty Days War, was largely fought in Thessaly. However a small force under the command of Prince Constantine attempted to advance on Ioannina but was repulsed at Pente Pigadia.[59] The Greeks were heavily defeated but the peace agreement signed in December 1897, while imposing heavy reparations, made only minor changes to the frontiers. The Turkish re-fortification of Ioannina seems to have occurred shortly after the events of 1897.[60] In 1912 these fortifications were put to the test. The countries of the Balkan alliance declared war on the Ottoman Empire on the 18th October and hostilities began immediately. The Turks were forced to fight on three fronts. Bulgarian troops advanced south into Thrace, the

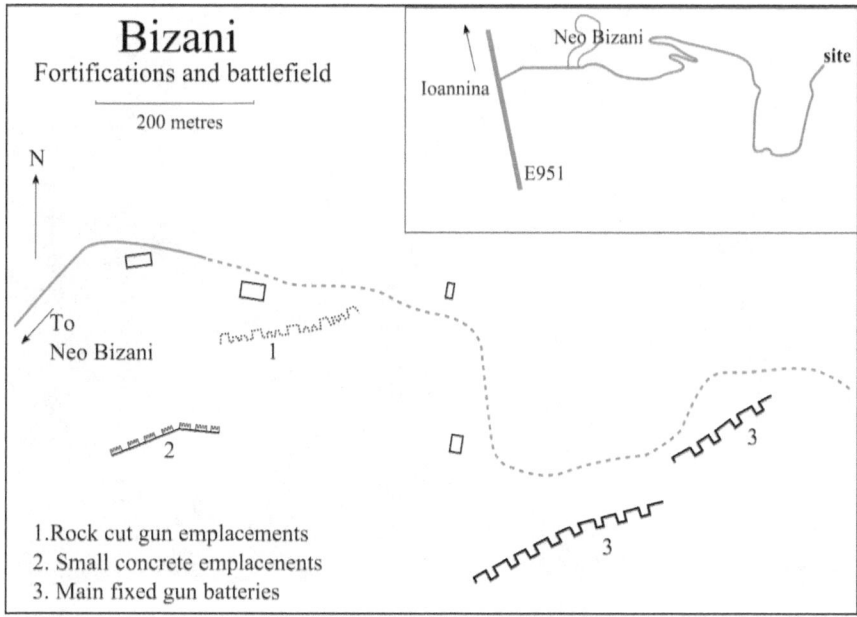

Serbs marched south and west into Macedonia while the main Greek force attacked Thessalonica from Thessaly. A smaller Greek force moved north from Arta towards Ioannina. By the 13th December the Turkish forces in Epiros had retreated inside the Yanya Fortified Area. The first Greek attack on the Bizani positions came the following day. Initial Greek success in capturing the high ground to the south of Bizani was reversed after eight days of fighting and they were forced to fall back some two kilometres.[61] A second attack at the end of January 1913 was inconclusive despite the arrival of reinforcements from Thessalonica. The final decisive battle began on the 4th March and is known as the Battle of Bizani, or the Third Battle of Yanya. Within two days Greek forces broke through the Turkish lines to the west and east of Bizani and Ioannina surrendered on the morning of the 6th March. Despite a heavy Greek bombardment the Bizani fort remained in Turkish hands until the formal surrender was signed.[62]

Bizani occupies the flat summit of a hill rising 300m above the plain. The position overlooks Ioannina ten kilometres to the north. The work was not a fort in the conventional sense but a dispersed system of permanent concrete gun emplacements with bunkers, searchlights and trenches surrounded by barbed wire entanglements.[63] Today the barbed wire has long corroded away and the trenches have disappeared into the landscape but the concrete emplacements for the Turkish gun batteries

Epiros

Figure 4.57 Fort Bizani: The eastern fixed battery.

Figure 4.58 Fort Bizani: The rear face of the western battery.

Epiros

Figure 4.59 Fort Bizani: Concrete emplacements on the hill summit.

survive along with the widely dispersed ruins of buildings in rubble masonry. These must have provided barracks and storerooms for the substantial garrison. Erickson gives the armament of the fort as thirty-two pieces of artillery and nineteen heavy machine guns. The main batteries face south and are concealed just behind the crest of the hill. The western battery consists of eight square emplacements constructed in concrete as a continuous indented line built into the slope of the hill. At a lower level the eastern battery is of the same concrete construction and has four gun positions. Both lines follow the undulating profile of the hill. Built into the concrete walls are arched openings presumably used as magazines. The twelve emplacements of these two batteries would have represented only a fraction of the fort's armament during the First Balkan War. The remainder was deployed in field fortifications as the Turks reinforced their original positions. At the highest point of the site another line of smaller emplacements, resembling a complex of slit trenches in concrete, may have been a machine gun position.

The site is easily reached from the main E951 south from Ioannina. Take the turning east to the village of Nea Bizani and continue beyond

Epiros

the village. The tarmac road climbs the hill and has now been extended to the edge of the fortified area. Close to the end of the road crude rock-cut emplacements can be seen excavated in the limestone. Dirt tracks wind between the ruined buildings to the prominent batteries on the southern edge of the area. The strategic importance of the position can be seen from the extensive views available.

Pente Pigadia

The old road from Arta to Ioannina ran on high ground to the east of the Louros gorge. Leake in 1809 described it as a carriage road, "paved in all the difficult places", and the only route passable all year from the coast to the plain of Ioannina.[64] A Turkish khan, or inn, stood at Pente Pigadia, the Five Wells, the highest point of the route at over 700m. In 1818 Ali Pasha built a small two-storeyed fort on the site. Pouqueville says simply that he fortified the khan and furnished it with cannon.[65] In the latter part of the 19C a new road was constructed along the banks of the Louros, still the route of the present E951. Although the old road fell into disuse the fort at Pente Pigadia remained of importance as a border post. After 1881 the border between Turkish Epiros and Greek

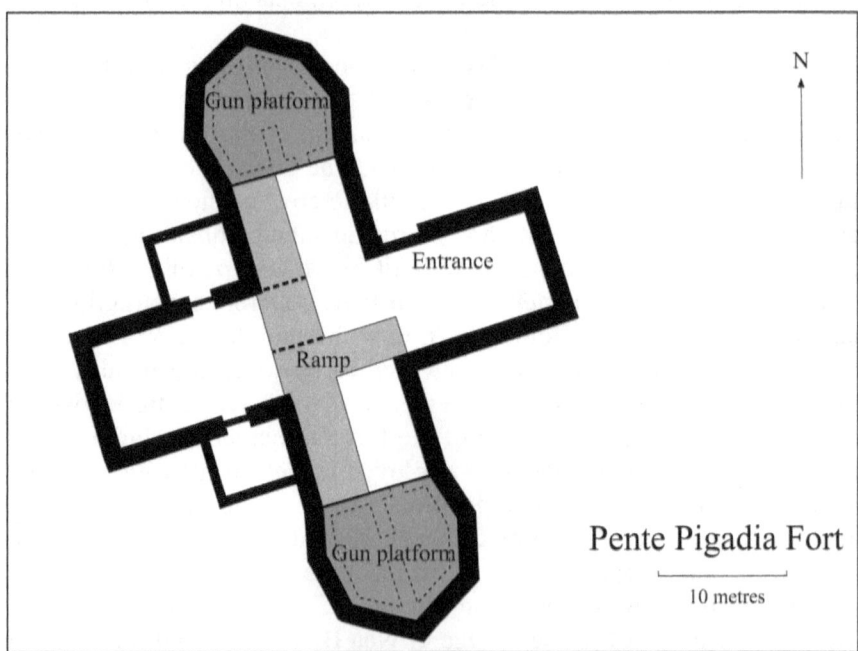

Epiros

Thessaly lay only ten kilometres to the east. During the Thirty Days War the Greeks advanced north from Arta towards Ioannina and were able to take Pente Pigadia without opposition. They were driven back almost immediately when Turkish reinforcements arrived. In 1912 the Greeks once again marched north and secured the Pente Pigadia area. This time the Turkish counter-attack was unsuccessful and they retreated behind their fortified lines around Ioannina. The battle is known to the Turks as the Battle of Beşpinar and to the Greeks as the Battle of Pente Pigadia.[66]

The fort still stands to its original two-storey height and although now roofless it is otherwise in relatively good condition. Despite being the scene of two battles, the fighting, which on both occasions was widely spread across the surrounding hills, seems to have left the fabric of the fort itself untouched. In plan the building resembles a Greek cross and is probably better described as a fortified barracks than a fort proper. Entry is via an arched door in the northeast angle of the cross. Externally this resembles the gates of the Kastro in Ioannina with a semicircular outer arch within a square façade surmounted by carved reliefs of Ali Pasha's symbols. The interior provided accommodation for the garrison on two floors. Only the joist holes remain to indicate

Figure.4.60 Pente Pigadia Fort: Overall view from the southeast.

Figure 4.61 Pente Pigadia Fort: View of the eastern arm of the fort showing the entrance with its flat inner arch, the joist holes of the upper floor and the tapered musketry slits.

the level of the wooden floors. The ends of the southern and northern arms of the fort are reinforced with multangular towers equipped with roof level gun platforms supported on heavy stone vaults. Only fragments of their parapets survive. A substantial T-shaped ramp that occupies much of the central section of the fort provided access to these platforms. The fort must have been roofed but how this was arranged to incorporate the gun ramps is not clear. At ground floor level the walls are pierced by regularly spaced tapered musketry slits. The upper floor has both narrow defence slits and a variety of larger openings that may have been simply windows. The fort is constructed of uniform roughly

Epiros

Figure 4.62 Pente Pigadia Fort: View of the internal ramps and the southern gun platform from the northern arm of the fort.

squared blocks with finer dressed stone used for the angles and around the wall openings. A continuous stringcourse runs completely around the building at the level of the first floor. Only traces of a second stringcourse at roof level survive. The entire fort seems to be the product of a single building phase. From the roof the remains of an earlier Turkish fort can be seen a little to the north, but only fragments of walls survive amidst a large area strewn with rubble. Although the earlier work is thought to date from 1760 it is not mentioned by Leake or other contemporary writers.[67]

A well-surfaced modern road now follows the course of the old route to Ioannina and passes within fifty metres of the fort. To reach the site from Ioannina follow the E951 south for seven kilometres beyond Bizani. Take the turning east then south towards Mirodafni. Pente Pigadia is approximately seventeen kilometres south of the junction. From Arta take the main road northwest to Filipiada then turn east through the village of Kampi. Beyond Kampi the road passes the 4C BC site of Orraon after seven kilometres. Pente Pigadia is a further seventeen kilometres to the north.

Notes

1. W. M. Leake, *Travels in Northern Greece, Vol. IV*, p. 48.
2. There is an intriguing reference to the topography of the hill in the United States Mediterranean Pilot of 1917. It states, "the castle has apparently been destroyed by an earthquake splitting the entire hill apart, leaving a deep perpendicular chasm dividing the fortress longitudinally." See United States Hydrographic Office, *Mediterranean Pilot, Vol. 3*, p. 429.
3. D. M. Nicol, *The Despotate of Epiros*, p. 228.
4. W. M. Leake, *Travels in Northern Greece, Vol. I*, p. 502.
5. G. Finlay, *The History of the Greek Revolution, Vol. I*, pp. 49-64.
6. Leake, *Travels in Northern Greece, Vol. I*, pp. 229-230.
7. Henry Holland, *Travels in the Ionian Islands, Albania, etc.*, p. 448.
8. Edward Lear, *Journals of a landscape Painter in Albania etc.*, p. 363.
9. A good idea of the appearance of the serai can be gained from the drawing made by Henry Holland in 1813. This shows the upper storey of the serai projecting boldly above the line of the ramparts. Holland, *Travels in the Ionian Islands etc.*, p. 451.
10. K. E. Fleming, *The Muslim Bonaparte*, p. 45.
11. Nicol, *The Despotate of Epiros*, p. 90.
12. The full text of this agreement and its ratification by the British is reprinted in C. P. De Bossett, *Parga and the Ionian Islands*, pp. 224-229.
13. The Treaty of Paris was in fact a series of treaties signed in November 1815. The United States of the Ionian Islands was defined by a document entitled; the Treaty between Great Britain and Russia respecting the Ionian Islands, signed on the 5th November 1815. Hansard, *The Parliamentary Debates from the Year 1803 to the Present Time, Volume 32*, p. 294.
14. De Bosset, *Parga and the Ionian Islands*, p. 74. The cessation of Parga to Ali Pasha was widely condemned across Europe at the time. The circumstances surrounding Maitland's negotiations were the subject of a famous legal case between De Bossett and Maitland heard in London in 1820.
15. De Bosset, *Parga and the Ionian Islands*, p. 45.
16. W. M. Leake, *Travels in Northern Greece, Vol. III*, p. 3.
17. The Italians had occupied Albania early in 1939 and from there they launched their initial invasion of Epiros in October 1940 after Metaxas' rejection of Mussolini's ultimatum. The attack was

quickly repulsed by the Greek army which pushed the Italians back north into Albania and actually briefly increased the territory under Greek control. The Germans attacked from Yugoslavia and Bulgaria on 6th April 1941 and by the end of the same month had overrun the entire country. By June of the same year a tri-partite occupation of the country had been established with Bulgarian control in western Thrace and Macedonia, a German occupation in Athens and Thessalonica and the Italians in possession of the bulk of the country including Epiros, Thessaly and the Peloponnese. See R. Clogg, *Concise History of Greece*, pp. 118-122.
18. N. Botzaris, *The Battle of Lepanto*, p. 75; Leake W. M., *Travels in Northern Greece, Vol. I*, p. 523.
19. De Bosset, *Parga and the Ionian Islands*, pp. 63-67.
20. ESCUTIS, *Muslim Presence in Epirus and Western Greece*, p. 418.
21. Mika Hakkarainen, *Venetian Presence in Thesprotia*, p. 227.
22. Hakkarainen describes Thesprotia divided into Venetian outposts on the coast and Ottoman territory inland with an undefined and disputed border area between. In particular there was no agreed demarcation line between Parga and Margariti. *Venetian Presence in Thesprotia*, pp. 223 and 226.
23. Niccolo Capponi, *The Victory of the West*, p. 304.
24. Treaty of London and the Treaty of Bucharest.
25. Miranda Vickers, *The Cham Issue: Albanian National and Property Claims in Greece*, pp. 2-3.
26. Balta, Yilmaz and Yasar, *Tsamouria – Nineteenth Century Ottoman Thesprotia*, p. 257.
27. The substantial remains of Gitana, or Gitani, are to be found on the north bank of the Kalamas one kilometre upstream from the modern barrage. Systematic excavation began in 1985 and has revealed the city's grid layout of buildings within a circuit of polygonal walls reinforced by square towers and divided into two sections by a strong crosswall. A theatre has been discovered outside the walls. The city was the political capital of the Thesprotian League and prospered until 167 BC when it was abandoned at the onset of the Roman occupation. See M. H. Hansen and T. H. Nielsen, *An Inventory of Archaic and Classical Poleis*, p. 345.
28. Hakkarainen, *Venetian Presence in Thesprotia*, p. 225.
29. Capponi, *The Victory in the West*, p. 244.
30. London Gazette, Issue 2097, December 1685.
31. The fragmentary ruins of the walls of Toroni occupy the Lygia peninsula five kilometres west of Igoumenitsa. The site was part of the

mainland territory of Kerkyra (Corfu) and was first settled in the Archaic period. The peninsula was fortified in three stages in the 5C BC. Only traces of the walls survive. See Hansen and Nielsen, *An Inventory of Archaic and Classical Poleis*, p. 349.
32. Named after Donatos the 4C bishop of Euroia. The location of Euroia remains the subject of debate.
33. Agios Donatos is one of several fortified sites in the Kokytos valley that date from the 4C BC. All occupy similar locations on spurs partially protected by natural cliffs on the eastern side of the valley. The most important lies some four kilometres to the south of Paramythia above the village of Chrysavgi. This is the ancient city of Elea, for a time the political capital of the Thesprotian League before this passed to Gitani. The site has been investigated and the grid layout of the city revealed. Substantial sections of polygonal walling up to seven metres in height survive. The site was gradually abandoned after 167 BC. A further five kilometres to the south above the village of Zervochori is a smaller fortress, confusingly also called Agios Donatos after the 17C church within its walls. See Mikko Suha, *The Walls of Agios Donatos Zervochoriou*.
34. Procopius, *De Aedificiis* 4.1.37-38 and 4.4. However writers from Leake onwards (*Travels in Northern Greece IV*, p. 65) have argued against treating Procopius as an accurate description of the extent of the works initiated by Justinian. See W. Bowden, *Thesprotia in the Context of Roman and Late Antique Epirus*, pp. 176-178.
35. The revolt was led by Dionysios, the Greek Metropolitan of Larissa, who was born in Paramythia. Although he was able to raise a small army and attacked Ioannina his uprising failed and ended in his own gruesome death. See Hakkarainen, *Venetian Presence in Thesprotia*, pp. 231-2.
36. Leake, *Travels in Northern Greece, Vol. IV*, p. 200.
37. These are respectively the northeast and southeast citadels. See Anna Comnena, *The Alexiad*, V.4.
38. B. Osswald, *Ethnic Composition of Medieval Ioannina*, p. 132.
39. Nicol, *The Despotate of Epiros*, pp. 84-86.
40. Nicol, *The Despotate of Epiros*, p. 203.
41. B. Osswald, *Monuments of the Medieval Castle of Ioannina*, p. 190.
42. Ali Pasha was born in Tepelini in Albania. Although his initial rise to prominence was as a brigand leader, he made various attempts to acquire a Turkish title and in 1783 succeeded in being appointed to the minor position of Pasha of Trikala. In 1786 he made himself

Pasha of Ioannina by a forged firman, or decree, backed by the threat of his troops camped outside the walls. His coup was eventually ratified by Sultan Abdul Hamid in 1788. See R. A. Davenport, *The Life of Ali Pasha of Tepelini*, pp. 48-56.
43. Davenport, *The Life of Ali Pasha of Tepelini*, p. 405.
44. Litharitsia was a substantial casemated bastion, or battery, of three of four storeys built against the slope of a rocky outcrop approximately 500m to the south of the Kastro. Its upper storey supported a second palace, or serai, built by Ali for himself in 1807. It also defended two further palaces nearby, built for his sons, Mokhtar and Veli. The whole complex formed virtually a third acropolis after the two within the Kastro. The bastion was shelled by the Turks in October 1820 destroying the palaces but its military function was unimpaired and it continued as an advance position until October 1821. The area occupied by the palaces is now a park. A conference and banqueting complex has been built on top of the surviving lower storeys of the bastion. See Davenport, *The Life of Ali Pasha of Tepelini*, p. 64 and Osswald, *The Monuments of the Medieval Castle of Ioannina*, p. 192.
45. B. Osswald, *The Monuments of the Medieval Castle of Ioannina*, p. 192.
46. E. J. Erickson, *Defeat in Detail. The Ottoman Army in the Balkans, 1912-1913*, p. 227.
47. Erickson, *Defeat in Detail*, pp. 303-4.
48. D. Konstantios, *The Kastro of Ioannina*, p. 18.
49. Nicol, *The Despotate of Epiros*, p. 154.
50. Konstantios, *The Kastro of Ioannina*, p. 31.
51. Leake, *Travels in Northern Greece, Vol. IV*, p. 137.
52. T. S. Hughes, *Travels in Sicily Greece and Albania, Vol. I*, p. 452.
53. Konstantios, *The Kastro of Ioannina*, p. 37.
54. Nicol, *The Despotate of Epiros*, p. 88, and Osswald, *The Monuments of the Medieval Castle of Ioannina*, p. 190.
55. The site of the tomb is now lost. See Nicol, *The Despotate of Epiros*, p. 154.
56. B. Osswald, *The Monuments of the Medieval Castle of Ioannina*, p. 188.
57. Konstantios, *The Kastro of Ioannina*, p. 27.
58. Davenport, *The Life of Ali Pasha of Tepelini*, p. 285.
59. H. W. Nevinson, *Scenes in the Thirty Days War Between Greece and Turkey*, pp.141-3.
60. Nevinson writing of the events of April 1897 calls Ioannina an

"unfortified town" at that date. Nevinson, *Scenes in the Thirty Days War*, p. 159.
61. This first attack is known as the First Battle of Yanya, Erickson, *Defeat in Detail*, pp. 293-8.
62. Erickson, *Defeat in Detail*, pp. 300-304.
63. R. C. Hall, *The Balkan Wars, 1912-1913*, p. 63.
64. Leake, *Travels in Northern Greece, Vol. IV*, p. 257.
65. F. C. H. L. Pouqueville, *Travels in southern Epirus, etc.*, p. 33.
66. Erickson, *Defeat in Detail*, pp. 232-234.
67. ESCUTIS, *Muslim Presence in Epirus and Western Greece*, p. 422.

Summary

Whilst the locations of the later military forts of northwest Greece were clearly dictated by the strategic needs of the time, many of the mediaeval castles of the area at first appear to have been placed in what are now remote isolated sites. However each was built in a position that had an obvious rationale in the context of the agricultural economy of the period. Many are re-built on ancient sites and for the same reasons. "Yet the citadel could not be too far removed from the farmlands it was meant to control. The ideal site was the tip of a spur, which ran out from the flank of a mountain and was linked to the main mass only by a narrow ridge".[1] Although Winter's description refers to early Iron Age sites it applies equally to the castles of the Despotate. The castles of Angelokastro, Dragomestre, Aetos, Barnakas, Nafpaktos, Thomokastro and Agios Donatos are all situated in locations that conform to this description. The small agricultural plains that each castle controlled are still farmed, often much more intensively with the use of modern irrigation. However the visual appearance of the castles themselves has changed dramatically in recent decades. With the exception of Rogoi, which Pouqueville described as already heavily overgrown in 1818, most of the mediaeval circuits have only recently been engulfed by trees and maquis vegetation.[2] Early photographs typically show the castle interiors and the surrounding hillsides virtually bare. The reforestation that has occurred is almost completely a 20C phenomenon.

The standard chronology of fortification in Western Europe describes a process of change from the high walls and towers of the pre-gunpowder age to the development of the angle bastion and eventually the independent polygonal fort. Before the deployment of gunpowder artillery, mediaeval castles and city defences gained their strength from high walls that prevented scaling and projecting towers providing flanking fire along the outer face of the wall. These features were successful because the siege engines of the period, although capable of throwing

Summary

relatively large projectiles, were not accurate enough to hit the same area of wall repeatedly. When the first gunpowder weapons were introduced these too had limited range and velocity, and initially fortifications were modified simply by adding gunports to existing structures. However as both manufacturing techniques and gunpowder improved, walls had to be thickened and were often heavily battered in an effort to deflect projectiles. Parapets also acquired curved surfaces for the same reason. To provide defenders with an offensive capability gun towers capable of mounting heavy cannon on their roof platforms were developed. By the early sixteenth century such towers had become projecting bastions built to the same height as the adjacent curtain walls thus forming one continuous gun platform. Round bastions gradually gave way to the angled arrowhead form. Walls became lower and thicker and were built predominately of earth with masonry facings. A ditch and outworks usually surrounded the circuit. The bastioned trace was to be the standard form of fortification for the next three hundred years becoming increasingly elaborate. Only with the advent of rifled artillery in the 19C was it finally superseded by detached polygonal forts built as a series of independent strongpoints around the area to be defended.

The fortifications of northwest Greece follow the above outline only until the beginning of the 16C. The early Byzantine circuits and their successors erected by the Despots of Epiros all conformed to the same pattern of high walls reinforced by round, square or beaked towers. The first adaptations for artillery were probably made by the Venetians who appeared in the northwest at the beginning of the 15C, acquiring Parga in 1401 and Nafpaktos in 1407. Their work at Nafpaktos, completed by 1470, pre-dates the development of the angle bastion and the town walls are reinforced with boldly projecting round towers that provided a solid platform with embrasures for cannon. The earliest works built specifically for artillery were constructed by the Turks at the Rio narrows on the Gulf of Corinth shortly after they seized Nafpaktos in 1499. The sea battery of the Castle of the Morea was housed in a heavily vaulted trefoil structure with flared gunports at ground level and another battery on the roof housed behind a massive parapet with curved, shot deflecting surfaces. When it was built it represented the leading edge of artillery fortification. Yet from this date Turkish military architecture changed little. A number of new polygonal gun platforms were added to the defences of Nafpaktos, but otherwise Turkish fortifications remained essentially unchanged throughout the sixteenth and seventeenth centuries. The Turks never adopted the bastioned system, the *trace italienne,* and when the Venetians re-conquered the area almost two centuries later,

Summary

they found themselves in possession of the same fortifications built after their defeat in the second Turco-Venetian war.

After 1700 the Venetians attempted to bring the fortresses of Greece up to date. Elsewhere in the Greek world, particularly on Corfu and Crete, they had developed elaborate fortifications over a long period with the expertise of centuries of Italian military engineering. On the mainland the restrictions of limited time and resources forced them to adapt the existing Turkish forts. In the northwest their major works were at Santa Maura and most notably at the Castle of the Morea. At the latter they added large angle bastions to the original Turkish land front with further protection provided by ravelins and a wide wet ditch. Their work here represents the most fully developed bastioned fort to be seen on the Greek mainland, although the limitations of the site precluded the construction of a symmetrical work. At Santa Maura the Venetians were forced to be more pragmatic. Here they thickened the original Turkish walls and added flanking outworks. Again they completely rebuilt the land front. The restrictions of the site seem to have allowed only small square bastions to be added to this front but it was reinforced by an elaborate system of outworks beyond the moat.

The Venetians maintained their remaining fortresses on the coast throughout the 18C, but the next great period of fortress building in the area began under Ali Pasha's regime after the fall of the Republic in 1799. Ali was a prolific fort builder but his works defy categorization in terms of the historical progression outlined above. They were built in a variety of idiosyncratic styles and seem to have been erected primarily to impress and intimidate the local population. His use of round and polygonal bastions gives some of his forts, particularly the Castle of Grivas and Fort St. George at Plagia, the superficial appearance of mediaeval castles. Where angle bastions were employed they are often small with very short flanks that do not fully enfilade the adjacent curtain. This is true of the Castle of St. Andrew in Preveza and the fort at Aktio. While the Venetians constructed solid terreplained ramparts Ali frequently built his apparently thick walls using a system of vaulting or arcading behind a relatively thin outer skin. Ioannina is a prime example where the walls of both the Kastro and the citadel within are hollow for almost their entire length. This method seems to have been adopted to provide a superficially imposing structure with the minimum use of materials. Finally there are a number of forts that appear to be experiments in form. The original sea-fort of Pantokratoras at Preveza has a pentagonal ground plan while the fort of Pente Pigadia is built in the form of a Greek cross. At Anthousa the core of the castle is simply a

Summary

large square gun platform. Ali frequently employed European military engineers and it is possible that they used these opportunities to build what would otherwise have remained theoretical designs.

The events of the Greek Revolution created only temporary field fortifications of which little survives. The walls of Mesolonghi for example are a symbolic re-creation of the defences of the famous siege rather than genuine survivals of the period. After 1832 the Turks fortified their new borders with simple gun towers and batteries on the northern shore of the Gulf of Ambracia. Their most substantial work was the rebuilding of the fort guarding the approaches to Preveza at Pantokratoras. This included a new sea-battery built with a low profile but in an anachronistic style. However with the final re-fortification of Ioannina at the end of the 19C under German military advice, the Turks succeeded in creating a completely modern line of defences that anticipated the field fortifications of the First World War. With the exception of a few concrete machine gun emplacements from the Second World War this was the last work of fortification in northwest Greece.

Notes

1. F. E. Winter, *Greek fortifications*, p. 6.
2. F. C. H. L. Pouqueville, *Travels in southern Epirus, etc.*, p. 32.

Chronology

Early history of the Region

14C BC	Mycenaean colonies established on northwest coast.
7C	Establishment of Elean and Corinthian colonies.
5C	Corfiot colony established at Toroni, Messenian colony at Nafpaktos.
431-404	Peloponnesian War.
426	Battle of Olpae.
4C	Creation of Aetolian and Akarnanian Leagues.
342-330	First unification of Epiros under the Molossian king Alexander I.
338	Nafpaktos occupied by Philip II after his victory over Athens and Thebes at the Battle of Chaironia.
297-272	Reign of Pyrrhus, first as king of the Molossians, then as king of Epiros.
272-240	Reign of Alexander II as king of the Molossians.
167	Romans sack seventy Molossian cities.
146	Corinth razed by Roman General Mummius.
44	Julius Caesar assassinated.
31 BC	Octavian defeats Anthony at Battle of Actium. Founding of Nikopolis.
293 AD	Emperor Diocletian creates provinces of Epirus Vetus and Epirus Nova.
324	Foundation of Constantinople.
380	Christianity becomes official religion of the Roman Empire.
395	Separation of Eastern and Western Empires.
410	Alaric, king of the Visigoths, sacks Rome.
474	Vandals sack Nikopolis.
474-491	Reign of Zeno as Byzantine Emperor. Probable date of

Chronology

	the Byzantine walls of Nikopolis.
491-518	Anastasius Byzantine Emperor.
527-565	Reign of Justinian.
867-886	Basil I Eastern Emperor.

The Normans in Sicily and their attacks on the Byzantine Empire

1035	William Iron-Arm and Drogo, eldest sons of Tancred of Hauteville, join in the revolt of the Lombards in Apulia against Byzantine control.
1040	By this date the Byzantines have lost most of Apulia to the Normans.
1042	Melfi chosen as Norman capital. William Iron-Arm elected count.
1046	Drogo succeeds his brother William.
1047	Holy Roman Emperor Henry III confirms Drogo as count of Apulia and Calabria.
1051	Humphrey, younger brother of Drogo, succeeds him.
1057	Robert Guiscard succeeds Humphrey.
1061	Robert Guiscard and brother, Roger, capture Messina (Sicily).
1071	Byzantines lose Bari, last possession in southern Italy, to Normans.
1071	Michael VII Doukas becomes Byzantine Emperor.
1072	Palermo falls to Robert Guiscard and his brother, Roger, who becomes count of Sicily (Roger I).
1078	Michael VII deposed. His son, Constantine, was engaged to Guiscard's daughter. When Constantine's right of succession was denied the engagement was broken.
1081	Guiscard attacks Byzantine Empire using Michael VII's deposition as justification. Defeats Alexius (Byzantine Emperor 1081-1118) at Battle of Dyrrhachium. Plunders Vonitsa.
1082	Guiscard occupies Corfu and Durazzo (Dyrrhachium).
1082	Bohemond defeats Greeks at Ioannina and besieges Arta. Restores and extends fortifications of Ioannina.
1082	Guiscard returns to Italy to aid Pope Gregory VII against Henry IV, king of Germany.
1083	Bohemond defeated by Alexius at Larissa.
1084	Guiscard sacks Rome. Byzantines recover territory in Epiros lost to Normans.

Chronology

1085	Guiscard occupies Corfu and Cephalonia. Dies 17th July 1085. Normans abandon attacks on Byzantines.
1091	Norman conquest of Sicily complete.
1099	Fall of Jerusalem to the First Crusade.
1101	Roger I dies.
1130	Roger II crowned king of the Kingdom of the Two Sicilies having acquired control of Calabria and Apulia.
1147-49	Normans again attack Byzantine Empire with no lasting results.
1154	Roger II succeeded by William I.
1166	Accession of William II as king of Sicily.
1185	William II attacks Byzantine Empire. Sacks Ioannina, captures Dyrrhachium and Thessalonica. Defeated en route to Constantinople.
1185	Cephalonia and Zante (Zakynthos) given to Margaritone of Brindisi, Grand Admiral of Sicily, as a reward for his services to William II.
1189	William II makes peace with Isaac II Angelus and abandons Byzantine conquests. Dies at Palermo having nominated Constance, daughter of Roger II, as his successor.
1190	Tancred, a grandson of Roger II, accedes to throne. Constance's husband, Henry, becomes Holy Roman Emperor (Henry VI) on the death of his father.
1191	Henry and Constance lead an army south into Italy to take the crown from Tancred. Expedition fails.
1194	Death of Tancred. Henry and Constance take crown of Sicily.
1194	Maio Orsini acquires Cephalonia and Zante by his marriage to the daughter of Margaritone of Brindisi.
1197	Death of Henry VI. Constance becomes regent for her son Frederick.
1198	Death of Constance. Frederick crowned king of Sicily.

The Despotate of Epiros

1204	Fall of Constantinople to the Fourth Crusade. Byzantine Empire divided between the Franks and the Venetians. Epiros allotted to Venice. Baldwin I becomes first Latin Emperor. Empires of Nicaea and Trebizond survive as fragments of the Byzantine Empire.

Chronology

1205	Michael I seizes Epiros.
1206	Venetians acquire Methoni and Koroni.
1209	Venetians develop Euboea as a colony.
1210	Michael gains agreement of Venetians to rule Epiros as their vassal.
1212	Venetians gain control of Crete.
1214	Michael breaks agreement with Venice, occupies Thessaly and attacks and captures Durazzo and Corfu.
1215	Michael dies and is succeeded by his half-brother, Theodore.
1220	Frederick becomes Holy Roman Emperor, Frederick II.
1224	Theodore seizes Thessalonica.
1225	Frederick marries Yolande of Jerusalem, heiress to the Kingdom of Jerusalem.
1227	Theodore crowned king of the Romans creating a second claimant to the throne of Byzantium.
1228	Frederick embarks on Sixth Crusade, recovers Jerusalem from the Ayyubids by treaty.
1229	Frederick crowned king of Jerusalem.
1230	Theodore defeated by Bulgarian Czar, John Asen. Michael II, the exiled son of Michael I, returns to Arta to claim Epiros.
1246	Thessalonica becomes part of Byzantine Empire of Nicaea.
1253	Michael II and his son, Nikephoros, are granted the title of Despot by John Vatatzes, Byzantine Emperor. Nikephoros is betrothed to Maria, the Emperor's daughter.
1257	Manfred of Sicily, son of Frederick II by his second wife, invades Epiros seizes Durazo, Valona, the coast of New Epiros and Corfu.
1258	Michael II gives his daughter, Helena, in marriage to Manfred. Her dowry is the area already in Manfred's hands. Gives his second daughter, Anna, to William of Villehardouin, Prince of Achaia.
1258	Kingship of Sicily seized by Manfred.
1258	Michael II and his allies, Manfred and William Villehardouin, attack Empire of Nicaea.
1259	Battle of Pelagonia. Emperor Michael VIII Palaiologos defeats Michael and his allies; invades Thessaly and Epiros and occupies major towns including Arta, Vonitsa and Ioannina. Michael II flees to Cephalonia.

Chronology

1261	Latins expelled from Constantinople. Byzantine Empire restored. Michael II returns from Cephalonia to Vonitsa and regains Arta and Ioannina.
1264	Michael II signs treaty with Byzantine Emperor, Michael Palaiologos. The Emperor's niece, Anna, is betrothed to Michael's son, Nikephoros.
1266	Manfred defeated and killed in battle by Charles of Anjou who had attacked the Kingdom of Sicily at the behest of Pope Urban IV. Charles becomes king of Sicily and Naples.
1267	Nikephoros becomes sole Despot on the death of Michael II.
1267	Charles acquires title to Manfred's territories in Epiros by Treaty of Viterbo.
1279	Nikephoros allies himself with Charles and becomes his vassal.
1280	Charles sends expedition against Byzantine Empire.
1281	Latin army defeated at Berat.
1282	Sicilian rebellion (the Sicilian Vespers) destroys Charles's fleet and expels him from Sicily.
1282	Byzantine Emperor Michael VIII dies.
1285	Death of Charles of Anjou.
1289	Charles II of Anjou assumes kingship of Naples.
1292	Byzantine Emperor, Andronikos II, attacks Ioannina and Arta. Nikephoros pays Florent of Hainault, prince of Achaia, and Richard Orsini of Cephalonia to help him defeat the Byzantine armies who sack Vonitsa during their retreat. Orsini arranges marriage of Nikephoros's daughter, Maria, held on Cephalonia as a hostage against the promised payment, to his son John.
1294	Thamar, second daughter of Nikephoros, marries Philip of Taranto, son of Charles II. Thamar's dowry includes the castles of Vonitsa, Nafpaktos and Angelokastro.
1295	John Orsini and Maria take up residence in Arta. Nikephoros grants Lefkas to John.
1296	Death of Nikephoros. His wife, Anna, becomes regent for her young son, Thomas.
1304	Anna refuses to accept Philip of Taranto as suzerain. Charles II organises expedition against Anna using the Angevin strongholds of Vonitsa and Nafpaktos as bases. Arta and Rogoi successfully resist attacks. Tho-

mas recovers Vonitsa and Nafpaktos for the Despotate.

1306	Philip of Taranto invades Epiros with little success but recovers Vonitsa and Nafpaktos.
1307	Thomas makes peace with the Byzantine Emperor and marries Anna Palaiologina, daughter of Michael IX.
1309	Philip divorces Thamar. Charles II dies and is succeeded by his son, Robert of Anjou.
1313	Philip marries Catherine of Valois.
1314	Vonitsa captured by Byzantine commander, Syrgiannes.
1315	Syrgiannes attacks Arta. Thomas declares peace with Byzantine Empire is at an end. Imprisons his own wife.
1317	Nicholas Orsini succeeds his father, John, as count of Cephalonia.
1318	Thomas murdered by his nephew, Nicholas Orsini, who then marries Thomas's widow, Anna. Nicholas holds Arta but Ioannina declares allegiance to Constantinople. Nicholas makes peace with the Emperor who grants him the title of Despot.
1320	Nicholas's wife, Anna, dies. He attacks Ioannina unsuccessfully.
1323	Nicholas killed by his younger brother, John, who regains Ioannina by negotiation and reunites Despotate.
1325	John of Gravina, brother of Philip of Taranto, confiscates Cephalonia and Zante from Guido Orsini.
1328	Emperor Andronikos III grants John title of Despot.
1331	Walter of Brienne, son-in-law of Philip of Taranto, occupies Lefkas, recovers Vonitsa and forces John Orsini to accept suzerainty of kingdom of Naples.
1331	Philip of Taranto dies at the end of the year. His widow, Catherine of Valois, becomes regent for her son, Robert.
1337	John Orsini poisoned by his wife, Anna. She holds power briefly with her young son, Nikephoros.
1338	Emperor Andronikos III takes control of Despotate. Anna is exiled to Thessalonica. Emperor arranges the betrothal of Nikephoros to Maria, daughter of his Grand Domestic, John Cantacuzene. Opponents to direct control of the Despotate from Constantinople carry off Nikephoros to the court of Catherine of Valois in the Peloponnese.

Chronology

1339	Supporters of Nikephoros seize Arta, Rogoi and Thomokastro. Nikephoros sails from Glarentsa to Thomokastro. Emperor besieges the three castles.
1340	John Cantacuzene recovers all three centres of resistance by skilful negotiation and restores order to the Despotate. Nikephoros joins his mother in Thessalonica.
1341	Andronikos III dies. Civil war between rival candidates for Emperor breaks out. John Cantacuzene is proclaimed emperor in Thrace. John, son of Andronikos, is proclaimed emperor in Constantinople. Nikephoros's mother, Anna, escapes from Thessalonica and returns to Arta.
1342	Nikephoros marries Maria, daughter of Cantacuzene. John Angelos, a cousin of Cantacuzene, captures Anna and reasserts Byzantine control over the Despotate.
1343	Walter of Brienne grants Lefkas and Santa Maura castle to a Venetian, Graziano Giorgio.
1343-1348	Serbian ruler, Stephen Dušan, invades first Albania then all of Epiros and Thessaly except for Vonitsa and Santa Maura.
1347	End of Byzantine civil war. Canatacuzene crowned Emperor John VI in Constantinople.
1348	Stephen Dušan assigns Epiros to his half-brother, Symeon Uroš, who marries Thomais, sister of Nikephoros. Thessaly is assigned to Gregory Preljub.
1354	John Cantacuzene abdicates.
1355	Death of Stephen Dušan and Gregory Preljub. Symeon Uroš leaves Epiros to pursue claims in Serbia.
1356	Nikephoros invades Thessaly. Eirene, widow of Gregory Preljub, flees to Serbia with her son, Thomas Preljubovič. Nikephoros recovers Epiros.
1357	Robert of Taranto invests Leonardo Tocco as count of Cephalonia and Zante.
1359	Nikephoros dies attempting to put down an Albanian rebellion. Symeon Uroš returns and seizes Thessaly and then Epiros. Thomas Preljubovič is betrothed to Symeon's daughter, Maria.
1362	Leonardo Tocco seizes Lefkas and Vonitsa.
1362	Symeon accommodates Albanian incursions into southern Epiros by making Gjin Boua Spata despot of

Chronology

	Acheloos and Peter Losha despot of Arta and Rogoi.
1367	Symeon assigns Ioannina to Thomas Preljubovič.
1367 – 1370	Peter Losha makes annual attacks on Ioannina.
1374	Gjin Boua Spata unites the two Albanian Despotates on the death of Peter Losha.
1375	Death of Leonardo Tocco. Maddalena Buondelmonti, his widow, invites the Knights of St. John to take over the defence of Vonitsa, as her sons, Carlo and Leonardo, are still infants.
1379	Gjin Boua Spata occupies Nafpaktos.
1384	Thomas Preljubovič assassinated.
1385	Thomas's widow, Maria, marries Esau Buondelmonti, brother of Maddalena. The Byzantine Emperor, John V, grants him the title of Despot.
1386	Venetians acquire Corfu.
1388	Venetians acquire Nauplion and Argos.
1388	Carlo Tocco marries Francesca Acciajuoli.
1389	Decisive defeat of Serbia by the Turks at the Battle of Kossova. Gjin Boua Spata attacks Ioannina. Esau Buondelmonti repulses the Albanian attack with Turkish help.
1394	Esau's wife Maria dies.
1396	Esau marries Eirene, daughter of Gjin Spata.
1399	Carlo Tocco raises an army and attacks the Albanians in Akarnania. Gjin Spata is killed. His grandson, Muriki Spata, gains control of Arta while his brother, Sgouros, holds Angelokastro.
1401	Parga becomes a Venetian protectorate.
1401-1405	Carlo Tocco gains control of most of Akarnania.
1402	Carlo takes control of Barnakas. Esau Buondelmonti divorces Eirene.
1407	Venetians buy Nafpaktos. Carlo occupies Angelokastro.
1411	Death of Esau Buondelmonti. His nephew, Carlo Tocco, is invited to take control of the Despotate of Ioannina.
1413	Venetians acquire Sagiada
1414	Death of Muriki Spata. His mother Eirene, widow of Esau Buondelmonti, arranges for the division of Muriki's Despotate between his brother, Yaqub, and her son, Carlo Marchesano, by her previous marriage. Yaqub becomes lord of Arta, Carlo lord of Rogoi.

Chronology

1415	Venetians gain Navarino
1415	Byzantine Emperor, Manuel II, grants Carlo Tocco the title of Despot.
1416	Carlo Tocco seizes Arta. His brother, Leonardo, takes Rogoi. Despotate of Epiros is reunited.
1429	Death of Carlo Tocco. Despotate is again divided. Lefkas and Vonitsa are left to Carlo's widow, Francesca. Leonardo's son, Carlo II, inherits Ioannina and Arta as well as the three islands of Cephalonia, Zante and Ithaca. Carlo's illegitimate sons are granted the territory to the south of Arta.
1430	Sultan Murad II captures Thessalonica. Ioannina surrenders to the Turks. Carlo II pays tribute to the Turks to remain as lord of Arta.
1448	Cyriac of Ancona visits Epiros.
1448	Death of Carlo II. His eldest son, Leonardo, inherits the remnants of his territory.

Period of Turkish domination

1449	Arta taken by the Turks.
1453	Fall of Constantinople to the Turks.
1460	Turks take Angelokastro and Barnakas.
1461	Turks conquer Peloponnese.
1461	Fall of the Byzantine Empire of Trebizond.
1463 – 1479	First Turco – Venetian war.
1477	Turks make unsuccessful attack on Nafpaktos.
1479	Turks capture Vonitsa, Lefkas, Cephalonia and Zante.
1489	Venetians acquire Cyprus.
1499 – 1500	Second Turco – Venetian war.
1499	Venetians surrender Nafpaktos. Sultan Bayezid II constructs the Castle of the Morea and the Castle of Roumeli.
1500	Venetians lose Methoni, Koroni and Navarino to the Turks but gain control of the islands of Cephalonia, Ithaca and Zante.
1537	Third Turco – Venetian war.
1571	Turks take Cyprus from Venetians.
1571	Battle of Lepanto.
1669	Venetians lose Crete to the Turks.
1683	Turks besiege Vienna but are defeated.

Chronology

1684	Venice, Austria, Poland and the Papacy form a Holy League against the Turks.
1684	Morosini captures Lefkas, Mesolonghi, Vonitsa and Preveza.
1687	Venetians complete conquest of the Morea.
1699	Treaty of Karlowitz. Venetians forced to concede their conquests north of the Gulf of Corinth.
1715	Turks recover the Morea.
1716	Turks besiege Corfu and are defeated.
1717	Venetians recover Preveza and Vonitsa.
1718	Treaty of Passarowitz.
1770	Orloff revolt.
1783	Ali Pasha appointed Pasha of Trikala.
1788	Ali Pasha confirmed as Pasha of Ioannina.
1797	Fall of Venice to Napoleon. Ionian Islands assigned to France by the Treaty of Campo Formio.
1798	Napoleon invades Egypt. Turks and Russians declare war on the French and seize Zante, Cephalonia and Lefkas.
1798	Ali Pasha seizes Preveza for the Turks.
1799	Russians and Turks take Corfu after a four month siege.
1800	Septinsular Republic created by Russia and Turkey.
1802 – 1807	Russian control of Lefkas.
1803	Ali Pasha defeats Souliots.
1804-1810	Period of William Leake's travels in northern Greece.
1807	Russians defeated by the French at the Battle of Friedland. Treaty of Tilsit restores Ionian Islands to the French.
1809	British occupy Zante, Cephalonia and Ithaca.
1810	Lefkas taken by Major Church.
1811	Ali Pasha seizes Margariti.
1814	French surrender Corfu to the British.
1815	Treaty of Paris creates the United States of the Ionian Islands under British protection.
1819	Ali Pasha occupies Parga.

The Development of the Greek State

1821	Greek War of Independence begins.
1822	Death of Ali Pasha. First Constitution of Greece.
1824	Byron dies at Mesolonghi.

Chronology

1826	Mesolonghi falls to the Turks.
1827	Sir Richard Church appointed commander of Greek forces.
1827	Treaty of London. Turkish naval defeat by a British, French and Russian fleet at the Battle of Navarino.
1829	Mesolonghi re-captured by Greek forces.
1828-34	Nauplion first capital of Greece.
1832	Treaty of Constantinople confirms borders of the new Greek state.
1834	Athens becomes capital of modern Greece.
1864	Ionian islands become part of the Greek state.
1881	Thessaly and Arta district ceded to Greece.
1897	Thirty Days War.
1903	Construction of the Lefkas ship canal.
1912 - 1913	First Balkan War.
1913	Epiros becomes part of Greece except for an area incorporated into the new state of Albania.
1919	Greek occupation of Smyrna region of Turkey.
1920	Treaty of Sèvres grants Greece the right to administer the Smyrna area.
1922	Turkish counter attack and burning of Smyrna.
1923	Exchange of populations between Greece and Turkey formalised by a convention signed at Lausanne in January 1923.
1940	Greek forces temporarily re-occupy northern Epiros.

Glossary

Ashlar
Masonry of rectangular blocks of dressed stone, either quarry-faced or smooth-faced.

Bastion
A structure projecting from the circuit wall of a fortification to provide flanking fire along the face of the walls and to adjacent bastions. Typically refers to the arrow headed bastions of the Italian style with two faces and two flanks, but may be applied to any form of flanking tower in earlier periods.

Batter, battered
A battered wall has a sloping outer face such that the thickness of the wall diminishes with height.

Casemate
A chamber within the walls of a fortification. It may provide accommodation for the garrison or be equipped with gunports.

Caponier
A casemated work projecting into the ditch surrounding a fortification to provide flanking fire.

Cloisonné masonry
A style of masonry in which each rectangular block of stone is framed by thin red brick or tile.

Cordon
A continuous semi-circular moulding around the outer face of a wall usually at the level of the base of the parapet.

Glossary

Covered Way
An infantry walkway on the outer edge of a ditch shielded by its own parapet and hence covered from view.

Counterscarp
The outer wall of a dry moat or ditch.

Crenellation
A battlemented parapet consisting of alternating merlons and crenels. The merlon is the upright projection; the crenel the gap between two merlons from which weapons were fired.

Demi-bastion
A half bastion built with only one flank and hence providing defensive fire in only one direction along the face of the wall.

Embrasure
An opening in the parapet to allow a gun to be fired. To allow the gun to be aimed at various points in an arc, embrasure openings are usually splayed.

Enfilade
Fire directed from the flank of a bastion or tower along the face of a fortification.

Glacis
An open area beyond the ditch sloping gently downhill from the covered way and designed to leave any attacker in clear view.

Groin-vault
A type of cross vault formed by the intersection of two barrel vaults at right angles to each other.

Isodomic
Masonry of trapezoidal or rectangular (ashlar) blocks built in courses of equal height.

Külliye
A religious complex including a mosque, madrasah, baths and other community buildings.

Glossary

Merlon
The upright projection used to protect defenders on the rampart who could return fire through the adjacent crenel.

Madrasah
A school or college for the study of Islam or other subjects. Also spelt medrese, medresa etc.

Mihrab
A niche in the wall of a mosque that indicates the direction of Mecca.

Parapet
Wall used to protect the defenders on the ramparts of a fortification, either plain or provided with embrasures.

Polygonal
Masonry with the visible surfaces of the stones dressed with straight sides or joints, giving the block the appearance of a polygon. It may be built in rough courses or with a completely random appearance.

Pseudo Isodomic
Coursed masonry in the manner of Isodomic but with courses of unequal height.

Redan
A triangular outwork of two faces open at the rear.

Redoubt
Small square or polygonal outwork often placed some distance from the main fortification to impede the approach of an enemy force.

Revetment
Either a stone retaining wall constructed against the outer face of an earthwork rampart or a wall supporting a terraced hillside.

Salient
The angle of a bastion or other feature projecting outwards from the line of fortification.

Serai or Seraglio
Seraglio is a Turkish word for the quarters of the women. It is also used

Glossary

to denote a palace generally and is used interchangeably with serai.

Stringcourse
A thin projecting course of brickwork or stone running horizontally around the outer face of a wall. Used to emphasize the junction between floors or to define the base of the parapet.

Talus
A sloping mass of masonry at the base of a fortifications wall designed to impede scaling ladders, protect the base of the wall from siege engines or simply provide reinforcement against earthquake damage.

Terreplein or Terre-plein
Flat surface of a rampart below parapet level that forms a firing platform for guns.

Bibliography

Ambraseys, N. and Finkel, C., *Material for the Investigation of the Seismicity of the Eastern Mediterranean Region during the period 1690-1710*, EC project "Review of Historical Seismicity in Europe" (1989-1993). Available from:
http://emidius.mi.ingv.it/RHISE/i_12amb/i_12amb.html, 2003.

Andrews, K., *Castles of the Morea,* The American School of Classical Studies at Athens. Revised edition (2006).

Anna Comnena, *The Alexiad*, Translated by E.A Dawes.
Available from:
http://www.fordham.edu/halsall/basis/annacomnena-alexiad00.html

Baker. Lieut.-Col., *Memoir on the Northern Frontier of Greece,* Journal of the Royal Geographical Society Volume 7 (1837). Electronic version available from Google books.

Balta, E., Yilmaz, F. and Yasar, F., *Tsamouria – Nineteenth Century Ottoman Thesprotia*, in B. Forsén (ed.), Thesprotia Expedition I Towards a Regional History, Helsinki (2009).

Blaquire. E., *The Greek Revolution; its Origin and Progress*, London (1824). Electronic version available from Google books.

Bodnar, E. W., *Cyriac of Ancona Later Travels*, Harvard University Press (2003).

Botzaris, N., *The Battle of Lepanto,* Athens (2001).

Bowden, W., *Thesprotia in the Context of Roman and Late Antique Epirus*, in B. Forsén (ed.), Thesprotia Expedition I Towards a Regional History, Helsinki (2009).

Brockmüller, S., Vott, A., May, S.M., Brückner, H., *Palaeoenvironmental changes of the Lefkada Sound (NW Greece) and their archaeological relevance,* in: G. Gönnert, B. Pflüger, J.-A. Bremer (eds.), Von der Geoarchäologie über die Küstendynamik zum Küstenzonenmanagement, Coastline Reports 9, Leiden, (2007). Available from:

Bibliography

http://databases.eucc-d.de/files/documents/00000781_CR9_ Brockmueller_etal.pdf

Capponi, N., *Victory of the West,* De Capo Press (2006).

Castillo, D.A., *The Maltese Cross: a strategic history of Malta,* Westport (2006).

Chanson, H., *Historical Development of Stepped Cascades for the Dissipation of Hydraulic Energy*, Transactions of the Newcomen Society 72 (2001). Available from:
www.uq.edu.au/~e2hchans/reprints/newcom01.pdf

Churchill, W.J., *The Annales Barenses and the Annales Lupi Protospatharii: Critical Edition and Commentary,* Univ. of Toronto (1979). Available from:
www.billchurchill.com/Dissertation/ChurchillDissertation.pdf

Clogg, R., *Concise History of Greece*, Cambridge University Press (1992).

Crowson, A., *Venetian Butrint*, Butrint Foundation (2007).

Davenport, R.A., *The Life of Ali Pasha of Tepelini,* London (1837). Available from: http://archive.org/details/lifealipashatep00algoog

De Bossett, C.P., *Parga and the Ionian Islands etc.*, London (1821). Electronic version available from Google books.

Doukellis, P.N. and Fouache, E., *La centuriation romaine de la plaine d'Arta replacée dans le contexte de l'évolution morphologique récente des deltas de l'Arachtos et du Louros,* Bulletin de correspondance hellénique Volume 116 (1992). Available from:
http://www.persee.fr/web/revues/home/prescript/article/bch _0007-4217_1992_num_116_1_1710

Erickson, E.J., *Defeat in detail: the Ottoman Army in the Balkans, 1912-1913,* Westport (2003).

ESCUTIS Project, *The Muslim Presence in Epirus and Western Greece*, in Elevating and Safeguarding Culture Using Tools of the Information Society: Dusty traces of the Muslim culture, Athens (2008). Electronic version available from Google books.

Finlay, G., *History of Greece from its conquest by the Crusaders to its conquest by the Turks, and of the empire of Trebizond*, Edinburgh (1851). Available from:
http://archive.org/details/cu31924028326878

Finlay, G., *History of Greece under Ottoman and Venetian Domination*, Edinburgh (1856). Available from:
http://archive.org/details/historyofgreeceu00finluoft

Finlay, G., *History of the Greek Revolution*, London (1849). Available from: http://archive.org/details/historygreekrev00finlgoog

Fleming, K. E., *The Muslim Bonaparte: diplomacy and orientalism in Ali Pasha's Greece*, Princeton University Press (1999).

Geoffrey Malaterra, *The Deeds Done by Count Roger of Calabria and Sicily and of Duke Robert his Brother.* Available from: http://medievalsicily.com/Docs/03_Norman_Conquest/Malaterra%20all%20text%20revised.pdf

Gordon, T., *History of the Greek Revolution Volume II*, London (1832). Electronic version available from Google books.

Gregory, T., *The early Byzantine fortifications of Nikopolis in comparative perspective*, Proceedings of the First International Symposium on Nikopolis (1984). Available from:www.preveza.gr/index.php?option=com_docman&task=doc_details&gid=620&Itemid=309

Hakkarainen, M., *Venetian Presence in Thesprotia*, in B. Forsén (ed.), Thesprotia Expedition I Towards a Regional History, Helsinki (2009).

Hall, R.C., *The Balkan Wars, 1912-1913: prelude to the First World War*, London (2000).

Hammond, N.G.L., *Epirus: The Geography, the Ancient Remains, the History and the Topography of Epirus and Adjacent Areas*, Oxford (1967).

Hansen, M.H. and Nielsen, T.H., *An Inventory of Archaic and Classical Poleis*, Oxford University Press (2004).

Hellenkemper, H., *Die byzantinische Stadtmauer von Nikopolis in Epeiros*, Proceedings of the First International Symposium on Nikopolis (1984). Available from: www.preveza.gr/index.php?option=com_docman&task=doc_download&gid=619&Itemid=309

Heuzey, L., *Le Mont Olympe et L'Arcananie*, Paris (1860). Available from: http://archive.org/details/lemontolympeetl00tgoog

Holland, H., *Travels in the Ionian Islands, Albania, Thessaly, Macedonia during the years 1812 and 1813*, London (1815). Electronic version available from Google books.

Hughes, T. S., *Travels in Sicily Greece and Albania*, London (1820). Available from: http://archive.org/details/travelsinsicily01hughgoog

Ingrao, C.W., Samardzic, N., Pesalj, J., (eds.), *The Peace of Passarowitz, 1718*, Purdue University Press (2011).

Ionian University, *Inscriptions of the Ionian Islands* (Επιγραφικά Μνημεία Ιονίων Νήσων). Available from: www.ionio.gr/tab/culture/activities/projects/epigraphs/index.php

Jing, Z., and Rapp, G., *The Coastal Evolution of the Ambracian Embayment and Its Relationship to Archaeological Settings*, in J. Wiseman and K. Zachos (eds.), Landscape Archaeology in Southern

Bibliography

Epirus Greece I, American School of Classical Studies in Athens (2003).

Kanetaki, E., *The still existing Ottoman Hamams in the Greek territory*, Middle East Technical University Journal of the Faculty of Architecture (2004). Available from:
http://jfa.arch.metu.edu.tr/content/view/13/29/

Karabelas, N.D., *Το κάστρο της Μπούκας (1478-1701)*, Proceedings of the Second International Symposium for the History and Culture of Preveza, Preveza (2010). Available from:
http://oxford.academia.edu/NikosDKarabelas/Papers/513149/The_Castle_of_Bouka_1478-1701_._Fortified_Preveza_through_sources

Konstantios, D., *The Kastro of Ioannina*, Ministry of Culture Archaeological Receipts Fund (1997).

Lane-Poole, S., *Sir Richard Church Commander-in–Chief of the Greeks in the War of Independence*, London (1890). Available from:
www.archive.org/details/sirrichardchurch00lanerich

Langenbach, R., *From Opus Craticium to the Chicago Frame: Earthquake Resistant Traditional Construction*, International Journal of Architectural Heritage Volume I (2007). Available from:
http://www.tandfonline.com/doi/pdf/10.1080/15583050601125998

Lawrence, A.W., *A Skeletal history of Byzantine Fortification*, Annual of the British School at Athens Vol. 78 (1983), pp. 171-227.

Leake, W.M., *Travels in Northern Greece vols. I-IV*, London (1835). Facsimile reprint Amazon.co.uk.

Lear, E., *Journals of a landscape Painter in Albania etc.*, London (1851). Available from:
www.archive.org/details/journalsoflands00learuoft

Leland, T., *The Orations of Demosthenes*, London (1829). Electronic version available from Google books.

Livy, *History of Rome*. Available from:
http://www.archive.org/details/livy01bakegoog

Locke, P., *The Franks in the Aegean 1204 – 1500*, London (1995).

London Gazette archives, Available from:
http://www.london-gazette.co.uk.

Lurier, H.E., *Crusaders as Conquerors: The Chronicle of the Morea*, Columbia University Press (1964).

Martin, R.M., *History of the British Colonies, Volume V, Possessions in Europe*, London (1835). Electronic version available from Google books.

Miller, W., *Essays on the Latin Orient*, Cambridge (1921).
Available from: http://archive.org/details/essaysonlatinori00milluoft

Miller, W., *The Latins in the Levant,* New York (1908). Available from: http://archive.org/details/latinsinlevanta00millgoog
Milright, M., *An Introduction to Islamic Architecture,* Edinburgh University Press (2010).
Mure, W., *Journal of a Tour in Greece and the Ionian Islands,* London (1841). Available from: http://archive.org/details/journalatouring00muregoog
Murray, W.M., *The Coastal Sites of Western Akarnania, a Topographical – Historical Survey,* University of Pennsylvania (1982).
Murray, W.M., and Petsas, P.M., *Octavian's campsite memorial for the Actian War,* The American Philosophical Society (1989).
Negris, P., *Vestiges Antiques Submergés,* Athens (1904). Reprinted Aries Publishers, 1980.
Nevinson, H.W., *Scenes in the Thirty Days War Between Greece and Turkey,* London (1898). Available from: http://www.archive.org/details/scenesinthirtyd01nevigoog
Nicol, D.M., *The Despotate of Epiros 1267 – 1479 A contribution to the history of Greece in the Middle ages,* Cambridge University Press (1984).
Nicol, D.M., *The Reluctant Emperor: A Biography of John Cantacuzene,* Cambridge University Press (1996).
Norwich, J.J., *A History of Venice,* London (1983).
Norwich, J.J., *Byzantium,* London (1993).
Osswald, B., *From Lieux de Pouvoir to Lieux de Memoire: The Monuments of the Medieval Castle of Ioannina through the Centuries,* in Gudmundur Hálfdanarson, (ed.), Discrimination and tolerance in Historical perspective, Pisa (2008). Available from: http://www.cliohworld.net/onlread/3/Osswald_From.pdf
Osswald, B., *The Ethnic Composition of Medieval Epiros,* in Ellis and Klusáková (eds.), Imaging frontiers, contesting identities, Pisa (2007). Available from: http://www.cliohworld.net/onlread/5/44.pdf
Pepper, S., *Ottoman military architecture in the early gunpowder era: a reassessment,* in James D. Tracy (ed.), City Walls: The Urban Enceinte in Global Perspective, Cambridge University Press (2000).
Polybius, *The Histories.* Available from: http://penelope.uchicago.edu/Thayer/E/Roman/Texts/Polybius/
Pouqueville, F.C.H.L., *Travels in southern Epirus, Acarnania, Aetolia, Attica, etc,* London (1822). Download available from Google books.
Pratt, M., *Britain's Greek Empire,* London (1978).
Pritchett, W.K., *Studies in Ancient Greek Topography Part VI,* University of California (1989).

Bibliography

Procopius, *De Aedificiis*. Available from: http://penelope.uchicago.edu/Thayer/E/Roman/Texts/Procopius/Buildings/home.html

Procopius, *History of the Wars Books VII and VIII*, trans. Dewing, H.B., Cambridge, Mass. (1928). Available from: http://archive.org/details/procopiuswitheng05procuoft

Pseudo-Scylax, *The Periplous or Circumnavigation*.
See: Shipley, G., Pseudo-Skylax's Periplous: The Circumnavigation of the Inhabited World - Text, Translation and Commentary, University of Exeter Press (2011).

Queißer, J., *Entwicklung landschafts-verträglicher Bauweisen für überströmbare Dämme*, Universitätsverlag Karlsruhe (2006).
Available from: http://uvka.ubka.uni-karlsruhe.de/shop/download/1000004379

Renvtzos, I., Giannoulis, N. and Kallinikos, J., *State, Society and Market in Preveza: Historical Time and Historical Centre in a Small Greek Town*, Seventh International Conference on Urban History (2008).
Available from: http://library.panteion.gr:8080/dspace/bitstream/123456789/516/1/rRENTZOS.pdf

Smith, W., *A Dictionary of Greek and Roman Geography Volume I*.
Available from: http://www.archive.org/details/dictionaryofgree01smituoft

Smyris, G., *Καστρα και Οχυρωσεις Του Αμβρακικου Κολπου*, http://www-ioa.epcon.gr/baseis/agr/agr/g_smiris1.htm

Sodini, J.P., *The Transformation of Cities in Late Antiquity within the Provinces of Macedonia and Epirus*, Proceedings of the British Academy Vol. 141 (2007).

Suha, M., *The walls of Agios Donatos Zervochoriou*, University of Helsinki (2007). Available from: https://oa.doria.fi/bitstream/handle/10024/29643/thewalls.pdf

The Treaty of Campo Formio. Available from: www.napoleon-series.org/research/government/diplomatic/c_campoformio1.html

United States Hydrographic Office, *Mediterranean Pilot Volume 3*, Washington (1917). Available from: http://archive.org/details/mediterraneanpi00offigoog.

Vickers, M., *The Cham Issue: Albanian National and Property Claims in Greece*, Conflict Studies Research Centre (2002). Available from: https://da.mod.uk/colleges/arag/document-listings/balkan/G109

William of Apulia, *The Deeds of Robert Guiscard*. Available from:

Bibliography

http://medievalsicily.com/Docs/03_Norman_Conquest/William%20of%20Apulia%20graham%20loud%20trans.pdf

Winter, F.E., *Greek fortifications,* University of Toronto Press (1971).

Wolfe, J., *Observations on the Gulf of Arta,* Journal of the Royal Geographical Society Volume 3 (1833). Electronic version available from Google books.

Woodhouse, W. J., *Aetolia, Its Geography, Topography and Antiquities,* Oxford (1897). Available from: http://archive.org/details/aetoliaitsgeogra00wood

Yewdale, R.B., *Bohemond I, Prince of Antioch,* Princeton University (1917). Available from: www.archive.org/details/bohemondiprinceo00yewduoft

Index

Abdul Hamid, Sultan, 10, 274
Achaia, Achaian, 4, 14 n.3, 18, 63; Roman province, 2
Acheloos, district, 6, 70; river, 2, 16, 18, 68, 69, 70
Acherontas or Acheron river, 1, 187 n.5, 191, 238; gorge, 191, 198, 200, 206
Actium (Aktio, Punta), cape, 98, 99, 102, 127, 129, 145; Battle of, 88, 127; temple of Apollo, 99
Adriatic sea, 3, 4, 7, 8, 103, 104, 221
Aetolia, Aetolians, 1, 2, 3, 16, 18, 127, 146, 158, 168
Aetos castle, 5, 18, 72, 74, **78-81**, 277
Aghia, 221, 222
Agrinio, 67, 86 n.27, 87 n.42
Agios Donatos castle (Aidonat Kalesi), 191, **238-243**, 274 n.32, 274 n.33, 277
Akarnania, 1, 2, 3, 5, 6, 13, 16, 72, 74, 75, 78, 82, 87 n.42, 102, 117, 127, 141 n.7, 167, 168, 246
Aktio, fort, **99-102**, 105, 279;
Albania, Albanians, 1, 2, 5, 6, 7, 10, 14, 15 n.10, 15 n.15,
16, 18, 69, 70, 159, 190 n.30, 191, 194, 195, 198, 230, 231, 232, 238, 239, 244, 246, 272 n.17, 274 n.42
Alcmaeon, 143
Alexander, fort, **125-126**
Alexander, king of the Molossians, 1, 146
Alexander II, successor to Pyrrhus, 1, 146, 158
Ali Pasha of Ioannina (or Tepelini), 9, 10-11, 15 n.14, 89, 90, 94, 99-100, 105, 117, 121, 122, 140 n.3, 141 n.4, 159, 164, 167, 168, 170, 175, 183, 189 n.30, 192, 194-195, 197, 202, 204, 207-208, 209, 215-219, 221-222, 224, 228, 230, 231, 233, 238, 244, 248, 249, 253, 257-260, 263, 268, 269, 272 n.14, 279; Pasha of Ioannina, 10, 274 n.42; Pasha of Trikala, 10, 274 n.42; and Souliots, 191, 198, 238
Alyzeia, 81
Ambracia (Ambrakia), 1, 143, 156, **157-160**, 165, 167, 173, 189 n.21
Ambracia, gulf of, 1, 13, 78, 88, 90, 94, 127, 129, 143,

Index

155, 167, 173, 188 n.12, 191, 280
Ambrakos, 143, 145, **156-157**, 188 n.16
Amcazade Köprülü Hüseyin Pasha, Grand Vizier, 27
Amphilochia (Karavasaras), 143, 168, 169, 174
Amphilochian Argos, 143, 158, 188 n.20
Anaktoria, 1, 173
Anastasius, Byzantine Emperor, 132
Anatoliko, Aitoliko, 11, 16, 64, **67-68**, 69
Andronikos II, Byzantine Emperor, 4, 244
Andronikos III, Byzantine Emperor, 5, 69, 193, 246
Anemogiannis, Giorgos, 23
Angelokastro, 5, 6, 16, 18, **69-72**, 74, 79, 82, 86 n.33, 246, 277; church of Agios Georgios, 70
Anthousa, castle and village, 191, **221-228**, 280
Antirio, 44, 45, 50
Arachthos river, 143, 156, 157, 160, 188 n.12, 188 n.14, 188 n.16, 264
Archontochori, 78, 81
Argos (Peloponnese), 7
Arsinoe, 86 n.33
Arta, 1, 3, 4, 5, 6, 11, 13, 14, 143, 155, 156, **157-159**, 167, 173, 188 n.16, 189 n.22, 192, 193, 194, 244, 246, 248, 264, 265, 268, 269, 271; castle of, 5, 143, 157, **159-167**, 174, 249
Arta - Volos border line, 13, 155, 248
Artolithia, 195
Astakos, 13, 18, **72-78**, 81, 86 n.35
Athens, 8, 11, 13, 18, 273 n.17
Austria, Austrians, 8, 9, 105
Avariko, 198, 200
Avars, 18
Baltic sea, 10
Bambini, 78
Bari, 2
Barnakas, castle, 5, 6, 18, **81-84**, 277; village, 87 n.47
Basil I, Byzantine Emperor, 2, 146
Bastia (see Sagiada)
Baties (Kastro Rizovouni), 1, 143, 145, 187 n.5
Bayezid II, Sultan, 16, 23, 44, 50, 102
Berenikia, 88
Berlin, Congress of, 13,
Bizani, Fort (Fort Bijan), 192, **264-268**, 271; Battle of, 14, 265, 271
Blaquire, Edward, 64
Bohemond, son of Robert Guiscard, 2-3, 159, 244, 260
Bonaparte, Napoleon, 9, 88-89, 104, 105, 159, 175, 207
Boua, Dimo, 69
Bouchetion, 1, 143, **145-154**, 156, 157, 187 n.4, 187 n.5
Bouka, castle of, 90, 140 n.3, 141 n.4,
Britain, British, 10, 13, 52, 61, 102, 105, 107, 109-110, 117, 142 n.10, 155, 191, 207-208, 221-222, 272 n.12
British Protectorate of the Ionian Islands, 105, 207

Index

Bucharest, treaty of, 14
Bulgaria, Bulgarians, 3, 14, 249, 264, 273 n.17
Buondelmonti, Esau, 6, 246
Buondelmonti, Maddalena, 15 n.7
Butrinto, Butrint, 7, 8, 9, 15 n.10
Byron, Lord, 64, 67
Byzantine Empire, 2, 3, 4, 5, 7, 16, 18, 69, 146, 159, 169, 173, 188 n.16, 193, 207, 238, 244, 246
Caotorta, Paulo, 210
Campo Formio, treaty of, 9, 105, 159
Candia, 8
Cantacuzene, John, 146, 168, 193, 207
Cephalonia, 4, 5, 6, 8, 9, 10, 14 n.4, 15 n.7, 102, 105, 173, 189 n.28
Cervantes, 23
Chaironia, Battle of, 18
Chameria, 230
Chania, 8
Chaones, 1
Charadrus, 145, 187 n.4
Charles I of Anjou, king of Sicily, 4
Charles II, king of Naples, 4, 5, 18, 69, 141 n.8, 146, 173
Chios, 8
Chronicle of the Morea, 88, 146
Church, Sir Richard, 13, 16, 18, 65, 74, 77, 105, 168
Cleopatra, 127
Constantine, Prince, 264
Constantine I, Roman Emperor, 2
Constantine, Fort, **125-126**, 141 n.7
Constantinople, 2, 3, 4, 5, 7, 18, 19, 102, 152, 159, 175, 238, 244; Theodosian Walls, 135
Constantinople, treaty of, 13, 155
Corfu (Kerkyra), 1, 3, 4, 7, 8, 9, 10, 15 n.10, 64, 104, 105, 158, 191, 207-208, 210, 221, 222, 233, 273 n.31, 279
Corinth, Corinthians, 1, 2, 141 n.7, 142 n.13, 143, 156, 157, 158, 173
Corinth, Gulf of, 1, 7, 8, 16, 19, 44, 45, 50, 63, 64, 159, 278
Crete, 7, 8, 15 n.8, 264, 279
Croatia, 8
Cyprus, 8, 229
Dalmatia, 7
Davis, Henry, Major-General, 110
De Bosset, Charles Philipe, 208, 209, 220, 272 n.14
Despotate of Epiros, 3-6, 7, 14, 15, 16, 18, 67, 69, 74, 86 n.32, 88, 102, 146, 159, 173, 193, 194, 238, 244, 246, 277
Dionysios, Metropolitan of Larissa, 248, 274 n.35
Domboetis, Seraphim, Metropolitan of Nafpaktos, 26
Don Juan of Austria, 19
Doria, Andrea, Genoese Admiral, 44, 50
Dorians, 18
Dragomestre, 5, 13, 18, **72-78**, 79, 86 n.37, 277
Dušan, Stephen, 5, 69, 194, 246
Echinades islands, 72
Egypt, Egyptian, 9, 11, 12, 13, 65, 89, 105

Elatria (Palaiorophoros), 1, 143, 145, 187 n.5
Elea, ancient city of Thesprotia, 274 n.33
Elis, Elean, 1, 14 n.1, 143, 145, 146, 156, 187 n.2, 187 n.5
Ephyra, 1, 191
Epiros, 1, 2, 3, 4, 5, 6, 7, 8, 9, 10, 11, 13, 14, 69, 90, 143, 145, 146, 157, 159, 188 n.12, 188 n.16, 191, 192, 194, 200, 208, 229, 231, 233, 238, 244, 246, 249, 264, 268, 272 n.17; Epiros Vetus, 2; Epiros Nova, 2,
Euboea, 7, 8
Filiates, 230, 239
First Balkan War, 14, 90, 105, 192, 249, 264, 267
Florent of Hainault, 4
Fourth Crusade, 3, 16, 18, 152, 159, 244
France, French, 9, 10, 13, 52, 61, 88-89, 104, 105, 117, 122, 142 n.10, 155, 159, 183, 190 n.30, 207, 221-222, 233, 263
Franks, 3, 4, 7, 85 n.9, 102, 152, 159
Frederick II, Holy Roman Emperor, 4
Friedland, Battle of, 9, 105
Geoffrey of Villehardouin, 14 n.3
Georgouleika, 84, 87 n.47
Germany, German, 15 n.15, 52, 179, 248-249, 273 n.17, 280
Gitana, Gitani, 233, 273 n.27, 274 n.33
Glarentza, 193
Glosses (Barnakas), 81, 82; ancient dam of, 84, 87 n.46, 87 n.47
Glyki, 191, 206, 238
Goltz, General van der, 249
Gomenitsa, Gumenizza (see Igoumenitsa)
Gordon, Thomas, 64
Goths, 2
Greece, Greek State, 2, 5, 10, 11-13, 14, 15 n.15, 18, 90, 100, 105, 143, 188 n.12, 208, 230-231, 249, 264, 269
Greek War of Independence (Greek Revolution), 11, 16, 64-65, 67, 74, 155, 168, 173, 248, 280
Grimani, Francesco, 52, 54, 55, 63
Grivas, Castle of, **117-122**, 125, 279
Guillame de Champlitte, 14 n.3
Guiscard, Robert, 2-3, 159, 173, 189 n.28, 244
Helena, daughter of Michael II, wife of Manfred, 4
Heuzey, Leon Alexandre, 169-170
Holland, Henry, 198, 272 n.9
Holy League, 8, 50, 103, 229, 233
Hungary, Hungarian, 8,
Huns, 2
Ibrahim Pasha, son of Mehmet Ali of Egypt, 11, 12, 13, 65
Igoumenitsa, 1, 191, 229, 233
Illyria, 2, 3
Inebahti (Nafpaktos), 19
Ioannina (Turkish Yanya), 1, 3, 4, 5, 6, 10, 11, 13, 14, 15 n.6, 173, 192, 194, 198, 238, **244-264**, 268, 279, 280; Ali Pa-

Index

sha's citadel and seraglio, **257-260**, 265, 269, 271, 274 n.35; Ali Pasha's tomb, 260; Aslan Pasha mosque, 262; Bohemond's tower, 259-260; Byzantine circuit, 248, 249; Fetihe mosque, 260; Litharitsia, 248, 259, 264, 275 n.44; moat, 249; Molos gate, 251; Northeast citadel, 261-262; Skala gate, 253, 255, 257; Thomas tower, 252

Ionian islands, 8, 9, 10, 13, **88**, 102, 103, 104, 105, 141 n.4, 159, 198, 207, 208, 272 n.13

Istria, 7

Italy, Italians, 2, 4, 9, 15 n.15, 102, 159, 218, 228, 233, 244, 272 n.17

Ithaca, 8, 10, 102, 105

Julius Caesar, 127

Justinian I, Byzantine Emperor, 18, 132, 142 n.16, 238, 274 n.34

Kabasalis, John, 79

Kalamas, river, 191, 233, 273 n.27

Kalamos, island of, 84

Kandila, 81, 84

Kariotes, Lefkas, 125

Karlowitz, treaty of, 8, 19, 45, 50, 64, 88, 90, 159, 175

Kastritsa, 264

Katochi, 18, **68-69**

Kerkyra (see Corfu)

Kiafas, castle and village of, 11, 191, **198-206**

Kokytos, river, 238, 274 n.33

Komaros, port of Nikopolis, 129, 131

Konope, 70, 86 n.33

Koroni, 7, 13, 44, 85 n.9

Koronisia, 145, **155-156**, 157, 188 n.16

Krinai, 189 n.20

Kryoneri, 67, 86 n.27

Kugni, hill of, 206

Laskara castle, 145, 155

Lausanne, convention on exchange of populations, 231

Leake, William Martin, 19, 55, 73, 74, 86 n.40, 90-91, 100, 156, 157, 159, 175, 184, 187 n.4, 188 n.14, 189 n.29, 190 n.30, 195, 198, 200, 202, 204, 205, 208, 238, 242, 259, 268

Lear, Edward, 200

Lefkas, 6, 8, 9, 10, 11, 15 n.7, 88, 102, **103-107**, 117, 122, 125, 141 n.7, 142 n.10, 142 n.13, 207, 246

Lefkas canal, 102, 106, 107, 110, 126, 141 n.7, 142 n.13

Leopold I, Holy Roman Emperor, 8

Lepanto (see also Nafpaktos), 19, 44

Lepanto, Battle of, 19, 23, 24, 221, 229

Limnaia, 13, 143, **167-173**

Loeben, treaty of, 9

London, treaty of (1827), 13

London, treaty of (1913), 14

Losha, Peter, 6, 246

Louros river, 129, 145; gorge, 268

Macedon, Macedonia, 1, 3, 14, 146, 158, 265; Roman province, 2

Mahmud II, Sultan, 11, 248

Maison, General in command

307

Index

of French forces, 13
Maitland, Sir Thomas, 208, 272 n.14
Malta, Knights of, 44
Manfred, son of Frederick II, 4
Manuel II, Byzantine Emperor, 6, 246
Margariti, castle and village, 10, 191, **229-233**, 238, 239, 273 n.22
Margaritone of Brindisi, 14 n.4
Maria, daughter of Nikephoros, wife of John Orsini, 4, 67
Maria, daughter of Symeon Uroš, 6
Marino, Aloisio, 113, 117, 142 n.11
Mark Antony, 127
Mazoma lagoon, 127
Mehmet Ali, ruler of Egypt, 11
Menidi, 155
Mesolonghi, 8, 11, 12, 13, 16, **64-67**, 68, 74, 86 n.27, 88, 168, 280
Messenia, Messenians, 1, 18, 44
Methoni, 7, 12, 44, 85 n.9
Michael I Comnenus Doukas, 3, 5, 86 n.32, 159, 167, 244
Michael II Comnenus Angelos Doukas, 3, 4, 69, 86 n.32, 159, 167, 173
Michael IX, Byzantine Emperor, 5
Molossi, Molossian, 1, 2, 146, 238
Monastiraki, 82
Monemvasia, 12
Monteleone, Don Santo, 228
Montenegro, 14, 249
Morea (see Peloponnese)

Morea, castle of, 7, 13, 16, 44, **50-63**, 102, 278, 279; Turkish bathhouse, 56
Morosini, Francesco, 8, 16, 19, 44, 64, 74, 103, 113, 117, 142 n.11, 159, 175, 233
Mukhtar Pasha, son of Ali Pasha, 10
Murad II, Sultan, 6, 246
Mure, William, 69
Mytikas, Akarnania, 78, 81, 84, 87 n.45
Mytikas, Preveza, 129
Nafpaktos, 1, 5, 7, 8, 10, 13, 16, **18-44**, 45, 50, 63, 67, 74, 78, 277, 278; Baba Tsaous mosque, 42; Botzaris tower, 24; Fetihe mosque, 23; Turkish Külliye, 27-28; Vezir mosque, 28
Nauplion, 7, 12, 44
Navarino, 7, 13
Navarino, Battle of, 13, 52
Nea Kerassous, 145, 148
Necromanteio, 191, 238
Negroponte (see Euboea)
Nerikos, 141 n.7, 142 n.13
Nicaea, Empire of, 3, 4, 86 n.32
Nikephoros I Comnenus Angelos Doukas, 3, 4, 5, 18, 69, 86 n.32, 102, 173
Nikephoros II, son of John II Orsini, 5, 6, 146, 193
Nikopolis, 2, 81, 88, 98, **127-140**, 145, 146, 158, 168, 188 n.20; Alkison Basilica, 140; Basilica of Doumetios, 135; Bishop's Palace, 135; Byzantine Nikopolis, **132-140**; Forum, 133, 140; Nymphaea, 131, 140; Odeion, 133, 140;

Index

Roman Nikopolis, **129-131**; Stadium and theatre, 129, 140; Victory monument, 129, 140, 142 n.15
Normans, 2-3, 192, 244
Octavian, 2, 88, 99, 127, 129
Olpae, Battle of, 158, 188 n.20
Olympia, 14 n.1
Orloff Revolt, 64
Orsini Maio, 14 n.4
Orsini, John I, son of Richard, 4, 102
Orsini, John II, son of John I, 5, 173, 193, 244, 246
Orsini, Nicholas, son of John I, 5, 207, 244; killed by brother John II, 5
Orsini, Richard, son of Maio, 4
Oswald, Brigadier, 105, 142 n.10
Otho, king of Greece, 67
Ottoman Empire (see Turkey)
Pandosia, 1, 187 n.5
Pamvotitha, lake, 244, 264
Pantokratoras Fort, 90, **94-99**, 155, 279, 280
Papacy, 8, 19
Paramythia, 15 n.6, 191, 230, 237, 238, 239, 274 n.35
Parga, castle and town, 5, 7, 8, 9, 10, 11, 15 n.6, 191, 198, **207-221**, 222, 229, 230, 272 n.14, 273 n.22, 278
Paris, treaty of, 10, 105, 207, 272 n.13
Passarowitz, treaty of, 9, 88, 104, 175, 233
Patras, Patrae, 18, 19, 44, 86 n.27
Pelagonia, Battle of, 4, 173
Peloponnese, 7, 8, 10, 11, 12, 13, 16, 44, 45, 50, 52, 74, 103
Peloponnesian War, 18, 158
Pente Pigadia, 264; Battle of, 269; fort, 192, **268-271**, 279
Peratia, 122, 125
Persians, 158
Petros of Koritsa, 198
Phidokastro (see Ambrakos)
Philip II of Macedon, 18
Philip of Taranto, son of Charles II, 5, 18, 69, 79, 173
Photike, 238
Pindos mountains, 244
Pirgos Ragiou, 191, **233-237**
Pisani, Andrea, 175
Plagia, 122, 125, 279
Poland, Poles, 8
Psathotopi, 157
Pouqueville, 48, 268, 277
Preljub, Gregory, 5-6
Preljubovič, Thomas, 6, 238, 246, 252, 260
Preveza, 8, 9, 11, 13, **88-93**, 99, 104, 105, 127, 129, 141 n.4, 143, 145, 155, 173, 175, 190 n.30, 248; Castle of St. Andrew, 90, 92, 99, 100, 279; Castle of St. George, 92, 94, 99; Pefkakia bastion, 92, 93, 99
Punta, 99
Pyrrhus, 1, 88, 146, 158, 167
Reshid Pasha, Turkish commander in the Greek War of Independence, 12, 13, 65
Rhodes, Knights of St. John, 175
Rio, 7, 44, 45, 50, 63
Riniasa (see Thomokastro)
Riza, 195, 198

Robert of Taranto, son of Philip, 15 n.7
Rogoi Castle, 5, 6, 143, **145-154**, 157, 173, 187 n.4, 193, 246, 277; church of the Assumption, 152
Rome, Roman, 1, 2, 18, 127, 129, 146, 158, 238
Roumeli, castle of, 7, 16, **44-50**, 63
Russia, Russian, 9, 10, 13, 64, 105, 117, 125, 141 n.4, 141 n.7, 189 n.30, 207, 221, 272 n.13
Sagiada, 7, 233
Sagredo, Augustino, 63, 117
Salamis, Battle of, 158
Salona (Amphissa), 65
Salaora, Salagora, 157, 188 n.16
Samoniva, 198, 200, 206
Santa Maura, castle of, 8, 64, 74, **88**, **102-117**, 120, 122, 141 n.7, 142 n.10, 233, 279
Sapienza, 44
Schulenburg, Count, 104
Second Balkan War, 14
Septinsular Republic, 9, 10, 105, 141 n.4, 189 n.30, 207
Serbia, Serbians, 5, 6, 14, 16, 69, 194, 246, 249, 265
Sicilian Vespers, 4
Sicily, 4, 14 n.4, 105
Slavs, 2, 18
Smyrtoula (Nikopoli), 129
Sobieski, John, king of Poland, 8
Sollion, 142 n.13
Souli, Souliots, 10, 11, 191, 195, 198, 200, 205, 206, 238
Spain, Spanish, 19, 55

Sparta, 18, 158
Spata, Gjin Boua, 6, 18, 19, 70, 246
Spata, Paul, son of Sgouros, 7, 19
Spata, Sgouros, brother of Gjin Boua, 70
Saint George Fort, Plagia, **122-125**, 279
Saint Luke the Evangelist, 152, 188 n.11
Strabo, 127, 141 n.7, 187 n.4, 187 n.5
Stratos, 86 n.42, 167
Teotochi, Count Marco, 209
Thamar, daughter of Nikephoros I, wife of Philip of Taranto, 5, 18, 69, 173
Theodore I Comnenus Doukas, 3, 14 n.4, 86 n.32, 159
Thesprotia, Thesproti, 1, 230, 231, 273 n.22, 272 n.27, 274 n.33
Thessalonica, 3, 4, 14, 159, 246, 265, 273 n.17
Thessaly, 3, 5, 6, 10, 13, 14, 69, 189 n.12, 246, 264, 265, 269, 273 n.17
Thirty Days War, 13, 264, 269
Thomas, Despot of Epiros, son of Nikephoros, 5, 67, 173, 191, 193; murdered by Nicholas Orsini, 5
Thomokastro, 5, 191, **193-198**, 277
Thrace, 14, 264, 273 n.17
Thucydides, 86 n.35, 167, 188 n.20,
Tilsit, treaty of, 10, 105, 117, 122, 207
Tocco Leonardo I, 15 n.7, 173,

Index

175
Tocco, Carlo I, son of Leonardo I, 6, 67, 69, 70, 79, 82, 194, 238, 246
Tocco, Carlo II, son of Leonardo II, 6, 246
Tocco, Leonardo II, brother of Carlo I, 6, 246
Tocco, Leonardo III, son of Carlo II, 6
Tocco, Menuno, third son of Carlo I, 79
Toroni, 1, 191, 234, 273 n.31
Transylvania, 8
Trebizond, Empire of, 3
Trojan War, 143
Trypa, hill of, 200
Turkey, Turks, 6, 7-9, 10, 11, 12, 13-14, 15 n.14, 16, 18, 19, 20, 24, 27-28, 44-45, 50, 52, 64-65, 68, 69, 70, 74, 79, 82, 85 n.9, 88-90, 102-105, 107, 117, 141 n.4, 143-145, 146, 152, 157, 159, 168, 175, 188 n.12, 190 n.30, 191, 192, 194, 198, 200, 207, 208, 221, 229, 230, 231, 233, 234, 237, 238, 244, 246, 248-249, 264, 268, 269, 273 n.22, 275 n.44, 279
Turkish fortification, 19-20, 22-23, 26, 30-31, 32, 35, 37, 38, 43, 44-49, 52-58, 63, 90, 106-109, 113, 115, 155, 165, 167, 168, 180, 182, 183, 187, 192, 206, 231-232, 233-237, 238, 265-267, 271, 278, 280
United States of the Ionian Islands, 10, 272 n.13
Uroš, Symeon, 5, 6, 69, 246
Valtos, Valton, 167, 168
Vandals, 2, 132
Vasilopoulo, 78
Vatatzes, John, Nicaean Emperor, 3, 86 n.32
Vathy, Preveza, 129
Veli Pasha, son of Ali Pasha, 10, 275 n.44
Venice, Venetians, 3, 7-9, 10, 11, 15 n.10, 16, 19-20, 44-45, 64, 67, 74, 85 n.9, 88, 90, 99, 102-104, 141 n.4, 141 n.7, 146, 159, 175, 189 n.30, 207-208, 209, 221, 229, 233, 273 n.22
Venetian fortification, 20-24, 26-27, 28, 30, 32, 35, 37, 38, 43-44, 50-52, 55-56, 58-63, 106-117, 122, 166, 167, 182, 187, 191, 209-213, 221, 278-279
Vienna, 8
Viterbo, treaty of, 4
Volos, 13
Vonitsa, 5, 6, 8, 9, 11, 13, 15 n.7, 18, 82, 104, 143, **173-187**, 189 n.28, 189 n.29, 189 n.30, 246; suburb of Recinto, 176, 183, 187; Church of the Panayia, 176, 183; Church of Ayia Sophia, 186
Walter of Brienne, 174
William II, king of Sicily, 14 n.4
William of Villehardouin, 4, 14 n.3
Woodhouse, William John, 70, 86 n.34
Zante, 6, 8, 9, 10, 14 n.4, 15 n.7, 102, 105, 207
Zeno, Byzantine Emperor, 132

www.ingramcontent.com/pod-product-compliance
Lightning Source LLC
Chambersburg PA
CBHW021832220426
43663CB00005B/220